TWENTIETH CENTURY VIEWS

The aim of this series is to present the best
in contemporary critical opinion on major
authors, providing a twentieth century perspective on their changing status in an era
of profound revaluations.

Maynard Mack, *Series Editor*
Yale University

BEN JONSON

BEN JONSON

A COLLECTION OF CRITICAL ESSAYS

Edited by

Jonas A. Barish

A SPECTRUM BOOK

Prentice-Hall, Inc., *Englewood Cliffs, N. J.*

Table of Contents

BEN JONSON

Introduction

by Jonas A. Barish

I

Probably no major author in English has suffered such a catastrophic decline in popularity since his own day as has Ben Jonson. Certainly none has been so punished for the crime of not being Shakespeare. Jonson was from the beginning tied to the kite of Shakespeare criticism, or perhaps it would be more exact to say that he was dragged captive behind the triumphal chariot of Shakespeare worship. In the seventeenth century it was fashionable, and profitable, to compare them, as Dryden did, to set them side by side as the two giants of the English theater, to discuss their respective virtues and evaluate their respective merits. By the time the century was over criticism had rendered its verdict: Shakespeare's pre-eminence would henceforth pass unchallenged. But by this time the luckless Jonson was yoked to Shakespeare in an odious tandem from which two centuries of subsequent comment would scarcely suffice to extricate him.

During the eighteenth century Jonson remained much appreciated as a writer for the stage. His chief plays held the theater fairly steadily till about 1785. But during this same period his good name was being poisoned in print by the editors of Shakespeare, who discovered early that a convenient and safe way to praise "their" poet was to abuse Jonson. The well-authenticated tradition of Jonson's conviviality gave way to a fraudulent countermyth: that Jonson, throughout his life, harbored an envenomed dislike of Shakespeare, whom he lost no opportunity of reviling and ridiculing, despite the fact—so ran the tale—that it was Shakespeare to whom he owed his start in the theater.

This insecure edifice of fantasy rested on a few bricks of fact. Jonson had, to be sure, regarded his own kind of drama as superior to Shakespeare's. He had poked fun at the rambling chronicle play, at the meandering romance. He had alluded slightingly to the "servant-monster" in *The Tempest,* and had dismissed *Pericles* as a "mouldy tale." [1] He

---

[1] For "servant-monster" see the Induction to *Bartholomew Fair,* line 127; for *Pericles,* the "Ode to Himself," composed after the failure of *The New Inn,* line 21.

was to pay for these sallies by being charged with conspiratorial malice, and by having his works ransacked for ill-natured allusions. The prologue to *Every Man In His Humour* was read not as a critical manifesto but as a savage diatribe (an "insolent invective") against Shakespeare, wherein every rift was loaded with rancorous ore. It was not enough that Jonson should be satirizing the history plays of York and Lancaster: when he speaks of the popular medley in which an infant is born, grows to manhood, and ends as an oldster, all within the space of a single afternoon, he must needs be sneering at *The Winter's Tale*—Perdita, evidently, being the ancient greybeard in question. The lines on the creaking throne, the nimble quib, the roll'd bullet and tempestuous drum, must in turn be "pointed at" *King Lear* and *The Tempest*. For where else in Elizabethan drama could one find storms and thunder? Jonson being so addicted to this style of virulent allusion, it followed that Morose's despairing wish, in *Epicene,* to attend a play that was nothing but fights at sea, with drum, trumpet, and target, rather than stay married a moment longer to a rasping shrew of a wife—this cry of misery could only be a furious onslaught on *Antony and Cleopatra.* And it must also have been Jonson, with his fever to pillory Shakespeare, who composed the prologue to *Henry VIII,* where the spectator who comes for a bawdy tale or a noise of targets is teasingly warned that he will be disappointed. How did Jonson come to write a prologue to a play by his "enemy"? Critical ingenuity rose triumphantly to the answer: he did so with the collusion of Shakespeare's associates, who smuggled the offensive lines into the play after its author had retired to Stratford-on-Avon and could no longer defend himself. "Jonson, in all probability, maliciously stole an opportunity to throw in his envious and spiteful invective before the representation of his rival's play." [2]

Once a fable of this sort finds proper soil, it sprouts like a weed; it burgeons, and runs wild. The eighteenth century critics—those who were involved—competed with each other in ascribing ignoble motives to Jonson. They charged him not only with parody but with plagiarism, with scurvy attacks on his fellow players, with a want of decency and decorum. They imagined, and gloated over, scenes of discomfiture in

---

[2] Thomas Davies, *Dramatic Miscellanies* (London, 1784), I, 191. The phrase "insolent invective" also comes from Davies (II, 37), as does the expression "pointed at" (II, 35), in connection with the presumed allusions to Shakespeare.

Most of the charges against Jonson rehearsed in this paragraph may be found assembled (and heatedly attacked) in W[illiam] Gifford, ed., *The Works of Ben Jonson* (London, 1816), I, i-ccxci, where the interested reader should look first. See also Octavius G. Gilchrist, *An Examination of the charges maintained by Messrs. Malone, Chalmers, and others, of Ben Jonsons enmity . . . toward Shakespeare* (London, 1808).

In my summary I have made no attempt to reproduce the actual order in which the charges were made, but rather to give an idea of the aimless crisscross of pseudo-reasoning that lies behind most of them.

which he was forced to acknowledge Shakespeare's superiority.[3] Attempting to account for the gifts he received from noble friends—money, books, hospitality—one critic reached a sage diagnosis: blackmail. The noble friends were afraid of being lampooned in Jonson's next satire; they were paying him to keep his mouth shut.[4]

Other writers, less scrupulous, crossed the borderline from misinterpretation into forgery, in order to defame Jonson. A certain Robert Shiells, a Scotsman, in 1753 reprinted Jonson's *Conversations* with Drummond of Hawthornden in an edition of Cibber's *Lives of the Poets*. Evidently judging that Drummond had not expressed himself with sufficient virulence, Shiells silently interpolated into Drummond's reminiscences an apocryphal sentence of his own: "[Jonson] was in his personal character the very reverse of Shakespear, as surly, ill-natured, proud, and disagreeable, as Shakespear with ten times his merit was gentle, good-natured, easy, and amiable." [5] Since, for the next half-century, Drummond's memoir was known only in Shiells's version, all the literate world who cared about the matter could assume that this sentence represented the opinion of one who had known Jonson personally, and well. It became possible for Isaac D'Israeli to say in 1814, apropos of the *Conversations*, that "if I err not in my recollection, I believe that he [Jonson] has not spoken favourably of a single individual!"! [6]

Shiells, however, had already been outdone in inventiveness by the Shakespearean actor Macklin. In *The General Advertiser* for 1748, Macklin published a letter purporting to describe a pamphlet from the reign of Charles I, bearing the quaint title, "Old Ben's Light Heart made Heavy by Young John's Melancholy Lover." The burden of the pamphlet is another elaborate canard about Jonson. Jonson is presented as insatiable in his malice against Shakespeare, hounding him in life, and after death persecuting his disciples, in the present case Ford. "Ben," affirms Macklin, with that familiarity by which the eighteenth century critics strove to convey their contempt,

> Ben was by nature *splenetic and sour;* with a share of envy. . . .
> This raised him many enemies, who towards the close of his life endeavoured to dethrone *this tyrant,* as the pamphlet stiles him, out of the dominion of the theatre. And what greatly contributed to their design, was the *slights* and *malignances* which the *rigid* Ben too frequently threw out against the *lowly* Shakspeare, whose fame since his death, as appears by the

---

[3] For these particular charges see Davies, *Dramatic Miscellanies,* I, 155; II, 51-55, 111-114.
[4] See Gifford, *Works of Jonson,* I, xcii-xciii, citing Chalmers.
[5] Theophilus Cibber, *The Lives of the Poets of Great Britain and Ireland* (London, 1753) , I, 241. See Gifford, *Works of Jonson,* I, xl.
[6] *Quarrels of Authors* (London, 1814), III, 305.

pamphlet, was grown too great for Ben's *envy* either to *bear* with or *wound*. It would greatly exceed the limits of your paper to set down all the *contempts* and *invectives* which were uttered and written by Ben, and are collected and produced in this pamphlet, as unanswerable and shaming evidences to prove his *ill-nature* and *ingratitude* to Shakspeare, who first introduced him to the *theatre and fame.*[7]

And this letter too was destined to be cited and recited by the editors of Shakespeare as crushing proof of Jonson's malevolence, until Malone demonstrated that the pamphlet was a hoax from beginning to end, compounded out of tears and flapdoodle by Macklin in order to puff his own forthcoming revival of a play by Ford. Even so, there were those who could not bring themselves to disbelieve its authenticity. Malone, himself infected with anti-Jonsonism, had exposed it only with apology, and reluctance, knowing that in the eyes of a proper Shakespearean any mitigation of the charge against Jonson was tantamount to an attack on Shakespeare.

What has happened—to transpose the matter into terms which the editors in question would neither have understood nor approved—is that they have come to see in Shakespeare a Christ figure, and in Jonson both the Judas and the mob demanding blood. Jonson's "slights" and "malignances," his "sneers," "contempts," and "invectives," constitute his direct persecution, his scourging and buffeting, of Shakespeare. The Judas kiss is his famous dedicatory epistle to the 1623 Folio, in which he addresses Shakespeare as "beloved master" and exalts him above Sophocles—for had not Dryden himself pronounced these verses "sparing" and "invidious"?[8]

Why the case against Jonson should have been carried to such extremes is not clear. One contributory factor, doubtless, was the tendency for eighteenth century scholars to view Elizabethan literary life unhistorically, in terms of its Augustan counterpart. Mistaking the Globe for Drury Lane, and Paul's Walk for Grubstreet, they credited Jonson, or discredited him, with the waspish behavior they had come to expect of their own contemporaries in the theatrical world.

To the extent to which they articulated their own motives, the critics aimed to deify Shakespeare, to show that in the precise degree to which Jonson was raucous, hostile, and vindictive, Shakespeare was gentle, mild, and forbearing. The hidden analogy with Christ insured that every act of aggression on Jonson's part would redound to Shakespeare's greater glory. But this ostensible purpose, however perverse in itself, concealed, one suspects, a deeper one: the desire to find a suitable victim

[7] *The Plays and Poems of William Shakespeare* [ed. James Boswell] (London, 1821), I, 403.
[8] Alexander Pope, ed., *The Works of Shakespeare* (London, 1725), I, xii. See Gifford, I, cclii.

to maul and mangle. Macklin, as the excerpt from his letter shows, is not really interested in exalting Shakespeare. He is interested in calumniating Jonson, for it is *that* that gratifies him. The elaborate tenderness for Shakespeare that expresses itself by inventing calumnies against Jonson seems, at length, sadistic; it masks precisely the ferocity that is projected onto Jonson. It comes at last to have about it, in however attenuated form, the atmosphere of a witch-hunt, or a lynching-party.

II

Jonson's champion, when he finally arrived, was the redoubtable Gifford, a scholar with a hot temper and a flair for polemics equal to Jonson's. In preparing his edition of Jonson's collected works—the first of its kind to make much pretense to scholarship—Gifford regarded it as a prime duty to cleanse Jonson's memory from the blackening it had received at the hands of the editors of Shakespeare. In a prefatory memoir of Jonson's life, and then more systematically in an essay entitled "Proofs of Ben Jonson's Malignity, from the Commentators on Shakespeare," [9] Gifford reviews the charges against Jonson, one by one, and reduces the bulk of them to absurdity. He could not quite make a clean sweep. Jonson had, beyond a doubt, on a few occasions spoken caustically of Shakespeare. But he could topple the whole rickety structure of Jonson's conspiratorial hatred and send it crashing into Lethe. When James Boswell (the Younger) reissued Malone's Shakespeare in 1821, he prefaced it with a defense of Malone against Gifford. But while vindicating his friend from the imputation of dishonesty, he granted that where Jonson was concerned Malone had been trained in a school of prejudice, and that in this domain, unhappily, the zeal for truth that inspired his researches on Shakespeare flickered more fitfully.[10]

Gifford, in any case, effectively silenced the chorus of detraction against Jonson as a man. He could do nothing, however, to relieve him, as an artist, from the comparison with Shakespeare that by now had become a conditioned reflex, though this too was a topic on which he had expounded with eloquence:

Shakspeare wants no light but his own. As he never has been equalled, and in all human probability never will be equalled, it seems an invidious employ, at best, to speculate minutely on the precise degree to which others fell short of him. Let him with his own Julius Caesar *bestride the narrow world like a colossus;* that is his due; but let not the rest be compelled to *walk under his huge legs, and peep about to find themselves dishonourable graves.*[11]

[9] *Works of Jonson,* I, ccxlix-ccxci.
[10] *Plays and Poems of Shakespeare,* I, xxxi.
[11] *Works of Jonson,* I, ccxii-ccxiii.

But even without Shakespeare, the onset of romanticism was destined to eclipse Jonson. The eighteenth century, while undermining his reputation as a man, had continued to enjoy his plays. With the close of the century and the rise of a new sensibility, Jonson ceased to be a live force in the theater and became a dead author, an anatomy, useful for exposing the errors of the past, but requiring much pickling. The romantic notion of the artist conflicted with the Jonsonian image at every point. The artist as seer, as warbler of native woodnotes wild, as dreamer, as nocturnal wanderer, as sensuous interpreter of the physical world, or decipherer of a mystical one; the artist as beautiful and ineffectual angel, as wind or sensitive plant—none of these roles suited Jonson. Everything that Shelley's skylark or Keats's nightingale was, Jonson was not. By his own choice he remained *perdix*, the partridge, a drab bird, an earth-dweller, fearful of high places and undistinguished as a melodist. His poetic creed stressed such prosy qualities as workmanship, rather than inspiration, judgment rather than lyric excitement. Nineteenth century comment on Jonson harps on his deficient powers of flight and song. Jonson, says Hazlitt, could not soar: "His genius . . . resembles the grub more than the butterfly, plods and grovels on, wants wings to wanton in the idle summer's air, and catch the golden light of poetry." [12] Note that Hazlitt, in describing Jonson's shortcomings, gives a sample of the way Jonson should have written. "Wants wings to wanton in the idle summer's air"—here is the critic showing the poet how. If only Jonson, implies Hazlitt, had been able to say things like *that,* it had been vain to blame and useless to praise him.

The complaint from John Addington Symonds at the other end of the century is similar: Jonson could not sing. True, he possessed learning, energy, persistence, and other estimable traits. But,

Jonson paid the penalty of these extraordinary qualities. It follows from what I have said of his work that he put nothing into his plays which patient criticism may not extract: the wand of the enchanter has not passed over them. There is no music which we hear but shall not capture; no aërial hues that elude description; no "scent of violets hidden in the grass"; no "light that never was on sea or land"; no "casements opening on the foam of perilous seas in faery lands forlorn." These higher gifts of poetry, with which Shakespeare—"nature's child"—was so richly endowed, are almost absolutely wanting in Ben Jonson. [13]

Behind Symonds' criticism, as behind that of A. W. Schlegel, whom he is paraphrasing, [14] lies the notion that poetry exists to capture the in-

[12] *Lectures on the English Comic Writers* (London, 1819), p. 71.
[13] *Ben Jonson,* English Worthies (New York, 1898), p. 61.
[14] See *A Course of Lectures on Dramatic Art and Literature,* trans. John Black, rev. A. J. W. Morrison, Bohn Standard Library (London, 1846), p. 461.

effable, to set snares for the invisible. Jonson, who dealt by preference with everyday realities of the most palpable sort, was by such criteria hardly recognizable as a poet at all.

Jonson as poet was chided for his failure to chant, to soar, to cast spells; Jonson as playwright was reproached with a failure to create life-like and endearing characters. Romanticism, with its interest in individual personality, was beginning to cherish psychological portraiture in the drama. At the same time, while wishing to hear the unique accent of the individual soul, it wished also to hear the still sad music that bound soul to soul. Shakespeare satisfied on both counts, Jonson on neither. Shakespeare's characters possessed some of the mysteriousness of real people; they seemed part of nature rather than literature. One wanted to know where they had come from and what happened to them afterward. And even at their most depraved, even when they most villainously declared their alienation from other men, they managed to express in a dozen ways their common bond with the rest of humanity.

Jonson offered no such satisfactions. His characters—so it was charged —were not individuals, but blueprints of types, or else, on the contrary, they were so frantically individual, so rampantly eccentric, that they ceased to seem human altogether. They were islands that never had and never could form part of the mainland. Moreover they belonged not to life but to literature, and to a labored, unspontaneous sort of literature at that. They did not strike one as "extemporary creations thrown off in the heat of the pen";[15] they seemed "made up" rather than "real." They never prompted one to ask how many children they might have had, or what their childhood might have been like. And far from striking chords of sympathy in readers, they tended to provoke a fascinated repugnance, or a derisive dismissal. They were not, furthermore, the sort of people one wished to live among. Nineteenth century readers thought of themselves, precisely, as living among the characters of fiction. They inquired into their good breeding and their family connections. In Jonson, as Hazlitt witheringly observed, one always finds oneself in low company.[16] Even the least prejudiced critics—Coleridge, Ward, and Swinburne—confessed themselves revolted by the rankness of Jonsonian realism, and dismayed by the absence of "goodness of heart" in his personages, his lack of a "cordial interest" in his own dramatic creations.[17]

It follows that when Jonson was praised, as he sometimes was, he was likely to be praised for odd reasons. Coleridge endorsed *Sejanus* and

---

[15] Isaac D'Israeli, *Amenities of Literature* (Paris, 1842), II, 183.

[16] *English Comic Writers*, p. 75. Hazlitt continues, "His [Jonson's] comedy, in a word, has not what Shakespeare somewhere calls 'bless'd conditions.'" To which one is sorely tempted to retort, "Bless'd fig's-end!"

[17] Coleridge, *Notes and Lectures upon Shakespeare and Some of the Old Poets*, ed. Mrs. H. N. Coleridge (London, 1849), I, 278, 270-271; Adolphus William Ward, *A History of English Dramatic Literature to the Death of Queen Anne* (London, 1875), I, 567-568; Swinburne, *A Study of Ben Jonson* (London, 1889), pp. 60, 29.

Catiline for their usefulness as versified history. Ward reckoned it as
one advantage of the plot of *Poetaster* that it allowed Jonson to parade
his learning. And Swinburne noted approvingly that *Volpone* contained
"a savour of something like romance." [18] To praise Jonson, one had to
turn him into a schoolmaster, or an exhibitionist of learning, or a purveyor of exoticism. Needless to say, none of these rather desperate shifts
afforded a sound basis for appreciation. As long as criticism of the drama
continued to center on character—as long as readers continued to judge
dramatic personages as though they were about to invite them to supper,
insisting that they have good hearts and good table manners—Jonson
was doomed to play satyr to Shakespeare's Hyperion.

In the various ways in which the critics taxed Jonson, they did not so
much say wrong things as inflate right things out of all reasonable proportion. Even the eighteenth century editors, who turned Jonson into
a hobgoblin, started from something real: the intense sense of personality
that radiates from everything he wrote. On this score he forms an authentic contrast to Shakespeare. Shakespeare effaces himself nearly to the
point of anonymity. Jonson always conveys the sense of his own comba-
tive presence. He hectors his audiences, he harangues his readers, he
stands before the recipients of his verse epistles "passionately kind and
angry" [19] as the occasion requires. He forces us, in short, to react to him
as a man. Too many readers have been driven by Jonson's assertiveness
into taking up postures of defense. Postures of defense, however, once
grown habitual, are difficult to distinguish from postures of attack. They
become postures of attack. Hence, no doubt, the tone of personal outrage
in which Jonson's unfriendly critics often discuss him. Hence, also, perhaps, the fact that the partisan of Jonson is likely to breathe a little fire
and brimstone—Gifford, for instance, whose proneness to passionate controversy was notorious.

III

It was easy, in any case, for the post-Romantic generations to draw up
a heavy indictment against Jonson. But the evidence of Jonson's genius
kept rising to confound the indicters, and to demand a reassessment.
T. E. Hulme's now celebrated essay on classicism and romanticism—
probably written by 1914, though not published till well after its author's
death, in 1924—showed the way the critical winds would blow.[20] It reminded the literate community that there was more in books than the

[18] Coleridge, *Notes and Lectures*, I, 282; Ward, *Dramatic Literature*, I, 564; Swinburne,
Ben Jonson, p. 35.
[19] *Conversations with Drummond of Hawthornden*, line 687.
[20] See *Speculations*, 2d ed. (London, 1954), pp. 111-140.

romantics, in their most extravagant reveries, had dreamed of: that such qualities as wit, plainness, and flintiness of texture might legitimately inhabit the house of art. Although Hulme did not speak directly of Jonson, he presaged the moment when Jonson's critics would cease complacently enumerating his defects, and turn to a positive reassessment of his virtues, as others would do for Donne, Marvell, Pope, and Dryden.

Before Hulme's essay was published, another new voice had spoken, that of T. S. Eliot, reviewing, first in *The Times Literary Supplement* and then in *The Athenaeum*, a study of Jonson that rehearsed much the old case against Jonson in much the old tone of voice. Eliot's reviews, later combined into a single essay, constituted a genuine fresh look, the unconstrained responsiveness of an alert intelligence surveying well-travelled ground. The romantics had looked on Jonsonian terrain and seen only a wasteland. Eliot looked again, and found himself in a land of plenty. He started, as a practicing poet might well start, with an inspection of Jonsonian dramatic verse. From the most unpromising play in the Jonson canon, *Catiline*, he disinterred two scenes which he labelled successes. He then proceeded to define as closely as he could the nature of the success, to point out that the vitality of Jonsonian verse lay in "the design of the whole" rather than piecemeal in single lines. With this demonstration Eliot freed Jonson from the tyranny of the "touchstone" method of appreciation, with its exclusive interest in nuggets, its clamor for "memorable" lines. Having done so much, he moved to consider Jonsonian comedy more at large, fishing out one by one the moldiest terms in the critical armory—"humours," "satire," "caricature"—scrubbing them off and returning them clean of outline and distinct of meaning. Though doubtless as much a symptom of the new climate as a cause, Eliot's essay must in any case be accounted the most significant piece of writing on Jonson since the seventeenth century. Together with Eliot's other essays on seventeenth century poets, it disintoxicated a generation of readers still drugged, as Hulme would have said, on romanticism. It renewed their responsiveness to such Jonsonian virtues as craftsmanship and hard comic sense, and it became, as a result, the indispensable starting-point for all subsequent comment on Jonson.

To Eliot's essay must be added another milestone, the collected edition of Jonson's works by C. H. Herford and Percy and Evelyn Simpson. This monument of scholarship, which engrossed the energies of three eminent scholars for nearly a lifetime, provided, for the first time, authoritative texts of all Jonson's known works, and a critical apparatus of staggering fullness and richness. It made Jonson available, and by its very presence it constituted a defense. In his biographical sketch in the opening volume, C. H. Herford presented a Jonson unblurred by bardolatry and undistorted by angry partisanship. His survey of Jonson's creative achievement displays similar virtues: he refuses to parrot clichés about Jonson, but refuses also to be stampeded into unconventional statements for the sake of unconventionality. Unfortunately, nineteenth century presuppositions about drama often impair the relevance of his judgments. At crucial moments he tends to fall back on the inappropriate criterion of psychology as a measure of excellence, or to embark on the mistaken, and misleading, quest for "sympathetic" characters in the jungle of Jonsonian dramatic personages. Herford's virtues and weaknesses may be sampled together in the Introduction to *Every Man Out of His Humour,* reprinted below.

Since Eliot's essay, and thanks to the labors of Herford and Simpson, Jonson criticism has at last commenced to grow green. It cannot yet, however, be said to be wholly flourishing, and one reason lies in the nature of Jonson's appeal, of which Eliot had this to say:

> The immediate appeal of Jonson is to the mind; his emotional tone is not in the single verse, but in the design of the whole. But not many people are capable of discovering for themselves the beauty which is only found after labor; and Jonson's industrious readers have been those whose interest was historical and curious, and those who thought that in discovering the historical and curious interest they had discovered the artistic value as well. When we say that Jonson requires study, we do not mean study of his classical scholarship or of seventeenth century manners. We mean intelligent saturation in his work as a whole. . . .[21]

It must be admitted that Jonson's most industrious readers continue to be largely those whose interest is historical and curious. This is not exclusively true of Jonson, but it is particularly true of him. He remains the special domain of scholars, from whose ranks the critics more strictly speaking emerge. It is chiefly the haunters of libraries and academies who have been able to achieve the intelligent saturation in Jonson's works as a whole that Eliot desiderates, because the rapid changes in language and culture have pushed Jonson out of the reach of readers without special instruction. Jonson criticism, in consequence, often has an antiquarian tinge about it. The critic has arrived at Jonson partly through a preoccupation with history, or language, or "seventeenth century manners." And his most fruitful efforts on Jonson's behalf have often been glossorial. Jonson's plays, of course, are not riddles, and his poems are not Chinese puzzles. He does not, as a rule, stand in need of the sort of explication that can make an impenetrable-looking poem by Donne burst out into sudden blaze. Still, judicious "placing" of Jonsonian drama in its proper contexts, such as that performed in some of the essays below, can cast sudden illumination, and bring out color and high relief in what at first seems merely tame or flat.

Likewise, the quest begun by Eliot, and pursued by younger critics, for structural principles in Jonsonian drama other than the threadbare

[21] *Selected Essays 1917-1932* (New York, 1932), p. 128. See below, p. 15.

and nearly unusable ones of "intrigue" and "character" (understood in their old-fashioned senses), has begun to bear fruit in studies of symbolism, significant allusion, and generic form. Jonson has benefited from the twentieth century rediscovery of form, from the reawakened attention to total structure, which the last century generally neglected. Just as the Romantics and their successors valued the striking line more than the "design of the whole" in a poem, so they valued also the striking scene, the passionate crisis, more than the total design of a play. They favored authors like John Webster, not only because of their occasional sublimities, but because the sublimities so often rose abruptly out of nothing, like architectural ruins in a landscape. The eighteenth century had anthologized the "beauties" of its favorite authors; the romantic critics compiled treasuries of their favorite scenes from Elizabethan drama. But the eighteenth century had also had Dr. Johnson, who reproached Shakespeare for concluding his plots too casually, for dismissing his characters with too little regard for poetic justice. It was to a similar concern for conclusions and cadences that Eliot restored twentieth century criticism when he insisted on the total design, and his followers have returned to Jonson with renewed respect for the "labored art" that impressed Jonson's contemporaries. Jonson, in his own critical pronouncements, stressed decorum—the subordination of details to the whole—and in his works he strove to construct harmonious unities, to make the parts fit, and the end crown all. His plays are, as a result, through-composed to a degree unique among writers of his period. It was by virtue of constructive mastery that Dryden accorded him first place among English comic playwrights, and one of the most rewarding tasks of twentieth century criticism has been to take up where Dryden left off, to discover where, and how, and to what degree, Jonson fulfilled his own prescription for excellence.

In the pages below the reader will hear one discordant note. If Eliot's essay long ago earned pride of place as the classic of appreciation of Jonson, Edmund Wilson's essay, "Morose Ben Jonson," seems likely to raise itself by merit to the bad eminence of the classic of demolition. Eliot hoped to forestall prejudice by signalling to the reader some of the riches of Jonson's dramatic universe. Wilson undertakes to buttress prejudice by making himself, in effect, a spokesman for the prejudiced. He finds new terms for old repugnances by investing them in the intimidating vocabulary of psychoanalysis. He certifies Jonson to us as an anal erotic. More familiarly, more particularly, Jonson was a pedant, a word-hoarder, a niggard; a spiteful, envious person; his characters do not seem real, as Shakespeare's do; he cannot sing of love; his lyric gift is small.

If it is an editor's duty to include a piece as lively and challenging as Wilson's in a collection like the present one, it is also a duty to caution the unwary. Of Wilson's thesis one may say first that it should be taken for what it is, a conscious attempt to set forth Jonson's deficiencies in full glare. It constitutes an anatomy in which healthy tissue is passed over in silence, for the most part, and diseased tissue lingeringly dissected. Much is said about Jonson's peevishness, but nothing that might account for the affection and regard in which he was held, throughout his life, by so many fellow authors and noble patrons.

One may say further of Wilson's ingenious psychograph that it promotes, if it does not perpetrate, a confusion between the artist's emotional problems and his art. For every symptom of maladjustment the patient receives a black mark as an artist. But this is too simple, as who should know better than the author of *The Wound and the Bow*? Just as few authors will survive the comparison with Shakespeare to which Jonson is perpetually being subjected, so few will survive such an inquest into their psychic health. Hang all that offend that way, and one will soon be forced to "give out a commission" for more authors. No doubt, neurotic habits may warp creative activity, transmit themselves cripplingly from the artist to his art. But the emotionally deranged may also enjoy metaphysical intuitions that normal men struggle to conceal from themselves, as Sartre observed of Baudelaire.[22] The fact that "miserliness" and "unsociability" and "a self-sufficient and systematic spite" form the subject of much Jonsonian theater—a highly exaggerated proposition, one may add—tells us little of what most concerns us: how does Jonson deal with his material? As soon as we ask the question we are led to perceive how Jonson wrung poetry from his bizarre themes, how he transmuted them into images of hallucinatory vividness, liberating them from "goodness of heart" and setting them free to perform a sort of *danse macabre*. Jonson gives us naked, unaccommodated greed, the thing itself, yet paradoxically wrapped in the intoxications of poetry, and made funny. What one responds to in his best comedies is the ferocious energy with which his driven characters perform their antics, the outpourings of language in which they express themselves, their ranting, their braying, their mincing, their affected posturing and rhapsodizing. A volcano is erupting, but a volcano kept under strictest control, and if the eruption resembles an anal expulsion, as Wilson claims, that does not alter the fact that genius has intervened, to impose order and measure and pattern on the explosion.

Similarly, to arraign Jonson for failing to investigate the "causes" behind his vixenish wives and impotent husbands, the "reasons" for Morose's aversion to noise, is to call him to account, as the romantic critics did, for something he never professed to offer, and which remains, in his world, irrelevant. Jonson does not, certainly, analyze his characters or psychologize over them. He incarnates, and sets in motion. He shows us, in Morose, not how such a man came to harbor such an obsession, but how, given the fact of the obsession, he behaves in the grip of it,

[22] Jean-Paul Sartre, *Baudelaire* (Paris, 1947), pp. 35-36.

how he teaches his persecutors to persecute him, and how the world may be trusted to react. With different neuroses Jonson would doubtless have written a different play; without neuroses he might perhaps have written a better one. The fact remains that the play he did write is rich, original, and unique. To question Jonson's psychic equilibrium in order to put him in his place as a writer is to revert, *mutatis mutandis,* to the technique of those eighteenth century editors who sounded the charge against his moral character in order to elevate Shakespeare. *Caveat lector.*

Probably no other caveat is needed, except a reminder that much valuable comment on Jonson could not, for various reasons, find a place here. Some of it was too technical or special; some of it too bulky, or resistant to excerption. Nevertheless, the essays below may be said to represent the state of Jonson criticism over the past forty years, both in its excellences and in its defects. If they succeed in leading the reader back to Jonson with a livelier sense of Jonson's qualities, they will have performed their main office; if they succeed in giving pleasure, they will have accomplished another. If they have the luck to stimulate fresh thought and provoke new interpretations, they will have deserved a niche in whatever paradise is reserved as the final resting-place for such volumes as these.

Ben Jonson

by T. S. Eliot

The reputation of Jonson has been of the most deadly kind that can be compelled upon the memory of a great poet. To be universally accepted; to be damned by the praise that quenches all desire to read the book; to be afflicted by the imputation of the virtues which excite the least pleasure; and to be read only by historians and antiquaries—this is the most perfect conspiracy of approval. For some generations the reputation of Jonson has been carried rather as a liability than as an asset in the balance-sheet of English literature. No critic has succeeded in making him appear pleasurable or even interesting. Swinburne's book on Jonson satisfies no curiosity and stimulates no thought. For the critical study in the "Men of Letters Series" by Mr. Gregory Smith there is a place; it satisfies curiosity, it supplies many just observations, it provides valuable matter on the neglected masques; it only fails to remodel the image of Jonson which is settled in our minds. Probably the fault lies with several generations of our poets. It is not that the value of poetry is only its value to living poets for their own work; but appreciation is akin to creation, and true enjoyment of poetry is related to the stirring of suggestion, the stimulus that a poet feels in his enjoyment of other poetry. Jonson has provided no creative stimulus for a very long time; consequently we must look back as far as Dryden—precisely, a poetic practitioner who learned from Jonson—before we find a living criticism of Jonson's work.

Yet there are possibilities for Jonson even now. We have no difficulty in seeing what brought him to this pass; how, in contrast, not with Shakespeare, but with Marlowe, Webster, Donne, Beaumont, and Fletcher, he has been paid out with reputation instead of enjoyment. He is no less a poet than these men, but his poetry is of the surface. Poetry of the surface cannot be understood without study; for to deal with the surface of life, as Jonson dealt with it, is to deal so deliberately that we too must be deliberate, in order to understand. Shakespeare, and smaller men also, are in the end more difficult, but they offer something at the start to encourage the student or to satisfy those who want nothing more; they are suggestive, evocative, a phrase, a voice; they offer poetry in detail as well as in design. So does Dante offer something, a phrase everywhere (*"tu se' ombra ed ombra vedi"*) even to readers who have no Italian; and Dante and Shakespeare have poetry of design as well as of detail. But the polished veneer of Jonson reflects only the lazy reader's fatuity; unconscious does not respond to unconscious; no swarms of inarticulate feelings are aroused. The immediate appeal of Jonson is to the mind; his emotional tone is not in the single verse, but in the design of the whole. But not many people are capable of discovering for themselves the beauty which is only found after labor; and Jonson's industrious readers have been those whose interest was historical and curious, and those who have thought that in discovering the historical and curious interest they had discovered the artistic value as well. When we say that Jonson requires study, we do not mean study of his classical scholarship or of seventeenth century manners. We mean intelligent saturation in his work as a whole; we mean that in order to enjoy him at all, we must get to the center of his work and his temperament, and that we must see him unbiased by time, as a contemporary. And to see him as a contemporary does not so much require the power of putting ourselves into seventeenth century London as it requires the power of setting Jonson in our London.

It is generally conceded that Jonson failed as a tragic dramatist; and it is usually agreed that he failed because his genius was for satiric comedy and because of the weight of pedantic learning with which he burdened his two tragic failures. The second point marks an obvious error of detail; the first is too crude a statement to be accepted; to say that he failed because his genius was unsuited to tragedy is to tell us nothing at all. Jonson did not write a good tragedy, but we can see no reason why he should not have written one. If two plays so different as *The Tempest* and *The Silent Woman* are both comedies, surely the category of tragedy could be made wide enough to include something possible for Jonson to have done. But the classification of tragedy and comedy, while it may be sufficient to mark the distinction in a dramatic literature of more rigid form and treatment—it may distinguish Aristophanes from Euripides—is not adequate to a drama of such variations as the Elizabethans. Tragedy is a crude classification for plays so different in their tone as *Macbeth, The Jew of Malta,* and *The Witch of Edmonton;* and it does not help us much to say that *The Merchant of Venice* and *The Alchemist* are comedies. Jonson had his own scale, his own instrument. The merit which *Catiline* possesses is the same merit that is exhibited more triumphantly in *Volpone; Catiline* fails, not because it is too labored and conscious, but because it is not conscious enough; because Jonson in this play was not alert to his own idiom, not clear in his mind as to what his temperament wanted him to do. In *Catiline* Jonson conforms, or attempts to conform, to conventions; not to the conventions of antiquity, which he had exquisitely under control, but to the conventions of tragico-historical drama of his time. It is not the Latin erudition that sinks *Catiline,* but the application of that erudition to a form which was not the proper vehicle for the mind which had amassed the erudition.

If you look at *Catiline*—that dreary Pyrrhic victory of tragedy—you find two passages to be successful: Act ii, sc. i, the dialogue of the political ladies, and the Prologue of Sylla's ghost. These two passages are genial. The soliloquy of the ghost is a characteristic Jonson success in content and in versification—

> Dost thou not feel me, Rome? not yet! is night
> So heavy on thee, and my weight so light?
> Can Sylla's ghost arise within thy walls,
> Less threatening than an earthquake, the quick falls
> Of thee and thine? Shake not the frighted heads
> Of thy steep towers, or shrink to their first beds?
> Or as their ruin the large Tyber fills,
> Make that swell up, and drown thy seven proud hills? . . .

This is the learned, but also the creative, Jonson. Without concerning himself with the character of Sulla, and in lines of invective, Jonson makes Sylla's ghost, while the words are spoken, a living and terrible force. The words fall with as determined beat as if they were the will of the morose Dictator himself. You may say: merely invective; but mere invective, even if as superior to the clumsy fisticuffs of Marston and Hall as Jonson's verse is superior to theirs, would not create a living figure as Jonson has done in this long tirade. And you may say: rhetoric; but if we are to call it "rhetoric" we must subject that term to a closer dissection than any to which it is accustomed. What Jonson has done here is not merely a fine speech. It is the careful, precise filling in of a strong and simple outline, and at no point does it overflow the outline; it is far more careful and precise in its obedience to this outline than are many of the speeches in *Tamburlaine.* The outline is not Sulla, for Sulla has nothing to do with it, but "Sylla's ghost." The words may not be suitable to an historical Sulla, or to anybody in history, but they are a perfect expression for "Sylla's ghost." You cannot say they are rhetorical "because people do not talk like that," you cannot call them "verbiage"; they do not exhibit prolixity or redundancy or the other vices in the rhetoric books; there is a definite artistic emotion which demands expression at that length. The words themselves are mostly simple words, the syntax is natural, the language austere rather than adorned. Turning then to the induction of *The Poetaster,* we find another success of the same kind—

Light, I salute thee, but with wounded nerves . . .

Men may not talk in that way, but the Spirit of Envy does, and in the words of Jonson envy is a real and living person. It is not human life that informs envy and Sylla's ghost, but it is energy of which human life is only another variety.

Returning to *Catiline*, we find that the best scene in the body of the play is one which cannot be squeezed into a tragic frame, and which appears to belong to satiric comedy. The scene between Fulvia and Galla and Sempronia is a living scene in a wilderness of oratory. And as it recalls other scenes—there is a suggestion of the college of ladies in *The Silent Woman*—it looks like a comedy scene. And it appears to be satire.

> They shall all give and pay well, that come here,
> If they will have it; and that, jewels, pearl,
> Plate, or round sums to buy these. I'm not taken
> With a cob-swan or a high-mounting bull,
> As foolish Leda and Europa were;
> But the bright gold, with Danaë. For such price
> I would endure a rough, harsh Jupiter,
> Or ten such thundering gamesters, and refrain
> To laugh at 'em, till they are gone, with my much suffering.

This scene is no more comedy than it is tragedy, and the "satire" is merely a medium for the essential emotion. Jonson's drama is only incidentally satire, because it is only incidentally a criticism upon the actual world. It is not satire in the way in which the work of Swift or the work of Molière may be called satire: that is, it does not find its source in any precise emotional attitude or precise intellectual criticism of the actual world. It is satire perhaps as the work of Rabelais is satire; certainly not more so. The important thing is that if fiction can be divided into creative fiction and critical fiction, Jonson's is creative. That he was a great critic, our first great critic, does not affect this assertion. Every creator is also a critic; Jonson was a conscious critic, but he was also conscious in his creations. Certainly, one sense in which the term "critical" may be applied to fiction is a sense in which the term might be used of a method antithetical to Jonson's. It is the method of *Education sentimentale*. The characters of Jonson, of Shakespeare, perhaps of all the greatest drama, are drawn in positive and simple outlines. They may be filled in, and by Shakespeare they are filled in, by much detail or many shifting aspects; but a clear and sharp and simple form remains through these—though it would be hard to say in what the clarity and sharpness and simplicity of Hamlet consists. But Frédéric Moreau is not made in that way. He is constructed partly by negative definition, built

up by a great number of observations. We cannot isolate him from the
environment in which we find him; it may be an environment which is
or can be universalized; nevertheless it and the figure in it consist of very
many observed particular facts, the actual world. Without this world the
figure dissolves. The ruling faculty is a critical perception, a commentary
upon experienced feeling and sensation. If this is true of Flaubert, it is
true in a higher degree of Molière than of Jonson. The broad farcical
lines of Molière may seem to be the same drawing as Jonson's. But
Molière—say in Alceste or Monsieur Jourdain—is criticizing the actual;
the reference to the actual world is more direct. And having a more
tenuous reference, the work of Jonson is much less directly satirical.

This leads us to the question of Humours. Largely on the evidence of
the two Humour plays, it is sometimes assumed that Jonson is occupied
with types; typical exaggerations, or exaggerations of type. The Humour
definition, the expressed intention of Jonson, may be satisfactory for
these two plays. *Every Man In His Humour* is the first mature work of
Jonson, and the student of Jonson must study it; but it is not the play
in which Jonson found his genius: it is the last of his plays to read first.
If one reads *Volpone,* and after that re-reads *The Jew of Malta;* then
returns to Jonson and reads *Bartholomew Fair, The Alchemist, Epicene*
and *The Devil Is an Ass,* and finally *Catiline,* it is possible to arrive at
a fair opinion of the poet and the dramatist.

The Humour, even at the beginning, is not a type, as in Marston's
satire, but a simplified and somewhat distorted individual with a typical
mania. In the later work, the Humour definition quite fails to account
for the total effect produced. The characters of Shakespeare are such as
might exist in different circumstances than those in which Shakespeare
sets them. The latter appear to be those which extract from the characters the most intense and interesting realization; but that realization has
not exhausted their possibilities. Volpone's life, on the other hand, is
bounded by the scene in which it is played; in fact, the life is the life of
the scene and is derivatively the life of Volpone; the life of the character
is inseparable from the life of the drama. This is not dependence upon a
background, or upon a substratum of fact. The emotional effect is single
and simple. Whereas in Shakespeare the effect is due to the way in which
the characters *act upon* one another, in Jonson it is given by the way in
which the characters *fit in* with each other. The artistic result of *Volpone*
is not due to any effect that Volpone, Mosca, Corvino, Corbaccio, Voltore have upon each other, but simply to their combination into a whole.
And these figures are not personifications of passions; separately, they
have not even that reality, they are constituents. It is a similar indication
of Jonson's method that you can hardly pick out a line of Jonson's and
say confidently that it is great poetry; but there are many extended passages to which you cannot deny that honor.

> I will have all my beds blown up, not stuft;
> Down is too hard; and then, mine oval room
> Fill'd with such pictures as Tiberius took
> From Elephantis, and dull Aretine
> But coldly imitated. Then, my glasses
> Cut in more subtle angles, to disperse
> And multiply the figures, as I walk. . . .

Jonson is the legitimate heir of Marlowe. The man who wrote, in *Volpone:*

> for thy love,
> In varying figures, I would have contended
> With the blue Proteus, or the hornèd flood. . . .

and

> See, a carbuncle
> May put out both the eyes of our Saint Mark;
> A diamond would have bought Lollia Paulina,
> When she came in like star-light, hid with jewels. . . .

is related to Marlowe as a poet; and if Marlowe is a poet, Jonson is also. And, if Jonson's comedy is a comedy of humours, then Marlowe's tragedy, a large part of it, is a tragedy of humours. But Jonson has too exclusively been considered as the typical representative of a point of view toward comedy. He has suffered from his great reputation as a critic and theorist, from the effects of his intelligence. We have been taught to think of him as the man, the dictator (confusedly in our minds with his later namesake), as the literary politician impressing his views upon a generation; we are offended by the constant reminder of his scholarship. We forget the comedy in the humours, and the serious artist in the scholar. Jonson has suffered in public opinion, as any one must suffer who is forced to talk about his art.

If you examine the first hundred lines or more of *Volpone* the verse appears to be in the manner of Marlowe, more deliberate, more mature, but without Marlowe's inspiration. It looks like mere "rhetoric," certainly not "deeds and language such as men do use." It appears to us, in fact, forced and flagitious bombast. That it is not "rhetoric," or at least not vicious rhetoric, we do not know until we are able to review the whole play. For the consistent maintenance of this manner conveys in the end an effect not of verbosity, but of bold, even shocking and terrifying directness. We have difficulty in saying exactly what produces this simple and single effect. It is not in any ordinary way due to management of

intrigue. Jonson employs immense dramatic constructive skill: it is not
so much skill in plot as skill in doing without a plot. He never manipu-
lates as complicated a plot as that of *The Merchant of Venice;* he has
in his best plays nothing like the intrigue of Restoration comedy. In
Bartholomew Fair it is hardly a plot at all; the marvel of the play is the
bewildering rapid chaotic action of the fair; it is the fair itself, not anything that happens in the fair. In *Volpone,* or *The Alchemist,* or *The
Silent Woman,* the plot is enough to keep the players in motion; it is
rather an "action" than a plot. The plot does not hold the play together;
what holds the play together is a unity of inspiration that radiates into
plot and personages alike.

We have attempted to make more precise the sense in which it was said
that Jonson's work is "of the surface"; carefully avoiding the word "superficial." For there is work contemporary with Jonson's which is superficial in a pejorative sense in which the word cannot be applied to Jonson—the work of Beaumont and Fletcher. If we look at the work of
Jonson's great contemporaries, Shakespeare, and also Donne and Webster
and Tourneur (and sometimes Middleton), they have a depth, a third
dimension, as Mr. Gregory Smith rightly calls it, which Jonson's work
has not. Their words have often a network of tentacular roots reaching
down to the deepest terrors and desires. Jonson's most certainly have not;
but in Beaumont and Fletcher we may think that at times we find it.
Looking closer, we discover that the blossoms of Beaumont and Fletcher's imagination draw no sustenance from the soil, but are cut and
slightly withered flowers stuck into sand.

> Wilt thou, hereafter, when they talk of me,
> As thou shalt hear nothing but infamy,
> Remember some of these things? . . .
> I pray thee, do; for thou shalt never see me so again.

> Hair woven in many a curious warp,
> Able in endless error to enfold
> The wandering soul; . . .

Detached from its context, this looks like the verse of the greater poets;
just as lines of Jonson, detached from their context, look like inflated
or empty fustian. But the evocative quality of the verse of Beaumont and
Fletcher depends upon a clever appeal to emotions and associations
which they have not themselves grasped; it is hollow. It is superficial with
a vacuum behind it; the superficies of Jonson is solid. It is what it is;
it does not pretend to be another thing. But it is so very conscious and
deliberate that we must look with eyes alert to the whole before we
apprehend the significance of any part. We cannot call a man's work
superficial when it is the creation of a world; a man cannot be accused

of dealing superficially with the world which he himself has created; the superficies *is* the world. Jonson's characters conform to the logic of the emotions of their world. They are not fancy, because they have a logic of their own; and this logic illuminates the actual world, because it gives us a new point of view from which to inspect it.

A writer of power and intelligence, Jonson endeavored to promulgate, as a formula and program of reform, what he chose to do himself; and he not unnaturally laid down in abstract theory what is in reality a personal point of view. And it is in the end of no value to discuss Jonson's theory and practice unless we recognize and seize this point of view, which escapes the formulae, and which is what makes his plays worth reading. Jonson behaved as the great creative mind that he was: he created his own world, a world from which his followers, as well as the dramatists who were trying to do something wholly different, are excluded. Remembering this, we turn to Mr. Gregory Smith's objection— that Jonson's characters lack the third dimension, have no life out of the theatrical existence in which they appear—and demand an inquest. The objection implies that the characters are purely the work of intellect, or the result of superficial observation of a world which is faded or mildewed. It implies that the characters are lifeless. But if we dig beneath the theory, beneath the observation, beneath the deliberate drawing and the theatrical and dramatic elaboration, there is discovered a kind of power, animating Volpone, Busy, Fitzdottrel, the literary ladies of *Epicene,* even Bobadill, which comes from below the intellect, and for which no theory of humours will account. And it is the same kind of power which vivifies Trimalchio, and Panurge, and some but not all of the "comic" characters of Dickens. The fictive life of this kind is not to be circumscribed by a reference to "comedy" or to "farce"; it is not exactly the kind of life which informs the characters of Molière or that which informs those of Marivaux—two writers who were, besides, doing something quite different the one from the other. But it is something which distinguishes Barabbas from Shylock, Epicure Mammon from Falstaff, Faustus from—if you will—Macbeth; Marlowe and Jonson from Shakespeare and the Shakespeareans, Webster, and Tourneur. It is not merely Humours: for neither Volpone nor Mosca is a humour. No theory of humours could account for Jonson's best plays or the best characters in them. We want to know at what point the comedy of humours passes into a work of art, and why Jonson is not Brome.

The creation of a work of art, we will say the creation of a character in a drama, consists in the process of transfusion of the personality, or, in a deeper sense, the life, of the author into the character. This is a very different matter from the orthodox creation in one's own image. The ways in which the passions and desires of the creator may be satisfied in the work of art are complex and devious. In a painter they may take the form of a predilection for certain colors, tones, or lightings; in a writer the original impulse may be even more strangely transmuted. Now, we may say with Mr. Gregory Smith that Falstaff or a score of Shakespeare's characters have a "third dimension" that Jonson's have not. This will mean, not that Shakespeare's spring from the feelings or imagination and Jonson's from the intellect or invention; they have equally an emotional source; but that Shakespeare's represent a more complex tissue of feelings and desires, as well as a more supple, a more susceptible temperament. Falstaff is not only the roast Manningtree ox with the pudding in his belly; he also "grows old," and, finally, his nose is as sharp as a pen. He was perhaps the *satisfaction* of more, and of more complicated feelings; and perhaps he was, as the great tragic characters must have been, the offspring of deeper, less apprehensible feelings: deeper, but not necessarily stronger or more intense, than those of Jonson. It is obvious that the spring of the difference is not the difference between feeling and thought, or superior insight, superior perception, on the part of Shakespeare, but his susceptibility to a greater range of emotion, and emotion deeper and more obscure. But his characters are no more "alive" than are the characters of Jonson.

The world they live in is a larger one. But small worlds—the worlds which artists create—do not differ only in magnitude; if they are complete worlds, drawn to scale in every part, they differ in kind also. And Jonson's world has this scale. His type of personality found its relief in something falling under the category of burlesque or farce—though when you are dealing with a *unique* world, like his, these terms fail to appease the desire for definition. It is not, at all events, the farce of Molière: the latter is more analytic, more an intellectual redistribution. It is not defined by the word "satire." Jonson poses as a satirist. But satire like Jonson's is great in the end not by hitting off its object, but by creating it; the satire is merely the means which leads to the aesthetic result, the impulse which projects a new world into a new orbit. In *Every Man In His Humour* there is a neat, a very neat, comedy of humours. In discovering and proclaiming in this play the new genre Jonson was simply recognizing, unconsciously, the route which opened out in the proper direction for his instincts. His characters are and remain, like Marlowe's, simplified characters; but the simplification does not consist in the dominance of a particular humour or monomania. That is a very superficial account of it. The simplification consists largely in reduction of detail, in the seizing of aspects relevant to the relief of an emotional impulse which remains the same for that character, in making the character conform to a particular setting. This stripping is essential to the art, to which is also essential a flat distortion in the drawing; it is an art of caricature, of great caricature, like Marlowe's. It is a great caricature, which is beautiful; and a great humour, which is serious. The "world" of Jonson is sufficiently large; it is a world of poetic imagination; it is somber. He did not get the third dimension, but he was not trying to get it.

If we approach Jonson with less frozen awe of his learning, with a clearer understanding of his "rhetoric" and its applications, if we grasp the fact that the knowledge required of the reader is not archaeology but knowledge of Jonson, we can derive not only instruction in two-dimensional life—but enjoyment. We can even apply him, be aware of him as a part of our literary inheritance craving further expression. Of all the dramatists of his time, Jonson is probably the one whom the present age would find the most sympathetic, if it knew him. There is a brutality, a lack of sentiment, a polished surface, a handling of large bold designs in brilliant colors, which ought to attract about three thousand people in London and elsewhere. At least, if we had a contemporary Shakespeare and a contemporary Jonson, it might be the Jonson who would arouse the enthusiasm of the intelligentsia. Though he is saturated in literature, he never sacrifices the theatrical qualities—theatrical in the most favorable sense—to literature or to the study of character. His work is a titanic show. But Jonson's masques, an important part of his work, are neglected; our flaccid culture lets shows and literature fade, but prefers faded literature to faded shows. There are hundreds of people who have read *Comus* to ten who have read the *Masque of Blackness*. *Comus* contains fine poetry, and poetry exemplifying some merits to which Jonson's masque poetry cannot pretend. Nevertheless, *Comus* is the death of the masque; it is the transition of a form of art—even of a form which existed for but a short generation—into "literature," literature cast in a form which has lost its application. Even though *Comus* was a masque at Ludlow Castle, Jonson had, what Milton came perhaps too late to have, a sense for the living art; his art was applied. The masques can still be read, and with pleasure, by anyone who will take the trouble—a trouble which in this part of Jonson is, indeed, a study of antiquities—to imagine them in action, displayed with the music, costumes, dances, and the scenery of Inigo Jones. They are additional evidence that Jonson had a fine sense of form, of the purpose for which a particular form is intended; evidence that he was a literary artist even more than he was a man of letters.

Tradition and Ben Jonson

by L. C. Knights

I hate traditions;
I do not trust them.
Ananias

Recent revivals of *Volpone* and *The Alchemist* occasioned some surprise—surprise that they were such good "theater." The general impression seems to have been that in these plays Jonson had, somehow, tri-
umphed over his "weight of classical learning," had in fact forgotten it,
and had provided some very good fun instead of his usual pedantries.
It may not be quite fair to the dramatic critics to suggest that their delight at being entertained instead of bored showed how little Jonson is
read, but certainly the reception given to those plays implied a still widespread misconception both of Jonson's intrinsic merits and of the extent
and kind of his indebtedness to the Classics.

Ben Jonson is a very great poet—more finely endowed, I think, than
any who succeeded him in the seventeenth century—and he read deliberately and widely. It was to be expected, therefore, that the effects
of his reading would be in some manner present in his verse. Dryden said
of him that he was a learned plagiary of all the ancients: "you track
him everywhere in their snow." But this, the common view, violently
distorts the sense in which Jonson is "traditional"; it not only makes
him appear to owe to the Greek and Latin writers a mere accumulation
of thoughts and phrases, it completely hides the native springs of his
vitality. The aim of this chapter is to correct the perspective, to show
that Jonson's art is intimately related to the popular tradition of individual and social morality.

A study such as this lies largely outside the field of strict literary criticism; but without a background of criticism to refer to it is impossible
to say anything at all, and I propose to begin (without more apology for
the indirect approach) by selecting one play and merely trying to explain
why I find it admirable.

"Tradition and Ben Jonson." From *Drama and Society in the Age of Jonson* by L. C.
Knights. Copyright 1937 by L. C. Knights. Reprinted by permission of Chatto and
Windus, Ltd, and Barnes & Noble, Inc.

Sejanus is chosen not only because it is commonly underrated, but because it is the first play in which Jonson finds his proper scope: the early "Humour" plays were mere experiments. Although here the typically Jonsonian method is deployed with less subtlety and richness than in, say, *Volpone,* the parallels between this "tragedy" and the later "comedies" are obvious and important.

The stuff of the play is the lust of political power and the pettiness that so often accompanies political greatness. The world with which we are presented is completely evil. Tiberius and Sejanus are equal in cruelty and cunning; Macro, the agent of Sejanus' overthrow, is, like others besides the principals, explicitly "Machiavellian"; the satellites and senators are servile and inconstant; the mob tears the body of the fallen favorite,

> And not a beast of all the herd demands
> What was his crime, or who were his accusers.[1]

The "good" characters are choric and denunciatory merely, representing no positive values. How carefully anything that might bring into play sympathetic feelings is excluded is seen in the treatment of Agrippina; the meeting of her adherents, for example, is described (II, ii) in terms that reduce it to a gathering of fractious gossips. And this exclusion operates in the smallest details—in Tiberius' remark about dedicating

> A pair of temples, one to Jupiter
> At Capua; th'other at Nola to Augustus,[2]

or in Sejanus' contempt for "all the throng that fill th' Olympian hall." [3]

But in drama substance and criticism of that substance are inseparable, and the world of *Sejanus* exists only in the light of a particular vision. The most obvious device for determining the angle of presentation is found in the vein of farce that runs throughout: there is a violent juxtaposition of contrasts. After the heroics of Sejanus' "love-making" Livia turns to her physician:

> How do I look to-day?
> *Eudemus.* Excellent clear, believe it. This same fucus
> Was well laid on.
> *Livia.*   Methinks 'tis here not white.
> *Eudemus.* Lend me your scarlet lady. 'Tis the sun
> Hath giv'n some little taint unto the ceruse. . . .
>
>   *(Paints her cheek.)*[4]

[1] V, x (III, 147) (the references in parentheses are to the volume and page of the Gifford-Cunningham edition of Jonson's *Works,* 1875).
[2] III, iii (III, 86).   [3] V, i (III, 113).
[4] II, i (III, 41).

Here, and in the other scenes of stylized farce (for instance, V, iii, or V, vii, where the secret is passed round) there are obvious theatrical possibilities. Perhaps the most effective scene would be the last, where the senators first cluster round Sejanus—indicating by their verbal *feu de joie* the kind of stylization demanded—then edge away as the drift of Tiberius' riddling letter becomes clear, leaving only Haterius, kept "most miserably constant" by his gout. But the whole of the last act, with its controlled confusion leading swiftly to an exciting climax, would act well; and for more subtle dramatic play we can turn to the scene (III, ii) where Tiberius and Sejanus maneuver against each other under cover of friendship; the variations gain from the surface rigidity of the characters.

The essential Jonsonian mode, however, is determined by something more fundamental than the separable elements of farce: it is determined by the verse—a dramatic medium in which exaggeration is controlled by a pervasively implicit sardonic mood. The exuberance of "Swell, swell, my joys . . ." (V, i) is followed by

> . . . 'Tis air I tread;
> And at each step I feel my advanced head
> Knock out a star in heaven.

It is "knock out"—the slight twist given to *"sublimi feriam sidera vertice"*—that finally determines our attitude. But a longer quotation is in place here. In Act II, scene ii, Sejanus addresses Drusus in soliloquy:

> Thy follies now shall taste what kind of man
> They have provoked, and this thy father's house
> Crack in the flame of my incensed rage,
> Whose fury shall admit no shame or mean.—
> Adultery! it is the lightest ill
> I will commit. A race of wicked acts
> Shall flow out of my anger, and o'erspread
> The world's wide face, which no posterity
> Shall e'er approve, nor yet keep silent: things
> That for their cunning, close, and cruel mark,
> Thy father would wish his: and shall, perhaps,
> Carry the empty name, but we the prize.
> On then, my soul, and start not in thy course;
> Though heaven drop sulphur, and hell belch out fire,
> Laugh at the idle terrors: tell proud Jove,
> Between his power and thine there is no odds:
> 'Twas only fear first in the world made gods.

In the sentiments, and in the vigorous development of a single dominant impulse, there is an obvious resemblance to *Tamburlaine*. But the attitude of sophisticated detachment toward the words, present in those words, suggests what Jonson had learned from *The Jew of Malta* (a relationship first stated in *The Sacred Wood*): with that play in mind we are not likely to accept Coleridge's verdict of "absurd rant and ventriloquism"—or not as he intended it. It is equally obvious that the speech is not by Marlowe, that in its combination of weight and vigor it looks forward to the finer poetry of *Volpone* and *The Alchemist*.

The means by which Jonson achieves that combination are here immediately apparent. The alliteration not only adds to the general critical-exaggerative effect, it secures the maximum of direct attention for each word:

> Sleep,
> Voluptuous Caesar, and security
> Seize on thy stupid powers.

More generally, we may say that whereas the auditory qualities of Shakespeare's verse arouse a vibrating responsiveness, help to create a fluid medium in which there is the subtlest interplay, the corresponding qualities in Jonson cause the words to separate rather than to coalesce. ("Separate," of course, is only a way of laying the stress.) Everything is said deliberately—though there is no monotony in the varying rhythm—and, following Jonson's own precepts for "a strict and succinct style," [5] with the greatest economy. The economy of course is not Shakespeare's. There are no overlaying meanings or shifts of construction; the words gain their effect by their solidity, weight, and unambiguous directness of expression. How poetically effective that weighted style can be is demonstrated again and again in the present play.

> There be two,
> Know more than honest counsels; whose close breasts,
> Were thy ripp'd up to light, it would be found
> A poor and idle sin, to which their trunks
> Had not been made fit organs. These can lie,
> Flatter, and swear, forswear, deprave, inform,
> Smile, and betray; make guilty men; then beg
> The forfeit lives, to get their livings; cut
> Men's throats with whisperings. . . .[6]

Jonson's metaphors and similes tend to fall into one of three classes. Many, perhaps the majority, are straight-forwardly descriptive. ("Metaphors far-fet," he said, "hinder to be understood.")

---

[5] *Discoveries,* cxxix.　　　　[6] I, i (III, 14).

> The way to put
> A prince in blood, is to present the shapes
> Of dangers greater than they are, like late
> Or early shadows.
>
> Did those fond words
> Fly swifter from thy lips, than this my brain,
> This sparkling forge, created me an armour
> T'encounter chance and thee? [7]

A second class is formed by those metaphors that, like the "race of wicked acts . . ." in Sejanus' soliloquy, heighten the effect of caricature. But Jonson's most striking figures are magnificently derogatory.

> Gods! how the sponges open and take in,
> And shut again! look, look! is not he blest
> That gets a seat in eye-reach of him? more
> That comes in ear, or tongue-reach? O but most
> Can claw his subtile elbow, or with a buz
> Fly-blow his ears?

Jonson's triumph, we have been told, is a triumph of consistency, and the habit of mind behind this last quotation provides the dominant tone of the play. I have already commented on the exclusion of irrelevant moods and associations, and there only remains to notice the characteristic linking together of words that usually invite sympathy or admiration with those demanding an exactly contrary response.

> Like, as both
> *Their bulks and souls* were bound on Fortune's wheel. . . .
>
> He . . . gives Caesar leave
> To hide his *ulcerous and anointed* face. . . .[8]

One does not need to look up the various suggestions of weight and clumsiness under "cob" in the Oxford Dictionary to feel the effect of "a cob-swan, or a high mounting bull" in the most famous speech from *Catiline*.

It should be plain by now that the appreciation of Jonson starts from

[7] This second image is bright and clear, but its surface quality is emphasized if we put beside it the line from *Henry V*,

> In the quick forge and working-house of thought,

where the rhythm, the double meaning of "quick" and the fused impression of swift movement and ordered labor evoke a far more complex activity of the mind.

[8] That the corresponding phrase in Tacitus is *"Facies ulcerosa ac plerumque medicaminibus interstincta,"* is, I think, irrelevant.

the appreciation of his verse: it could start from nothing else; but it does not seem to be realized how clogging are the discussions of "humours" which, in histories of English literature, fill up the pages on Jonson. His plays have the tightness and coherence of a firmly realized purpose, active in every detail, and a commentary on Jonson's technical achievements—the weight and vigor of his verse, the intensive scrutiny that it invites—is only one way of indicating his essential qualities.

Sejanus, like the other greater plays, is the product of a unique vision; but in stressing the uniqueness one has to avoid any suggestion of the idiosyncratic. It is not merely that the matter on which the poet works is provided by the passions, lusts, and impulses of the actual world, the firmly defined individual spirit which molds that matter springs from a rich traditional wisdom; it relies, that is to say, on something outside itself, and presupposes an active relationship with a particular audience.

The point can be made by examining a passage that is commonly recognized as "great poetry."

> See, behold,
> What thou art queen of; not in expectation,
> As I feed others: but possess'd and crown'd.
> See, here, a rope of pearl: and each more orient
> Than that the brave Ægyptian queen caroused:
> Dissolve and drink them. See, a carbuncle,
> May put out both the eyes of our St. Mark;
> A diamond, would have bought Lollia Paulina,
> When she came in like star-light, hid with jewels,
> That were the spoils of provinces; take these,
> And wear, and lose them: yet remains an ear-ring
> To purchase them again, and this whole state.
> A gem but worth a private patrimony,
> Is nothing: we will eat such a meal.
> The head of parrots, tongues of nightingales,
> The brains of peacocks, and of estriches,
> Shall be our food: and, could we get the phœnix,
> Though nature lost her kind, she were our dish.[9]

Mr. Palmer, supporting a general thesis that Jonson "wrote for a generation which had still an unbounded confidence in the senses and faculties of man. England had not yet accepted the great negation . . . ," remarks: "In the figure of Volpone Jonson presents the splendors of his theme. Was ever woman so magnificently wooed as the wife of Corvino?"[10] This is to miss the point completely. The poetic force of Vol-

---

[9] *Volpone,* III, vi (III, 249).   [10] *Ben Jonson,* pp. x and 175.

pone's wooing has two sources. There is indeed an exuberant description
of luxury—"Temptations are heaped upon temptations with a rapidity
which almost outstrips the imagination"—and the excited movement
seems to invite acceptance. But at the same time, without cancelling out
the exuberance, the luxury is "placed." We have only to compare passages
(from the early Keats, for example) in which the imagined gratification
of sight, taste, and touch is intended as an indulgence merely, to see how
this placing is achieved. It is not merely that the lines quoted have a
context of other swelling speeches (compare *Sejanus*), so that by the time
we reach them the mode is established, the exaggeration, which reaches a
climax at "phœnix," is itself sufficient to suggest some qualification of
Mr. Palmer's "splendors." The verse demands the usual scrupulous inspection of each word—we are not allowed to lapse into an impression of
generalized magnificence—and the splendors, in "caroused," "spoils of
provinces," "private patrimony," are presented clearly enough as waste.
"Though nature lost her kind," at least, implies a moral judgment; and
the references to Lollia Paulina and Heliogabalus (Gifford quotes
"Comedit linguas pavonum et lusciniarum"), which would not be un-
familiar to an Elizabethan audience, are significant.

The manner of presentation (relying on a response which later criticism
shows is neither obvious nor easy) suggests that the double aspect of the
thing presented corresponds to a double attitude in the audience: a
naïve delight in splendor is present *at the same time as* a clear-sighted
recognition of its insignificance judged by fundamental human, or divine,
standards. The strength of this attitude is realized if we compare it with
a puritanic disapproval of "the world" on the one hand, or a sensuous
abandonment on the other. It is the possession of this attitude that
makes Jonson "classical," not his Greek and Latin erudition. His classicism is an equanimity and assurance that springs—"here at home" [11]
—from the strength of a native tradition.

For Jonson's knowledge, and use, of the native literary tradition there
is, I believe, evidence of the usually accepted kind. One could consider
his references (explicit and otherwise) to earlier poets and prose-writers
from Chaucer onwards; his avowed interest in the *Vetus Comoedia;*[12]
the obvious "morality" influence in such plays as *The Devil Is an Ass*
and *The Magnetic Lady;*[13] the popular source of the jog-trot rhythms

[11]   And make my strengths, such as they are,
                            Here in my bosom, and at home.
                                  (*A Farewell to the World*)
[12] English, not Roman. See *Conversations*, 16.
[13] An influence that was active in other playwrights. It is some time since Sir Arthur
Quiller-Couch suggested that *Henry IV* was Shakespeare's rehandling of a morality play
("*Contentio inter Virtutem et Vitium de Anima Principis*"). The subject generally is
of more than academic interest; those who are interested can consider such different
plays as *Troilus and Cressida* (Pandarus is demonstrably "the Pander"), *Old Fortunatus*,
Michaelmas Term, or any of Middleton's comedies.

used for Nano, Androgyno, and the Vice, Iniquity. But when we are
dealing with a living tradition such terms are hopelessly inadequate, and
exploration can be more profitably directed, in the manner suggested by
the analysis above, toward Jonson's handling of his main themes, lust
and the desire for wealth and their accompanying vanities.

In *The Devil Is an Ass* the satire is more than usually direct. But the
play provides more than a succession of satiric comments on the first
period of intensive capitalistic activity in England; it formulates an
attitude toward acquisition. The word "formulates" is used advisedly.
The outlook is a particular one, is Jonson's own; but it is clear that the
satire presupposes certain general attitudes in the audience, and that it
builds on something that was already there. Fitzdottrel, immersed in his
schemes for making money, believes that he has surprised his wife making
love with Wittipol, and (II, iii) reproaches her:

> O bird,
> Could you do this? 'gainst me! and at this time now!
> When I was so employ'd, wholly for you,
> Drown'd in my care (more than the land, I swear,
> I have hope to win) to make you peerless, studying
> For footmen for you, fine-pace huishers, pages,
> To serve you on the knee. . . .
> You've almost turn'd my good affection to you;
> Sour'd my sweet thoughts, all my pure purposes.. . . .

Fitzdottrel is an ass and it is quite unnecessary to say that there is not a
hint of pathos, though it is easy to imagine the temptations of a nineteenth century novelist in such a scene. (Compare the exaggerated significance that is given to Mrs. Dombey's jewels—"She flung it down and
trod upon the glittering heap," etc.) The point is that Jonson evidently
relies upon his audience's immediately despising those "pure purposes";
what these are—the way in which the money acquired would be employed—is magnificently brought out in the Tailbush-Eitherside scene
(IV, i: "See how the world its veterans rewards . . ."). It is, of course, the
tone and manner of presentation that is commented on here. As one
learns to expect, that tone is consistent throughout and one has to be alive
to its implications even in the smallest particulars. The "Spanish lady" is

> such a mistress of behaviour,
> She knows from the duke's daughter to the doxy,
> What is their due just, and no more.

Here the scornful alliteration acts as a leveller (we have seen something
similar in *Sejanus*): Jonson, that is, takes his stand on a scheme that

shows duke's daughter and doxy in proper perspective. It was not merely
that Jonson as an individual "never esteemed of a man for the name of
a Lord";[14] his values were a part of the national life. We have only to
turn up Bunyan's account of By-End's ancestry and connections: "My
wife . . . came of a very honourable family, and is arrived to such a
pitch of breeding, that she knows how to carry it to all, even to prince
and peasant." The tone and method are identical.[15]

In *The Devil Is an Ass,* in *Volpone* and *The Alchemist* Jonson is
drawing on the anti-acquisitive tradition inherited from the Middle
Ages. But this account is too narrow; the tradition included more than
a mere distrust of, or hostility toward, riches. Understanding is, perhaps,
best reached by studying (with Volpone in mind) the speeches of Sir
Epicure Mammon. Each of them, it seems to me, implicitly refers to a
traditional conception of "the Mean." Mammon, wooing Doll, describes
their teeming pleasures:

> and with these
> Delicate meats set our selves high for pleasure,
> And take us down again, and then renew
> Our youth and strength with drinking the elixir,
> And so enjoy a perpetuity
> Of life and lust! And thou shalt have thy wardrobe
> Richer than nature's, still to change thy self.
> And vary oftener, for thy pride, than she.[16]

The reference to "nature," which gives the proper angle on "a perpetuity
of life and lust," is important. The accepted standard is "natural," and
although exact definition would not be easy we may notice the part
played by that standard throughout Jonson's work. An instance from
Volpone has been quoted. Mammon's folly is that he expects Subtle to

> teach dull nature
> What her own forces are.[17]

Similarly in the masque, *Mercury Vindicated,* the alchemists "pretend
. . . to commit miracles in art and treason against nature . . . a matter
of immortality is nothing"; they "profess to outwork the sun in virtue,

---

[14] *Conversations,* 14. I know that Jonson was capable of writing fulsome dedications:
but before we make much of that charge we need to inquire, in each instance, the
grounds of his praises. Many of the Elizabethan aristocracy had a decent sense of responsibility, literary and other.

[15] Dr. G. R. Owst's *Literature and Pulpit in Medieval England* (pp. 97-109) gives an
admirable account of the long popular and religious tradition behind Bunyan, reinforcing the conclusions that one would draw from reading *The Pilgrim's Progress* itself.

[16] *The Alchemist,* IV, i (IV, 120).   [17] *Ibid.* (IV, 116).

and contend to the great act of generation, nay almost creation." [18] The obviously expected response is similar to that given to the description of Mammon's jewels whose light shall "strike out the stars." Who wants to strike out the stars, anyway?

The Staple of News, that odd combination of morality play and topical revue, is generally spoken of as a "dotage"; but, apart from the admirably comic Staple scenes, it contains passages of unusual power, and all of these, we notice, are informed by the same attitude. In a speech of Pennyboy Senior's the anti-acquisitive theme (the play is mainly directed against the abuse of "the Venus of our time and state, Pecunia") is explicitly related to the conception of a natural mean:

> Who can endure to see
> The fury of men's gullets, and their groins?
> . . . What need hath nature
> Of silver dishes, or gold chamber-pots?
> Of perfumed napkins, or a numerous family
> To see her eat? poor, and wise, she requires
> Meat only; hunger is not ambitious:
> Say, that you were the emperor of pleasures,
> The great dictator of fashions, for all Europe,
> And had the pomp of all the courts, and kingdoms,
> Laid forth unto the shew, to make yourself
> Gazed and admired at; you must go to bed,
> And take your natural rest: then all this vanisheth.
> Your bravery was but shown: 'twas not possest:
> While it did boast itself, it was then perishing.[19]

We have seen something of the background that all these passages imply. That a sense of the mean, an acceptance of natural limitations, was a part of the inheritance of Jonson and his contemporaries, can be demonstrated from medieval and sixteenth century sermons and the writings of moralists. But it was not something imposed from above; it sprang from the wisdom of the common people, and it was only indirectly that it found its way into writing.[20] The anti-acquisitive attitude had been more explicitly formulated. It was not only a part of the life of the small local communities of the Middle Ages, it was the basis of the Canon Law on such subjects as usury. And although the age of

[18] (VII, 236-238). [19] *The Staple of News,* III, ii (V, 244).

[20] An essay by John Speirs on "The Scottish Ballads" (*Scrutiny,* June 1935) is relevant here. There it is remarked, for example, that in the Ballads, "The images of finery . . . possess a symbolic value as profound as in Bunyan ('. . . he that is clad in Silk and Velvet'). That finery is associated with folly, pride and death. It is Vanity."—The relation between popular thought and medieval sermon literature is brought out by Dr. Owst.

Jonson was also the age of Sir Giles Mompesson and Sir Arthur Ingram it was still, we remember, a commonplace, accepted by the worldly Bacon, that "The ways to enrich are many, and most of them foul." [21]

In a well-known passage in *Discoveries* Jonson speaks of following the ancients "as guides, not commanders": "For to all the observations of the ancients, we have our own experience; which, if we will use, and apply, we have better means to pronounce." [22] That this was not a mere assertion of independence (or a mere translation—see M. Castelain's learned edition) is shown by every page on which he seems to draw most directly on the classics. Wherever the editors suggest parallels with Horace or Catullus, Tacitus or Suetonius, the re-creation is as complete as in—to take a modern instance—Mr. Pound's *Propertius,* so complete as to make the hunt for "sources" irrelevant. When Fitzdottrel is gloating over the prospect of obtaining an estate on which his descendants shall keep his name alive, Merecraft, characteristically speaking "out of character," reminds him of the revolution of the times:

> *Fitzdottrel.*   'Tis true.
> *DROWN'D LANDS* will live in drown'd land.
> *Merecraft.*   Yes, when you
> Have no foot left; as that must be, sir, one day.
> And though it tarry in your heirs some forty,
> Fifty descents, the longer liver at last, yet,
> Must thrust them out on't, if no quirk in law
> Or odd vice of their own not do it first.
> We see those changes daily: the fair lands
> That were the client's, are the lawyer's now;
> And those rich manors there of goodman Taylor's,
> Had once more wood upon them, than the yard
> By which they were measured out for the last purchase.
> Nature hath these vicissitudes. She makes
> No man a state of perpetuity, sir.[23]

Here is the passage in Horace (*Satires,* II, 2) that the speech "derives" from:

> *nam propriae telluris erum natura neque illum*
> *nec me nec quemquam statuit: nos expulit ille,*
> *illum aut nequities aut vafri inscitia iuris,*
> *postremo expellet certe vivacior heres.*

[21] *Essays,* "Of Riches."
[22] *Discoveries,* xxi, *Non nimium credendum antiquitati.*
[23] *The Devil Is an Ass,* II, i (V, 58).

Even in the lines that come nearest to translation there is a complete transmutation of idiom: *"nequities"* has become "some odd vice," and "ignorance of the subtle law," the sardonically familiar "quirk in law." But as Horace is left behind the presence of everyday life is felt even more immediately, in "daily," "those rich manors there," and "goodman Taylor's," followed as these are by a kind of country wit about the yardstick. The strength of the passage—it is representative—lies in the interested but critical inspection of a familiar world.

In pointing to the idiom we are of course noticing very much more than "local color"; we are noticing ways of thought and perception. Jonson's idiom—his vocabulary, turns of phrase and general linguistic habits—might form a study in itself. It was Coleridge who spoke of "his sterling English diction" [24]—which seems a sufficient rejoinder to the description, "ponderous Latinism," applied by a recent anthologist of the seventeenth century. It is easy, as Gifford pointed out, to exaggerate the extent of Jonson's latinized formations when we forget the similar experimenting of his contemporaries. (And it was not Jonson who tried to introduce "lubrical," "magnificate," "ventosity," and the rest.) But whereas these have had too much attention, a more striking characteristic had had none. Important as Jonson was as a formative influence on the Augustan age, his English is not "polite"; it is, very largely, the popular English of an agricultural country. It is not merely a matter of vocabulary—"ging" (gang), "threaves," "ding it open": one could go on collecting—his inventive habits are of a kind that can still be paralleled in country life. There is the delighted recognition of those elements of caricature that man or nature supplies ready made: "It is now such a time . . . that every man stands under the eaves of his own hat, and sings what pleases him." [25] There are those derisive compounds: "Honest, plain, livery-three-pound-thrum." There is a predilection for alliterative jingles:

> You shall be soaked, and stroked, and tubb'd and rubb'd,
> And scrubb'd, and fubb'd, dear don.

And if this kind of clowning is thought unworthy of serious criticism we can point to the easy alliterative run of "the tip, top, and tuft of all our family," or half the speeches quoted from *Sejanus.* But even the pleasantries reveal a natural bent, and the boisterous coining of nicknames—"His great Verdugoship"—was more than a rustic habit; "old Smug of Lemnos," "Bombast of Hohenhein" (Vulcan and Paracelsus) indicate an attitude, similar to Nashe's,[26] of familiar disrespect toward textbook

---

[24] *Lectures on Shakespeare* (Bohn edition), p. 397.

[25] *Pleasure Reconciled to Virtue* (VII, 300).

[26] "The gods and goddesses all on a row, bread and crow, from Ops to Pomona, the first applewife, were so dumpt with this miserable wrack . . ." (*Nashe's Lenten Stuff*).

worthies. And the amazing fertility that reveals itself now in a popular
fluency

> —our Doll, our castle, our cinque port,
> Our Dover pier—

now in Volpone's mountebank oration, now in Mammon's description of
luxury, is an index of a native vigor that we recognize as "typically
Elizabethan." The more we study Jonson in minute detail the more
clearly he appears both intensely individual and—the paradox is justifiable—at one with his contemporaries.

The speech last quoted from *The Devil Is an Ass* has a further significance; it represents an outlook that is present even in such pure
entertainment as *The Silent Woman* (see Truewit on Time in I, i), and
that combines easily with hilarious comedy, as in Volpone's ludicrously
inadequate modesty:

> *Mosca.* That, and thousands more,
> I hope to see you lord of.
> *Volpone.* Thanks, kind Mosca.
> *Mosca.* And that, when I am lost in blended dust,
> And hundred such as I am in succession—
> *Volpone.* Nay, that were too much, Mosca.[27]

Merecraft's speech, that is, forms part of the permanent somber background of which we are made aware in all of Jonson's comedies. But the
insistence on mortality has the very opposite effect of the introduction
of a death's head at a feast; it is not for the sake of a gratuitous thrill.

> Nature hath these vicissitudes. She makes
> No man a state of perpetuity, sir.

It is the tone—the quiet recognition of the inevitable—that is important;
and the clearly apprehended sense of mutability heightens, rather than
detracts from, the prevailing zest.

It is here, I think, that a genuine "classical influence," or at least the
influence of Horace, can be traced.

> *iam Cytherea choros ducit Venus imminente luna,*
> *junctaeque Nymphis Gratiae decentes*
> *alterno terram quatiunt pede . . .*

[27] *Volpone,* I, i (III, 178).

> *pallida Mors aequo pulsat pede pauperum tabernas*
> *regumque turris.*[28]

The potency of the evocation of the nymphs' flying feet is not lessened because they are also the feet of Time. But even here it is plain that the Jonsonian attitude is not acquired but inherited. There is no need to stress the medieval and sixteenth century insistence on wormy circumstance (a good deal of it was pathological), but we need to keep in mind the way in which, in the popular literature of those periods, death and life are vividly juxtaposed.

And the ability to see life under two opposed aspects simultaneously was part of the natural equipment of the poets of the seventeenth century before the Restoration. It is expressed in Marvell, in the recognition of conflicting claims in the "Horatian Ode," in the concluding lines of the "Coy Mistress":

> And tear our pleasures with rough strife
> Through the Iron gates of Life.

The aspects of experience represented by "the Iron gates" would hardly be present in a nineteenth century "love poem," or, if present, would have a totally different intention and effect. It was in connection with Marvell, we remember, that Mr. Eliot defined Wit: "It involves a recognition, implicit in the expression of every experience, of other kinds of experience which are possible." [29] Jonson had not a metaphysic wit and he was not Donne, but it is a similar recognition, implicit or explicit, of the whole range of human life, that explains his tough equilibrium.

How little a mere classicizing can produce that equilibrium a final comparison may show. When Jonson's verse seems to catch an Horatian inflection it is not because he has assumed it:

> *dum loquimur, fugerit invida*
> *aetas*[30]

becomes, quite naturally,

> think,
> All beauty doth not last until the autumn:
> You grow old while I tell you this.[31]

On the other hand there is Landor:

[28] *Odes,* I, iv.   [30] *Odes,* I, xi.
[29] *Selected Essays,* p. 289.   [31] *The Devil Is an Ass,* I, iii (V, 31).

> occidit et Pelopis genitor, conviva deorum,
> Tithonusque remotus in auras. . . .
> . . . sed omnis una manet nox
> et calcanda semel via leti.[32]

Laodameia died; Helen died; Leda, the beloved of Jupiter went before.
. . . There is no name, with whatever emphasis of passionate love repeated,
of which the echo is not faint at last.[33]

In this affected mimicry the Horatian tone *("durum: sed levius fit patientia")*, all, in fact, that gives value to the recognition of a common night, has completely evaporated, and we are left with as orotund a piece of self-indulgence as ever found its way into anthologies. Jonson's tone is that of a man who has seen many civilizations, and is at home in one.

I have tried to show that, in Jonson's audience, we may postulate a lively sense of human limitations. When Mammon declared of the elixir that, taken by an old man, it will

> Restore his years, renew him, like an eagle,
> To the fifth age; make him get sons and daughters,
> Young giants; as our philosophers have done,
> The ancient patriarchs, afore the flood,
> But taking, once a week, on a knife's point,
> The quantity of a grain of mustard of it,

they had a right to laugh as our modern seekers after youth have not.[34] But it was not a sense that incapacitated from living in the present. One does not need to search for illustration of Jonson's lively interest in every aspect of his environment. Merecraft's speech comes from a play which, as we shall see, forms the most striking indictment of the newer forms of economic parasitism. It would be good to see *The Devil Is an Ass* acted; it would be good to see *Sejanus*—which has a contemporary relevance not merely because it is a study of tyranny ("We shall be marked anon, for our not Hail" [35]), but it would be better if one could feel assured that they were widely read. Jonson's permanent importance is beyond question, but the discipline that a thorough assimilation of his

---

[32] Horace, *Odes*, I, xxviii.

[33] *Imaginary Conversations*, "Aesop and Rhodope."

[34] *The Alchemist*, II, i (IV, 46). Gifford quotes Hurd (IV, 180): "The pursuit so strongly exposed in this play is forgotten, and therefore its humor must appear exaggerated." It would have pleased Gifford to refute Hurd by quoting from our newspapers and upper-class periodicals, with their appeals to "Banish middle age," etc.

[35] *Sejanus*, V, viii (III, 132).

work imposes is an especial need of the present day. It is not merely that poets might profitably study his verse as well as Donne's and Hopkins', Skelton's and "The Seafarer" (I am not suggesting anything so foolish as direct imitation); not merely that practitioners of "the poetic drama" might learn something of effective stylization (the result of an emotional discipline) from his plays: these matters, in any case, are best left to poets. But for all of us he is one of the main channels of communication with an almost vanished tradition. That tradition cannot be apprehended in purely literary terms, but we can learn something of it through literature, just as to feel our way into the technique of Jonson's verse is to share, in some measure, that steady, penetrating scrutiny of men and affairs.

An Introduction to Ben Jonson

by Harry Levin

I. Tradition

In the history of literature, Ben Jonson has gone down as a figure, rather than as a writer. Critics call him by his first name upon very slight acquaintance. The strength of this impression is a testimony to the malice of one of his friends, William Drummond of Hawthornden. The eighteenth century contributed to the confusion by producing a Johnson whose opinions were quite as emphatic and even more notorious. The nineteenth century, with its preference for personalities above achievements, put the final stamp on what was left of Ben Jonson's reputation. His unique personal prestige, the extraordinary number of his articulate friends and enemies, the fact that we know more about him than we need to know—these are the accidents that constrain him into playing the part of eccentric. What is actually eccentric is the development of English literature. By the standards of his time, Jonson never deviates from his defined intentions and assured technique, which constituted the nearest approximation England had yet made to an organized culture and an academic style. Saint-Evremond expressed the mind of the Restoration when he singled Jonson out for the select company of Aristotle, Horace, Corneille, Boileau, and other literary law-givers. A succession of revolutions has impaired their authority.

For the last two centuries Jonson's principal function has been to serve as a stalking-horse for Shakespeare. Others abide our question, Shakespeare transcends it; and if you would understand, point for point, the limitations he transcends, go read Jonson. Often an attempt is made to settle the problem on a quantitative basis—Shakespeare's characters are considered three-dimentional, Jonson's are reproached with incurable flatness. The retort to this kind of criticism is a stubborn insistence that, strictly speaking, no literary creation has any dimensions

"An Introduction to Ben Jonson." (Original title: "Introduction.") From *Selected Works of Ben Jonson,* ed. by Harry Levin. Copyright 1938 by Random House, Inc. Reprinted by permission of Random House, Inc. and the Nonesuch Library. A brief introductory passage of about two pages has been omitted.

at all. Another chapter in the history of taste and of studies has been compiled since the days when Jonson was damned by the canons of Shakespearean pantheism. Scholarship talks less about nature and more about the theater. Aesthetics requires a measure of abstraction. The old impatience with limitation has been replaced by a new appreciation of convention, which we take to be not only the form, but also the essence, of art.

No dramatist could have strayed very far from the crude psychology and constricting conditions that hedged in the Elizabethan stage. It is true that Shakespeare had an artifice against artifice, an unequalled capacity for conveying the impression that he was not subject to such limitations. So successful are his occasional touches of nature that we are still surprised when his personages act according to the exigencies of the plot, and not according to motives which we ourselves should acknowledge in their place. But this trick of transcendence is not to be reckoned with; all that can be said is that it succeeds sporadically, even in Shakespeare. Webster catches it now and then, Dekker and Heywood handle it rather inexpertly, and if Jonson is really responsible for the painter's scenes in *The Spanish Tragedy,* he had mastered it, too. There is no reason to condemn his usual method of characterization for dealing with encounters instead of experiences and appealing to judgment instead of sympathy. Jonson's characters move in the same world as those of Marlowe and Middleton, Nashe and Donne, lampooning courtiers and pamphleteering journalists. In this as in other respects, Jonson is closer than Shakespeare to the literature of his day, and by no means preoccupied with the literature of the past.

Jonson is commonly conceived as a man who wrote comedies because he had a theory about why comedies ought to be written. This formidable misconception is buttressed by Jonson's own words, in a tireless series of prefaces, prologues, and asides. To accept them is to take an author's rationalizations about his own work too seriously and to ignore the historical circumstances that they were designed to meet. The comedy of humours was not arrived at as a descriptive formulation for purely critical purposes; it was seized upon as a polemical weapon to answer the Puritan attacks on the stage. Jonson, Chapman, and other dramatists were exploiting a psychological novelty which had appeared at the turn of the sixteenth century, in order to ward off popular resentment against the satirical sharpness of their "wormwood comedies." The induction to *Every Man Out of His Humour* sets forth the full argument for comedy as a social purgative. It is perhaps as relevant to Jonson's work as psychoanalysis is to the dramas of Eugene O'Neill.

Like Aristotle's doctrine of catharsis which it strikingly resembles, Jonson's theory of humours is less analytic than apologetic, less a system of literary criticism than an exercise in ethical justification. Had Jonson regarded it as more than a convenient metaphor, he would have become entangled in the contradiction which brought the Spanish philosopher Huerte before the Inquisition. If you undertake to reform society by confronting it with its own picture, and that picture is so darkly deterministic that it precludes all possibility of reform, what then? Do you curb your reforming zeal? Do you moderate your behaviorism? Are you obliged to choose between philanthropy and misanthropy? Or are you simply a hard-working playwright, with a hardheaded and somewhat doctrinaire view of humanity, trying to protect your vested interests by beating the moralists at their own game? O cursèd spite!

If Jonson's too ample protestations can be construed to show him as a reformer, he does nothing to discourage the assumption that he is a pedant as well. Here the incentive may be a private one. We must bear in mind the bricklayer's apprentice who lived to receive an honorary degree from Oxford, the second-rate actor and patcher of second-hand plays who forged for himself the position of *arbiter elegantiarum* of English letters. Jonson was a dramatist before he was a scholar. Poetry was too literally its own reward, and he envied the status of acquaintances who had fallen back on the gospel or the law—Donne and Bacon, for example. The wars of the theaters, his repeated retirements from the loathèd stage, and the petulance and paralysis of his old age left him no solace but his books. As his audiences grew smaller, his own orientation widened; he improved his relations with the ancients and began to invoke posterity. Practical disappointments could only confirm him in the theoretical principles of a self-made humanist.

Gathering manuscripts and accumulating commentaries, enjoying the friendship of Camden, Cotton, Savile, and Selden, he sought to fit into a better regimen for a literary life than the Bohemian purlieus of the theater afforded. The *Discoveries* are chiefly remarkable as an evidence of this phase of Jonson's activity, as an armory of maxims and a storehouse of ideas, as a link between Jonson and his masters in rhetoric, Seneca and Quintilian, Vossius and Heinsius. The very titles of his occasional collections of verse and prose—*Underwoods, The Forest, Timber* —glance at the *Sylvae* of the polymaths of humanism. His failures, never clapper-clawed by the palms of the vulgar, were dressed up in annotated editions to catch the eye of the learned. The thin quarto of *Sejanus*, with its marginal freight of Latin citations, must have formed a curious item on an Elizabethan bookstall. Derisive echoes make us wonder at Jonson's presumption in daring to gather his plays into a folio volume and publish them under the insufferable designation of *Works*.

The cultivation of these outward and visible marks of erudition accomplished far more than its calculated effect. It persuaded readers that the *Works* smelled exclusively of the lamp and desensitized their perception against a swarm of other odors—fragrant, pungent, savory, and rank, as the case may be. Jonson does speak with much conviction when he is paraphrasing the classics, but it is doubtful if an indefinite number of hours in a library could have taught him to sketch in his detail so casually as this:

> Ha' not I
> Known him, a common rogue, come fiddling in
> To th' osteria, with a tumbling whore,
> And, when he has done all his forced tricks, been glad
> Of a poor spoonful of dead wine, with flies in't?

It would be strange if signs of Jonson's vast reading had not crept into his writing; it would be stranger if the Tyburn brand on his thumb, his military career in the Low Countries, his religious conversion, his dubious activities as a spy, and all his duels and amours had not given him opportunities for observation that are assimilated in the things he wrote. Next to extreme bookishness, undue realism is the quality for which Jonson has been most bitterly censured. At Saint John's College, Cambridge, he was looked down upon as "a meere Empirick, one that getts what he hath by obseruation, and makes only nature priuy to what he indites." He put down everything he read, according to one side, everything he saw according to the other.

These vicissitudes of opinion are resolved by a single consideration—Jonson, first and last, was pre-eminently a craftsman, planning and constructing his verse and prose as solidly as he had learned to lay bricks. That is why he has been mistaken for both a pedant and a reformer, why he has been miscalled an arrant translator and a mere empiric. The fact is that, like a good workman, he felt the weight of literary tradition while remaining within the current of contemporary life. He differs from his fellow writers not in aims and methods, but in being more conscious of the task of adaptation they jointly performed and in going about it more systematically. England had, for the first time, a legislator of Parnassus, to sit in the chair later occupied by Dryden, Pope, and Samuel Johnson. All of a sudden, it had seemed, there were not enough forms and concepts, not enough phrases and words, in the native stock, to express all the possibilities of which people were becoming aware. There had ensued a stage of borrowing and engrafting, of translation and experiment. What was now needed, and what Jonson definitely represented, was a vernacular classicism.

In this light, we are struck by the straightforward and pragmatic nature of Jonson's classical program. The efforts of scholars at the Universities, lawyers in the Inns of Court, and friends of the Countess of Pembroke had failed to revive tragedy in its pristine purity; schoolmasters, critics, and divines united to deplore the way in which Paul's Churchyard flouted the rules of rhetoric; English poets had abandoned the chase after the chimaera of quantitative meters. Ben Jonson entered the field as a professional man of letters. As one who thoroughly grasped

and had extensively practiced most of the bastard forms which had
sprung up, he knew how they could be clarified and made supple. As
the first of a line of neo-classicists, he wanted not to surrender to Greece
and Rome, but to rival them, to wed ancient form to modern substance.
He had hoped to achieve a perfect embodiment of this ideal in the
pastoral fragment of *The Sad Shepherd,* where his proclaimed purpose
was to garner

> . . . such wool
> As from mere English flocks his Muse can pull,

and therewith to fashion

> . . . a fleece
> To match or those of Sicily or Greece.

It is characteristic of the culture of the Renaissance at its ripest, that
it should seek to give classical precedent a local habitation and a name.
Horace's *fons Bandusiae* is transformed into Ronsard's *fontaine Bellerie.*
The tropes of Catullus,

> *Quam magnus numerus Libyssae harenae*
> *Lasarpiciferis jacet Cyrenis,*
> *Oraclum Jovis inter aestuosi*
> *Et Batti veteris sacrum sepulcrum;*
> *Aut quam sidera multa, cum tacet nox,*
> *Furtivos hominum vident amores,*

suffer a sea-change, in Jonson's paraphrase:

> All the grass that Rumney yields,
> Or the sands in Chelsea fields,
> Or the drops in silver Thames,
> Or the stars that gild his streams,
> In the silent summer nights,
> When youths ply their stol'n delights.

Sedate dignitaries from the pantheon of Natalis Comes are jostled out
of Jonson's masques by English worthies from Captain Cox's library;
the same blend of refined commonplace and homely folklore tinctures
the lyrics of Jonson's disciple, Herrick. The tribe of Ben was responsible
for fastening his favorite measure, the heroic couplet, upon English
poetry, where it prevailed with the tenacity of neo-classicism itself until, further straitened by an enforced sojourn in France, it became the

cell in which Pope was condemned to pace out his existence, five steps down and five steps back.

We can distinguish between what is classical and what is native in the traditions available to Jonson, but we have no means of measuring the extent to which they make themselves felt in his work. It would be futile to try to determine the preponderating element or to weigh them both in the clumsy balance of form and content. The norms of dramatic structure, in comedy and in tragedy, Jonson had obviously generalized from Latin models, more precisely from Plautus, Terence, and Seneca. Of the profound significance of the Roman satirists for the late Elizabethan mentality, particularly after downright imitation had been prohibited and the pent-up gall had burst forth on the stage, Jonson's "comical satires" are our main witness. Yet more than the materials of his plays is indigenous. The conventions of the English morality are respected in Jonson's casts and plots, in the *redende Namen* of his characters, in the beast-fable of *Volpone* or the gaping Hell-mouth of *The Devil Is an Ass*. And beneath his writing runs a broad substratum of journalism, of all the tracts, broadsides, and jestbooks that had granted literary recognition to the London underworld, before Jonson came along.

Finally, there is a plane upon which these opposing forces reach an equilibrium. The extremes of rhetoric and pamphleteering, the old and the new, foreign and domestic, and erudite and popular meet in an illusory half-world, wherein the *fallax servus* borrows the lath dagger of the Vice and Cato shakes his finger at Til Eulenspiegel. The whole farrago of types and themes becomes intelligible, from this distant vantage point, as the outside of a large, heterogeneous cultural movement. Across Europe, along the drift from Renaissance to Reformation, from Italy to Germany, stride two gigantic protagonists, the rogue and the fool. In the conflicts of humanistic learning and empirical experience, the war between theology and science, a literature is evolved which has the expansiveness of the picaresque and the inclusiveness of satire. It is the age of Erasmus, Brandt, Rabelais, and Cervantes. It is the time to cry "Ducdame" and call all fools into a circle.

Against the background of the Reformation, then, rather than that of the Renaissance, Jonson may be seen at his best. He was by birth and apprenticeship an Elizabethan, but the succeeding years are those he dominates, and the elegies of his lamenting "sons" would have been more impressive if they had not been issued in the year of the Bishops' War. For it is Jonson's career which most strongly marks the transition in English literature from sonnet to satire, from comedy of the court to comedy of the city, from poets who celebrated imaginary mistresses to poets who dedicated themselves to detraction, from the virtuous conduct to Castiglione's Courtier to the gross etiquette of Dedekind's Grobian. Jonson is the legitimate heir of the Renaissance, of the Elizabethan age, and of Christopher Marlowe—it took a third poetic craftsman, T. S.

Eliot, to discern that. When we come to examine the texture of Jonson's verse, we shall be grateful for this discernment. We must recognize this formal continuity, if only to appreciate how sharply it reverses its intellectual bearing. Marlowe belongs to one century and Jonson to another, and their respective attitudes toward human nature are as far apart as More's *Utopia* and Hobbes's *Leviathan*.

II. *Satire*

The richness of the Renaissance, about which so much has been said, is more than a metaphor. In what was, after all, the heroic age of mercantile enterprise, it should not astonish us to find a luster reflecting the influx of wealth from the Indies and of gold from the Americas. We breathe the glittering atmosphere of the Mediterranean, ever the center of fashion and luxury, in *The Jew of Malta, Othello,* and *Volpone,* while *Eastward Ho, The Tempest,* and *The Fair Maid of the West* have in them something of the saltier air of British adventure. Economic expansion, in England, is accompanied by an intensely universal feeling of nationwide participation, which finds cultural expression in the collections of the voyagers, in the Tudor translations, in the chronicle plays, in the idealized figure of the Virgin Queen. This exaltation and confidence, which suggests comparison with the American Dream, seems to lose its bloom in the last decade of Elizabeth's reign, just as the freshness of our own national ideals withered after the Civil War.

In the latter half of the sixteenth century, there was time for a new English aristocracy to grow up, and for a popular monarchy to leave off fostering democratic notions and assume more or less absolute pretensions. By the turn of the century, a mercantilist economy had dammed up the enormous flow of resources, and it was no longer easy to believe that all things were possible to any man. Patents and monopolies still changed hands; the great companies were setting out to establish the new plantations; projectors flourished, and made the court a hotbed of promotion and intrigue. Step by step, through the literature of these crucial years, we can watch the sentiment of expectation change to a sense of wariness, depression, and disillusionment. With increasing introspection, everything is anatomized. Newer and more analytic forms, such as the character and the essay, are devised; ancient modes, like satire and epigram, are borrowed to fit modern instances. The native hue of Elizabethan resolution is sicklied o'er with the pale cast of Jacobean melancholy. Nature, it is felt, is in decay; the times are out of joint; *difficile est satyram non scribere.*

That Ben Jonson should have viewed this change in the light of the historic contrast between the Roman Republic and the Roman Empire was inevitable. Exasperated by the demands of the groundlings, exhausted by the rivalry of Marston, Dekker, and other poetasters and professionals, he was led to adopt the idiom of the Silver Age and to address himself, in the tone of Martial and Tacitus, to the imperial theme. *Sejanus*, with its acid depiction of the caprice of princes and the folly of favorites, greeted the accession of the leading apologist for the divine right of kings, the future patron of Somerset and Buckingham. Small wonder that it brought Jonson to the Star Chamber. It is no accident that Shakespeare, in his Roman tragedies, and Chapman, in his French histories, were dwelling upon the problem of authority, or that the issues of *Coriolanus* and of *Sejanus* seem even more pregnant today. The concentrated indignation of Jonson's Roman elders, the glimpses of espionage and repression, the episodes of judicial murder, the mood of flattery and fear evoke as many echoes in our ears as the cry, "Lictors, resume the fasces!"

Significantly, both Jonson's tragic heroes are villains, so confirmed in their villainy that they need no motive; Sejanus resolves to debauch Livia before her husband has struck him, and Catiline does not wait for the election of Cicero to hatch his plot. If their efforts do not achieve the fullness of tragedy, it is Jonson's fault, for failing to counterweight them with anything but appeals to principles and exercises in rhetoric. Cicero, not Catiline, is remiss. It would be rash to conclude that the satiric spirit is hostile to tragedy. On the contrary, Jonson's tragedies come most to life when his courtiers are fawning or when his women, whose psychology is never more than cosmetic-deep, are gossiping. The very satire which called the story of Sejanus to Jonson's attention, Juvenal's tenth, is almost medieval in its stress upon tragic reversal of fortune. The tragedian of an age of satire, Seneca, was the unavoidable model for every Elizabethan dramatist who aspired to the buskin. Shakespeare himself was forced to describe the Trojan War and Homeric heroes as "Nothing but lechery! all incontinent varlets!" His Cleopatra gives more than a hint of how Jonson would have treated her:

> . . . the quick comedians
> Extemporally will stage us, and present
> Our Alexandrian revels. Antony
> Shall be brought drunken forth, and I shall see
> Some squeaking Cleopatra boy my greatness
> I' the posture of a whore.

The genius of tragedy is essentially the same as that of comedy, as someone mumbled through a haze of wine fumes, very early one morning in the house of Agathon. Of the tragedy of the Renaissance, disposed as it was to leave so little to fate, this is particularly true. Tragic suffering can be, and in the more remote past has been, blind and passive;

comic matters notoriously involve human agency. The slings and arrows of an outrageous fortune are not to be endured, revenge is sweet, revenge ripens into conspiracy, conspiracy passes over into intrigue, and the gap is bridged; the Elizabethans have proved at least that a similar dramatic technique will serve for tragedy and for comedy. Thus Tiberius and Sejanus, the Jew of Malta and his blackamoor, the arch-plotter Volpone and the parasite Mosca, are respectively related.

If tragedy can scoff, comedy can scorn. The comical satires are of the "biting" variety, not the "toothless." Professing to sport with human follies, not with crimes, Jonson too often took it upon himself to dispense poetic justice, to regulate his comical satires by a more rigorous ethic than life itself ever provides, to conjure up an inferno of punishments for his personal enemies. Some high-minded malcontent—an Asper or a Crites—like the melancholy Jaques and not unlike the sort of madman that Hamlet pretended to be, figures as Jonson's accredited representative, and is entrusted with the responsibility of scourging vice, untrussing affectation, and reconciling humours all around. Jonsonian comedy invariably tends in the direction of an arraignment; it must enact a trial and achieve an official resolution of the comic knot, whether by royal Cynthia or imperial Augustus, by court or Senate, or merely by a nonchalant interloper or humane jurist of the Bridlegoose breed.

In the riper comedies, the rules become more flexible. The final courtroom scene in *Volpone,* it is true, reverses the venal decision of the fourth act, but by that time our faith in lawyers and judges and Venetians and human beings has become corroded, and we sense the hollowness of the categorical imperative. In *Epicene,* the pretense is acknowledged, and we are invited to hear a false canon lawyer and a mock doctor of divinity hold a sham disputation. This discrepancy between law and life is the condition which governs *Bartholomew Fair.* "Think to make it as lawful as you can," pleads Dame Purecraft, and Rabbi Busy discovers scriptural sanction for the eating of pig. The bumpkin Cokes, while being edified by a ballad on the wretched end which befalls pickpockets, is robbed of his purse. In this select company of gamblers and bawds, only the half-witted Troubleall would insist upon warrant for what is done; in the very sink of enormities, the pompous Justice Overdo can find no one to expose but his own wife; in the topsy-turvy jurisdiction of Pie-powders, it is the reforming element—Overdo, the puritan Busy, and the angry man, Wasp—who land side by side in the stocks. Jonson could go no farther in reducing his own legalism to absurdity, except by haling into *The Staple of News* the trial of dogs which Aristophanes had originated and Racine would improve. These names are worth recalling, if they convey the generalization that parody of justice has always been a premise for comedy.

His object all sublime Jonson gradually relinquished to the genuine doctors and divines. With a more incisive perception of the conflict between interests and ideals, "the space between the breast and lips," he gave up the attempt to discipline his characters and they profited by their freedom. His uncompromising attitude toward his fellow men persisted, but he no longer described men as good and bad; they were simply fools and knaves, or, in Elizabethan parlance, gulls and coney-catchers. The eschatology of *The Alchemist* is based on this simplified scheme; after the three knaves have cozened their victims, one of them outwits the other two, who thereupon assume the status of fools, while the arch-knave is pardoned and permitted to baffle the one honest man of the piece. *The Devil Is an Ass*, as its name implies, is a study in comparative ethics, demonstrating that what is religiously regarded as the absolute in evil can only bungle along by contrast with what goes on above ground. "Hell is a grammar-school to this!" exclaims the chastened fiend, and departs on the back of the Vice, setting off an ineffectual firecracker, and leaving the field to Protagoras and Jeremy Bentham.

Because Jonson was enough of an Aristotelian to rank knowledge above virtue, and enough of a Machiavellian to delight in ingenuity for its own sake, it does not follow that he ever succeeded in banishing morality from his stage. In comedy, as well as tragedy, there must be a context of good and evil, but it can be defined socially rather than theologically. Pity and terror, accordingly, give way to insouciance and curiosity, and sometimes to contempt and cynicism. Comic writers start by making certain devastating assumptions about human nature, by questioning every man's honesty and every woman's virtue, even though they seldom push them to such drastic conclusions as *Mandragola, The Country Wife, Turcaret,* and *Volpone*. "Interpreteth best sayings and deeds often to the worst," says Drummond. These assumptions inhere in the tradition of classical comedy, as part of that perfectly Euclidean realm where there are so many coincidences and no surprises, where old men exist to leave legacies, clever parasites to get around them, beautiful orphans to be shipwrecked, and young men to go a-whoring.

Jonson had assimilated the latent antagonisms of this early comedy—fathers versus sons, philistines against poets, the city as opposed to the universities. When he came to print *Every Man In His Humour* in folio, he heightened the asperity of the elder generation by assigning Old Knowell a speech out of Juvenal on the depraving of youth through luxury and trade, and weakened the position of the younger generation by omitting Lorenzo Junior's defense of poetry. The Ovid of *Poetaster* becomes virtually the "marked man" of later romanticism, condemned first by his father to the study of law, and then by the Emperor to banishment. When Jonson came to composition with his audience, however, in *Epicene* and *Bartholomew Fair,* youth could expect indulgence and pantaloons or serious asses might tremble in apprehension of the fate of Malvolio. His scholars, dropping their academic accent, set up for wits; the city became the town, and they found their way around it without difficulty. It might have comforted the banished Ovid to learn that he had furnished the very language for this elegant new coterie of Truewits and Clerimonts.

Epicene, the most brittle of Jonson's comedies, was the most likely to win Pepys's plaudits and fit Dryden's canons. Frankly a thing of veneer, explicitly discouraging attempts to glance beneath its polished contours, it stands at an interesting halfway point between Plautine and Restoration comedy. Its courtly air and its emphasis on the relations between the sexes remind us that it was written for the boy-actors who had performed Lyly's plays, whereas Jonson's apprenticeship was served in the theater that had employed Marlowe, while *Sejanus* and *Volpone* were produced by Shakespeare's company. But the action of *Epicene* is not presided over by any Meredithian comic spirit. If it were not farce, it would be pathology. Was there ever a more disillusioned cavalier than Sir Dauphine Eugenie, setting out to win the collective favors of a bevy of women he totally despises? And in the attitude of the wits toward their monomaniac victim, there is more than a touch of sadism, of the "comedy of affliction."

For all its artificiality, *Epicene* was definitely set in London. From that time forth, Jonson cast aside the *fabula palliata* and took up the *fabula togata.* The change is merely a matter of nomenclature, since Jonson always followed the standard comic practice—from Menander to Minsky —of conceiving the comic stage as an intersection of city streets. Within this convention there is dramatic unity, as well as room for considerable movement. All that is needed are a few doors and windows, which Jonson, revising *Every Man In His Humour,* had no trouble in labelling "Moorfields" and "The Old Jewry." He never returned to the "fustian countries" where he had dallied before, or to the Rome which he had tried to use as a looking-glass for England. Italy, to an English eye the incarnate breeding-place of corruption, had seemed the appropriate setting for *Volpone*; it is a grim chauvinism which insists on laying the scene for *The Alchemist* at home:

> Our scene is London, 'cause we would make known,
> No country's mirth is better than our own.

The demands of realism are most fully satisfied by *Bartholomew Fair.* Although the most meticulously local of Jonson's plays, it is also the most broadly universal; for is not all the world a fair—paraphrasing Seneca, Jonson develops the conceit in his *Discoveries*—and do not men seek gilded roofs and marble pillars, even as children are attracted to cockleshells and hobby-horses? Under this more genial dispensation, humours diffuse into vapors, and vapors evaporate *in fumo.* Like a pilgrimage, a fair forms a comprehensive natural background against which all types and classes may be exhibited; like Chaucer, Jonson allows his characters to step out of the proscenium. Ursula, the pig-woman, challenges an odorous comparison with the Wife of Bath herself, let alone Elinor Rumming or Marion Tweedy Bloom. Here as always, realism thrives upon the implicit contrast between the way things are presented and the way literature has been in the habit of presenting those same things. What, then, could be a crueller falling-off than for Leander, having swum the Hellespont from Sestos to Abydos, to let a foul-mouthed ferry-man row him across the Thames from the Bankside to Puddle Wharf?

The plots of *Eastward Ho, Volpone,* and *The Alchemist* are more highly wrought, but not so farfetched as we might believe. Amid the traffic and speculation of the Renaissance, treasure-trove, legacy hunting, and alchemy were considered legitimate alternatives in the general pursuit of riches. If this crass afterthought robs Jonson's comedies of their fantasy, it binds them much more firmly to the life of their time. For they have a single theme, which may be underscored as the leading-motive of Jonsonian drama, and which is enunciated by its most authoritative spokesman in the mystic words, "Be rich!" Even through the disembodied parables of his final period, Jonson was playing with such subjects as the pursuit of the Lady Pecunia; and in the projector Merecraft, he created a prototype for the Mr. Micawbers and Robert Macaires and Mulberry Sellerses of bourgeois literature.

Gold is the core of Jonson's comedy, getting and spending are the chains which bind it together, and luxury furnishes the ornaments which cover its surfaces. It is further stipulated, by Volpone himself, that such gold must not be the reward of any productive endeavor. Both *Volpone* and *The Alchemist* hinge upon some monstrous device, a will or the Philosophers' Stone, but Jonson can bring to bear upon almost any situation a suspiciously circumstantial familiarity with all the ruses of craft and quackery. Insofar as it would be the nature of Volpone or Subtle to plot, whether on or off the stage, the motive of chicane becomes the determining factor in the strategy of Jonson's plays. In *Volpone,* perhaps even more than in *The Alchemist,* he has erected his most imposing hierarchies of collusion. In the later play he relaxes the two-edged ironies of fathers who disinherit sons and husbands who prostitute wives, in order to admit a procession of more earth-bound appetites, ranging from the petty desires of a lawyer's clerk to cut a figure, to the intransigent gluttony of Sir Epicure Mammon.

This fat knight is a Falstaff who has suddenly begun to babble like a Faustus. Hankering after fleshpots, his lordly talk is "all in gold"; "Silver I care not for." Out of the boundless opulence which his insatiate libido has already summoned up, he is even prepared to make an occasional benefaction—"And now and then a church." The limit of his lust is only measured by his gullibility; he observes Habsburg and Medici traits in Doll Common, and addresses her in the language which Faustus reserved for Helen of Troy. 'Tis pity she's a whore! Before he takes her upstairs, he is warned not to arouse her fanaticism by introducing topics of biblical controversy. "We think not on 'em," he replies. And their departure gives Face and Subtle the excuse to bring experiments to a fiasco and blame it upon Sir Epicure's impatient sensuality. "O my voluptuous mind!" he cries.

Marlowe consistently presented the voluptuary as a hero; to Jonson, he is always either a villain like Volpone or a dupe like Sir Epicure Mammon. Taking up, at Eliot's suggestion, Sir Epicure's moist-lipped recital of the delights he hopes to enjoy, and placing it alongside Gaveston's announcement of the entertainments he has prepared for Edward II, we can observe in each case a texture woven with equal richness and a comparable barrage of sensuous appeal. Jonson's accumulation of images is even denser and more various than Marlowe's, and its effect is utterly subversive. Jonson could not have expressed his reservations more explicitly, nor hit upon a more elaborate contrivance for turning to dust and ashes all the lovely fruit of the Renaissance imagination. Nothing has been neglected, but the intonation has changed, for he is consciously dealing in illusion. Marlowe to Jonson is as Hyperion to a satyr. Sir Philip Sidney had pimples, Jonson told Drummond, and advanced an appalling explanation of Queen Elizabeth's best-known trait.

The luxurious trappings of Jonson's verse are to be viewed, but not touched; they will either vanish away or taint whoever is brash enough to reach out for them. The limping jig of Volpone's deformed chorus rehearses the tale of Lucian's cock, whose crowing awoke its indigent master from dreams of banquets and visions of riches. The plague hangs over the house in which *The Alchemist* operates; brightness falls from the air. Sooner or later, of course, Jonson would rally to the cause of the expiring Renaissance, and the Ghost of Dionysius would bawl down Zeal-of-the-Land Busy in Leatherhead's puppet-show. He would have *Pleasure Reconciled to Virtue* in a masque, at any rate. Perhaps Jonson's asperity was due to the fact that he was a satirist by vocation and a Stoic by philosophical inclination. But vocation and inclination are the result of temperament; if Jonson had not been a scholar, he might have called himself a Puritan. And if he had never existed, there still would have been the Puritans, and other poets would have found it difficult not to write satire. Sir Toby Belch's question was a little beside the point. Malvolio was virtuous precisely because there were no more cakes and ale.

Jonson raised one question which neither Mandeville nor Rousseau would settle. Like his author, the miser of *The Staple of News* is a disciple of Seneca:

> Who can endure to see
> The fury of men's gullets and their groins?
> What stews, ponds, parks, coops, garners, magazines,

> What velvets, tissues, scarfs, embroideries,
> And laces they might lack? They covet things
> Superfluous still, when it were much more honour
> They could want necessary. What need hath Nature
> Of silver dishes or gold chamber-pots?
> Of perfumed napkins, or a numerous family
> To see her eat? Poor and wise, she requires
> Meat only; hunger is not ambitious.

Here, in his Stoic doctrine of nature, he is at variance with King Lear:

> O, reason not the need; our basest beggars
> Are in the poorest thing superfluous.
> Allow not nature more than nature needs,
> Man's life is cheap as beast's. Thou art a lady;
> If only to go warm were gorgeous,
> Why, nature needs not what thou gorgeous wear'st,
> Which scarcely keeps thee warm.

Jonson takes more for granted than Shakespeare does. He presupposes that life is fundamentally a compact, rational affair, needlessly complicated by impulse and artifice. To Shakespeare, all experience, however variegated, is of the same baseless fabric. The two poets, who worked so closely together, were as far apart as Heraclitus and Parmenides. Jonson adopts the attitude of society, Shakespeare the viewpoint of the individual, which is finally more real. Jonson's instrument is logic, Shakespeare's psychology; Jonson's method has been called mechanical, Shakespeare's organic. That is why we must criticize Shakespeare in terms of movement and warmth, Jonson in terms of pattern and color.

III. *Rhetoric*

It was an inescapable irony which compelled Jonson to spend his last twenty years as a purveyor of magnificence to the court. It was ironic that a Stoic should be a party to such an extreme form of conspicuous consumption as the masque; that a poet should be forced into competition not only with Inigo Jones, but—as *Neptune's Triumph* dramatizes the issue—with the cook, and at a far lower stipend than the dancing-master; that Ben Jonson should be called upon to provide what he himself ruefully brands

> . . . the short bravery of the night,
> . . . the jewels, stuffs, the pains, the wit
> There wasted, some not paid for yet!

But it was inescapable because Jonson had been overlooked by popular success; because he had to get what comfort he could from his official position as poet laureate; because his talent for decoration, his penchant for symbolism, his command of poetic convention, his play of allusion, his knowledge of the classics, and his interest in folklore needed an occasion to converge upon. Shakespeare's career proceeded, according to Edward Dowden's formula, out of the workshop into the world; Jonson's career went in the other direction.

All of his conscientious craftsmanship was insufficient to impose coherence on so synthetic a medium. To gather some slight conception of what it was all about, we find ourselves trying to envisage an aristocratic revue or an erudite Silly Symphony. Spain and France, in the persons of their ambassadors, quarrelled over invitations, precedence, and the King's right ear; Lanière and Ferrabosco contributed galliards and corrantos; the Queen, the Prince, the Lady Arabella, and other mummers disguised themselves as gypsies or heathen deities or parts of speech, and mounted the musicians' gallery to descend in some grandiose machine. From state papers, *viola da gamba* scores, and architects' elevations, we emerge as confused as Pocahontas must have seemed at the performance of *The Vision of Delight.* Thumbing through Jonson's part in these evanescent entertainments is like visiting a costumer's shop strewn with a musty assortment of bent farthingales, second-hand armor, faded wigs, and limp dominos.

If there is any special significance in the masque, it is apparent in the frequency with which a pastoral note is sounded, with which golden ages and happier eras are restored, or we are whisked away to unreal Arcadias and remote Hesperides. Behind the frivolity and superficiality of the *genre* lay at least one meaning—that the court and the city no longer shared any literary conventions, that there was less and less of the community of interest which had permitted the Globe and Blackfriars to present the same plays. Structurally, the relation between Jonson's masques and comedies is close, too close to have pleased the spectators of his last comedies. Yet Jonson's comedies, from first to last, have a tendency to crystallize, whenever opportunity offers, into a series of games, ceremonies, shows, songs, litanies, orations, and every sort of masque-like invention. The rites conducted by Sejanus, Volpone's medicine-show, Morose's invective against his barber, Dapper's interview with the Queen of Faery, Justice Clement's merry assizes, Littlewit's redaction of *Hero and Leander*—these episodes, besides fulfilling their dramatic function in the plays to which they belong, are independently reducible to formal pattern.

Beyond these internal harmonies, Jonson invites scrutiny as an engineer of plots. We have noticed that the recurrent trials point a moral; we must recognize that they also adorn a play, by supplying an external framework for the action and a ritual for some of the scenes. If we admit the parallel between promoting a confidence game and spinning a comic intrigue, we can appreciate the way Jonson utilized the get-rich-quick motive and the scheme of a hoax in his most successful comedies. His others are less so because they sacrifice situation to character. The lists of *dramatis personae,* in *Every Man Out of His Humour* or *The New Inn,* read like pages out of Earle and Overbury. The stage becomes so overloaded with sharply defined, carefully delineated supernumeraries, who have been called into being only to have their legs pulled, that it becomes all but impossible for a plot to get under way.

The difficulty of introducing his characters in a natural sequence of encounters was met by Jonson with a great deal of ingenuity. The plan of *Volpone,* turned to account again in *The Alchemist,* enables them to make their entrances one after another, without monotony or stiffness. The opening scene of *The Alchemist,* wherein the thieves, having fallen out, bespatter each other with abuse until the spectators have learned the past history, crimes, misdemeanors, and unendearing foibles of all three, is a triumph of exposition. The complicated intermarriages, the awkward progresses from house to house, and the Mephistophelian servants that comic dramatists allowed themselves in order to hold their plots together, Jonson was never quite ready to give up. But he did devise, in *Bartholomew Fair,* a new unity, which incorporates the three old ones into a more manageable partnership, based solely upon local color. The critical dialogue in which he sought warrant for his innovation in Horace's *Art of Poetry* did not survive the conflagration of his library, but we have today in the films ample evidence of the breadth and diversity of this method. Particularly in the journalistic milieu of *The Staple of News,* with his gift for recreating an atmosphere, Jonson seems to be striving toward a comic institution around which to build his play —a thinking-shop or a school for scandal.

Occasionally the hand of the puppeteer appears, the situation is obviously manipulated, and we smell a device. If Jonson had been less fond of those who are witty in themselves, he might have done more convincing portraits of those who are the cause that wit is in others. There are not enough fools positive and too many fools contingent. The dramatist relies upon the assistance of his characters to bring off his practical jokes. It is the difference between Socrates' basket and Falstaff's; Socrates is made a fool by Aristophanes, Falstaff by Mistress Ford and Mistress Quickly. It would not have occurred to Jonson to let well enough alone and allow circumstances to force Sganarelle to practice medicine. His ironies must be overseen by his personal representatives, ever alert to persuade the jealous Corvino to lend his wife to another, or to stir up a reluctant duel between Sir John Daw and Sir Amorous La Foole. Sometimes his fools are conscious of their folly and have good reason for persisting. Captain Otter, as a creature of humours, is a palpable fraud; he is a realistically drawn, thoroughly unpleasant broken-down gambler, who affects certain mannerisms which we have come to associate with the name of Jonson's pupil, Dickens, to ingratiate himself with his rich wife and her fine friends.

Because Jonsonian comedy can only succeed by subordinating parts to whole, its cast of characters is not its outstanding feature. Each has only his characteristic move, as in chess, and the object of the game is to see what new combinations have been brought about. Between the abstract idea of the plot and the concrete detail of the language is a hiatus. Nothing is lacking, but the various components can be distinguished without much trouble. In Corvino's phrase, it is too manifest. After the large masses have been sketched out in baroque symmetry, decoration is applied to the surfaces. What is said, frequently, does not matter, so long as something is said, and then Jonson is at special pains to make what is said interesting for its own sake. Surly's school-book Spanish and Doll's memorized ravings are simply blocked in. But when Mosca reads the inventory, or when Subtle puts Face through the alchemists' catechism, they too are saying something where—in the dramatic economy—they mean nothing, and their speeches take on the aspect of incantation. It is a trick which reaches its logical limit in *Epicene,* where everything spoken has a high nuisance value and the words themselves become sheer filigree. Beyond that point, they have the force of Molière's comic refrains. Lady Would-be's uncontrollable flow of recipes, prescriptions, literary opinions, and philosophical speculations, at cross-purposes with Volpone, demonstrates how conveniently this talking-machine technique bears out Bergson's theory of laughter.

To linger over the elements of pure design in Jonson's dialogue is to ignore its expressiveness as representation. The language itself is completely idiomatic, uninhibited by the formality of plot and characterization or the complexity of scenes and speeches. Because "Spenser writ no language," Jonson refused to tolerate him, and he could spare Marston nothing but a prescription to purge unnatural diction. His own occasional verse moves, like his drama, on the social plane and speaks in the familiar tones of human intercourse. Even self-communion, with Jonson, takes the form of a public address. Ode, epigram, elegy, epistle—nearly every poem is composed on something or to somebody, brandishing precepts and eliciting examples in the injunctive mood of Roman poetry. A poetic style suitable for these purposes had to be fittest for discourse and nearest prose. Whatever the restraints Jonson chose to accept, his handling of words never lost its flexibility; throughout the most tortuous stanzas his phrasing remains as English as Purcell's.

It would be hard to derive an inference about Jonson's dramatic verse from the comedies he wrote in prose, since *Epicene* and *Bartholomew Fair* are farther from one another than from any of the remaining plays. Neither the enamelled elegance of the one nor the rough-and-ready realism of the other accomplishes anything that Jonson has not been able to achieve in meter with the help of two fertile resources, enjambment and the broken line. He is so unwilling to pause every time five iambs have elapsed, that he now and then revives the classical stratagem of concluding a line in the midst of a word. And he is so fond of crisp dialogue that he often divides a single pentameter among three speakers, as in the staccato asides that punctuate the harangues of Tiberius or Voltore. Longer speeches strike up a syncopation between the shifting colloquial rhythms and the sustained stresses of blank verse. Face's praise of Spaniards is rendered in a string of four-foot clauses, so that the iterated phrase leaps across the page and then creeps back again:

> Ask from your courtier to your inns-of-court man,
> To your mere milliner. They will tell you all,
> Your Spanish jennet is the best horse; your Spanish
> Stoop is the best garb; your Spanish beard
> Is the best cut; your Spanish ruffs are the best
> Wear; your Spanish pavan the best dance;
> Your Spanish titillation in a glove
> The best perfume. And for your Spanish pike
> And Spanish blade, let your poor Captain speak.

The cadence is individualized to catch the breathlessness of Celia's appeal for mercy or reverberate with the finality of Volpone's revelation.

It is typical of Jonson, as of Dryden and the baroque in general, that rhythmic arrangement should take precedence over actual sound. High, astounding terms are relatively rare. Already a rationalistic bias is perceptible; writers seem less eager to use words for their own sake and more anxious to employ them for what they signify. Jonson had the custom of setting down everything he proposed to say in prose and versifying it in a subsequent operation. Hence his poetry is primarily pictorial and only then musical, it addresses the visual rather than the auditory instincts, it appeals—as the writing of a poet who gave up the stage for the printing-press—to the eye instead of the ear. Like his personifications of Fancy and Wonder in *The Vision of Delight,* Jonson's eye had the power to summon up an infinite variety of vistas. Like a good apothecary, he was never without an ounce of civet with which he might sweeten his imagination at will. "He hath consumed a whole night in lying looking to his great toe,"—if we are to believe Drummond—"about which he hath seen Tartars and Turks, Romans and Carthaginians, fight in his imagination."

Graphic speech is the generic trait with which even Jonson's ugliest ducklings are well endowed. The stolid Corvino indulges in unsuspected flights of conceit and the sullen Ananias reveals a flamboyant strain of polemical eloquence. Kitely's jealousy of his wife prompts him to deliver an exhaustive survey of the wiles of amorous deception. To dismiss the threat of punishment, Voltore invokes a swarm of luridly ridiculous tortures upon the prostrate person of his client. In introducing Drugger as an honest tobacconist, Face cannot resist the temptation to add some dozen or sixteen lines covering the various sharp practices of dishonest tobacconists that Drugger utterly eschews. Dramatic action is supplemented by the potential drama of these three speeches. In each instance a set of images picks up the situation where the business leaves off, and projects it to the most extravagant bounds of possibility. Uniformly Jonson's style is stamped with the brilliance of his iconoplastic talents.

The imagery surprises us by being so tangible, by presenting its objects not as fanciful comparisons but as literal descriptions. They are seldom glimpsed through the magic casement of metaphor, through the intervention of rhetoric. The rich jewel in the Ethiop's ear belonged to Juliet only by metaphysical parallel; Jonson would have slashed off the ear, conveyed the jewel to Volpone's coffers, and dangled it before Celia as the price of her virtue. Heaping up sensuous detail in thoroughgoing Elizabethan fashion, he ordinarily contrives to bring it within the immediate grasp of his tantalized characters. The result is that the theme of his plays and their poetic realization are more closely knit together. Examining the content of Jonson's images, Caroline Spurgeon has discovered that the largest single category is drawn from the usages and conditions of society and that he returns more consistently than any of his rivals to the subject of money. A further consequence of this restriction of materials is a kind of heightening of the commonplace, more proper to the humorous than to the lyrical imagination. Deprived of other figures of speech, Jonson relies much on hyperbole. That is not the only quality of style he shares with Aristophanes and Rabelais.

The poetry of misplaced concreteness and solid specification is an instrument of the satirist; he is adept at mastering the tricks of a trade and enumerating technical data; his swift, disintegrating glance takes in all the ingredients of Goody Trash's gingerbread. A profusion of images is not the best way to communicate feeling. Selection is more likely to produce the poignant response; accumulation bewilders at first and invites analysis in the end. When Jonson's intention is not satirical, his "wit's great overplus" dilutes the effect of his verse. In one line,

> Ditch-delivered by a drab,

Shakespeare can concentrate an impact that Jonson labored through the long and learned *Masque of Queens* without quite attaining. Ultimately his facility at image-making becomes self-conscious and, as it were, poetical. It carries him into the region of the conventionally beautiful and leaves him among the curlèd woods and painted meads. It ominously foreshadows the time when poets will work with a repertory of standard items and critics will ponder the distinction between imagination and fancy.

Satirists are well aware that appearances deceive, yet it is with appearances that satirists are chiefly concerned. Jonson delights in exhibiting façades, because they both impress us and make us uneasy about what lies behind them. Every once in a while a masochistic fascination leads him to explore the obverse of beauty, to give way to the fly-blown fancies of *The Famous Voyage,* to betray a revulsion worthy of Swift.

> Though art's hid causes are not found,
> All is not sweet, all is not sound.

It is never simple for literature to report the senses directly. In the Renaissance especially, it was hard to reconcile perceptions and principles; attempts oscillate from the sheer apprehension of Marlowe to the sublimated allegory of Spenser. Between these poles there is room for voluptuousness, scientific curiosity, asceticism, prurience—all the degrees and mixtures of intellectualized sensibility that we see in *Ovid's Banquet of Sense, The Metamorphosis of Pygmalion's Image, Nosce Teipsum,* or "The Ecstasy." As an Elizabethan, Jonson too had been perplexed by the problem. As a Stoic and satirist, he was able to make his own rejection. As a professional man of letters, he had to keep on writing through a period when immanent emotions and confident attitudes were being reduced to questions of literary technique.

In his fecundity and in his artificiality, in his virtues and in his faults, Jonson remains the craftsman. When he appraises the idle apprentice Shakespeare, he speaks with the authority of a fellow craftsman, and—after a few precise couplets of prefatory remarks, acknowledgments, and qualifications—deliberately turns on the lyric strain:

> I therefore will begin. Soul of the age!
> The applause, delight, the wonder of our stage!

And he proceeds to a workmanlike and reasonably impassioned estimate. Because he was in the habit of discussing his craft concretely, he could not fail to be interested in Plutarch's comparison of poetry and painting. It is no mere chance that any effort to describe his own work falls repeatedly into the vocabulary of the fine arts. If we are looking for a single impression of Ben Jonson, it is of the Flemish painters that we are finally mindful—of crowded street scenes and rich interiors, of sharp portraiture and lavish ornament, of the gloss and the clarity and the tactile values that are the tokens of mastery.

Morose Ben Jonson

by Edmund Wilson

When Swinburne published his study of Ben Jonson hardly sixty years ago, he indignantly called attention to the fact that English scholarship, which had shown such devotion to the texts of the Greek and Latin classics, should never, in two centuries and a half, have produced a decent edition of so important an English writer. That complaint can no longer be made—though the definitive edition of Jonson by C. H. Herford and Percy and Evelyn Simpson, brought out by the Oxford University Press, has been slow in appearing and is not yet complete. The first two volumes were published in 1925, and the eighth has only just come out. This, containing Jonson's poems and prose, is the last instalment of the text Jonson, but it is to be followed by two volumes of commentaries, which ought to be particularly valuable, since no writer is more full of allusions, both topical and learned, than Jonson, and his work has never been properly annotated. There has not appeared, from this point of view and from that of clearing up the text, a serious edition of Jonson since that of William Gifford in 1816. This new one is a model of scholarship, handsomely printed and interestingly illustrated—in some cases, with hitherto unpublished drawings made by Inigo Jones for the décors and costumes of Jonson's masques.

Except, however, for the first two volumes, which assemble biographical materials and contain historical and critical essays on Jonson's various works, the Herford-Simpson edition is not especially to be recommended to the ordinary nonscholarly reader who may want to make the acquaintance of Jonson. It presents the original text with the seventeenth century punctuation and spelling and with no glossary and no notes except textual ones. The books are, besides, expensive, and the earlier volumes are now hard to get—so the approach to this beetling author remains, as it has always been, rather forbidding and fraught with asperities. The best reprinting of the Gifford edition is also expensive and out of print. The three volumes of selections in the Mermaid Series are full of perplexing misprints, which drop out words or substitute wrong

"Morose Ben Jonson." From *The Triple Thinkers*, revised ed. (Charles Scribner's Sons, 1948), by Edmund Wilson. Copyright 1938, 1948 by Edmund Wilson. Reprinted by permission of the author.

ones, and equipped with inadequate notes that turn up often on the wrong pages. The two volumes in the Everyman's Series include only Jonson's plays, and they are printed in a small dense type that makes them uncomfortable reading; there is a glossary, but it is incomplete. The only breach that I know in the hedge that seems to have sprung up around Jonson, as if his editors had somehow been influenced by their bristling and opaque subject, has been made by Mr. Harry Levin in his *Selected Works, of Ben Jonson* (published by Random House). Here, in a clear readable text of his own and with a brilliant introduction, Mr. Levin has got together most of the best of Jonson for a compact and well-printed volume. There is an obstacle, though, even here, for he has furnished no notes and no glossary, and with Jonson, the explanation of a literary reference or the key to a phrase of slang is often absolutely indispensable for the understanding of a passage.

But it is not merely that Jonson's text itself has been a little hard to get at. It is rather that lack of demand has not stimulated popular editions. *Volpone* can still hold an audience—though it took a German adaptation to bring it back into fashion; and *The Alchemist* has been recently done both in New York and in London; but, among a thousand people, say, who have some knowledge and love of Shakespeare, and even some taste for Webster and Marlowe, I doubt whether you could find half a dozen who have any enthusiasm for Jonson or who have seriously read his plays. T. S. Eliot, admitting the long neglect into which Ben Jonson's work had fallen, put up, in *The Sacred Wood,* a strong plea for Jonson as an artist, and thus made a respect for this poet *de rigueur* in literary circles. But one's impression is that what people have read has been, not Jonson, but Eliot's essay. The dramatist himself, a great master for the age that followed his own, is still for ours mostly a celebrated name, whose writings are left unexplored. What I want to do here is to attack the problem of Jonson's unpopularity from what I believe to be a new point of view, and to show that his failure as a drawing attraction, in either the theater or the study, is bound up in a peculiar way with his difficulties as an artist.

It is a fault of Eliot's essay, so expert in its appreciation of the best-woven passages of Jonson's verse, that it minimizes his glaring defects. If you read it without reading Jonson, you will get a most plausible picture of a special kind of great writer, but this picture is not exactly Jonson. What is suppressed is all that Bernard Shaw meant when, telling off the Elizabethan dramatists, he characterized Ben Jonson as a "brutal pedant"; and, in grappling with Jonson's shortcomings, we cannot perhaps do better than begin by facing squarely those qualities which made it impossible for Shaw—who admired, though he patronized, Shakespeare—to take seriously the comic writer who had, up to Shaw's own appearance, achieved the greatest reputation in English dramatic literature. The point is that Shakespeare, like Shaw, however much they differ in their philosophies, has an immense range, social and moral, in understanding a variety of people. To an intelligent and sensitive man of any school of thought, Shakespeare appears sensitive and intelligent. But Ben Jonson, after Shakespeare, seems neither. Though he attempts a variety of characters, they all boil down to a few motivations, recognizable as the motivations of Jonson himself and rarely transformed into artistic creations. Shakespeare expands himself, breeds his cells as organic beings, till he has so lost himself in the world he has made that we can hardly recompose his personality. Jonson merely splits himself up and sets the pieces—he is to this extent a dramatist—in conflict with one another; but we have merely to put these pieces together to get Jonson, with little left over. In the theater, he aims at several styles, as he tries for a multiplicity of characters, but the variety here, too, is mainly a mere technical matter of metrics and vocabulary, where Shakespeare can summon voices that seem to come from real human throats.

Jonson also lacks natural invention, and his theater has little organic life. His plots are incoherent and clumsy; his juxtapositions of elements are too often like the "mechanical mixtures" of chemistry that produce no molecular reactions. His chief artifices for making something happen are to introduce his characters in impossible disguises and to have them play incredible practical jokes. Nor has he any sense of movement or proportion: almost everything goes on too long, and while it continues, it does not develop. Nor is his taste in other matters reliable. His puns, as Dryden complained, are sometimes of a stunning stupidity; and when he is dirty, he is, unlike Shakespeare, sometimes disgusting to such a degree that he makes one sympathetic with the Puritans in their efforts to clean up the theater. His reading of Greek and Latin, for all the boasting he does about it, has served him very insufficiently for the refinement and ordering of his work, and usually appears in his plays as either an alien and obstructive element or, when more skillfully managed, as a padding to give the effect of a dignity and weight which he cannot supply himself. He is much better when he lets himself go in a vein that is completely unclassical.

It is surely, then, misleading for Eliot to talk of Jonson's "polished surface," to call him a "great creative mind," who "created his own world," and not to warn you of the crudities and aridities, the uncertainty of artistic intention and the flat-footed dramatic incompetence, that you will run into when you set out to read him. None of his plays, with the exception of *The Alchemist*, really quite comes off as a whole. The three others of the best four of his comedies, though they all suffer from the faults I have mentioned, have elements of genuine humor and passages of admirable writing. But the story of *The Silent Woman* is revolting in its forced barbarity (Jonson's murderous practical jokes have their own analogue in literature in the booby-traps of Rudyard Kipling);

Volpone, which reaches at moments a kind of heroic magnificence in exploiting its sordid and cruel themes, suffers, also, though somewhat less, from being based upon practical joking, and it is badly let down at the end by an improbable conventional conclusion; and, as for *Bartholomew Fair,* with some terribly funny scenes and a rich pageant of London low-life, there is in it so much too much of everything that the whole thing becomes rather a wallow of which the Pig-Woman and her pigs are all too truly the symbol. Contrast it with Hogarth's *Southwark Fair* (the product, to be sure, of a more disciplined age), equally confused and crowded, but so much better composed, so much sharper and firmer in outline. With *The Alchemist,* Jonson did ring the bell. This comedy is concentrated and well-constructed. There is no element of false morality to blur Jonson's acrid relish of the confidence games of his rogues: the cynicism is carried right through. The verse, which invests with style, which raises to distinction and glitter till it gives a ring almost like poetry, the slang of the underworld and the jargon of its various chicaneries, is an original achievement of Jonson's, which is only sustained in this one play. And, though there are one or two labored devices, the invention is more resourceful and the dialogue more spontaneous than in any of Jonson's other comedies. Yet this play, one of the funniest in English, is not really an example of high comedy as either a play of Molière's or a play of Aristophanes' is. Ben Jonson is not enough of a critic—that is, he has not enough intelligence—for either Molière's kind of interest in character and human relations or Aristophanes' kind of interest in institutions and points of view. *The Alchemist* is a picaresque farce, fundamentally not different from the Marx brothers. And it shows Jonson's poverty of themes that, when he had earlier attempted a tragedy, he should have arrived at a similar story. *Sejanus,* which takes us to the Roman Senate and inside the court of Tiberius, is also a chronicle of the intrigues of rogues who begin by working together but later sell each other out.

This is a too offhand summary of Jonson's work, but I want to get at him in another way.

Ben Jonson seems an obvious example of a psychological type which has been described by Freud and designated by a technical name, *anal erotic,* which has sometimes misled the layman as to what it was meant to imply. Let me introduce it simply by quoting from the account of it in a handbook of psychoanalysis, *The Structure and Meaning of Psychoanalysis* by William Healy, A. F. Bronner and A. M. Bowers. The three main characteristics of this type are here paraphrased from Freud as follows: "(a) orderliness . . . in an over-accentuated form, pedantry; (b) parsimony, which may become avarice; (c) obstinacy, which may become defiance and perhaps also include irascibility and vindictiveness." Now, Jonson had all these qualities. He was a pedant, whose cult of the classics had little connection with his special kind of genius. There is something of the "compulsive," in the neurotic sense, about his constant citing of precedents and his working into the speeches of his plays passages, sometimes not translated, from the Greek and Latin authors (though it was common for the Elizabethans to stick in scraps from Seneca or Ovid), as if they were charms against failure. That he always did fear failure is evident; and the arrogance, irritability, and stubbornness which are also characteristic of this Freudian type have obviously, in Jonson's case, their origin in a constant anxiety as to the adequacy of his powers. The more he defies his audience, vindicates himself against his critics (though at the same time he puts himself to special pains to propitiate the vulgar with vulgarity and to impress the learned with learning), in his innumerable prologues, inductions, interludes between the acts, epilogues, dramatic postscripts, and apologies added to the printed texts—the more he protests and explains, declaims at unconscionable length his indifference to and scorn of his detractors, the more we feel that he is unquiet, not confident. He is offsetting his internal doubts by demonstrations of self-assertion.

The hoarding and withholding instinct which is the third of the key traits of this type Jonson also displays to a high degree. This tendency is supposed to be based on an atttiude toward the excretatory processes acquired in early childhood. Such people, according to Freud, have an impulse to collect and accumulate; they feel that doing so gives them strength and helps them to resist the pressures that their elders are bringing to bear on them. Sometimes they simply concentrate on storing up; sometimes they expend in sudden bursts. They are likely to have a strong interest in food both from the deglutitionary and the excretatory points of view; but the getting and laying by of money or of some other kind of possession which may or may not seem valuable to others is likely to substitute itself for the infantile preoccupation with the contents of the alimentary tract. Now, Jonson certainly exemplified this tendency, and he exhibited it in a variety of ways. His learning is a form of hoarding; and allied to it is his habit of collecting words. He liked to get up the special jargons of the various trades and professions and unload them in bulk on the public—sometimes with amusing results, as in the case of the alchemical and astrological patter reeled off by the crooks of *The Alchemist,* and even of the technique of behavior of the courtiers in *Cynthia's Revels,* but more often, as with the list of cosmetics recommended by Wittipol in *The Devil Is an Ass* and, to my taste, with the legal Latin of the divorce scene in *The Silent Woman,* providing some of his most tedious moments. The point is that Ben Jonson depends on the exhibition of stored-away knowledge to compel admiration by itself. And the hoarding and withholding of money is the whole subject of that strange play *Volpone.* Volpone is not an ordinary miser: he is a Venetian "magnifico," whose satisfaction in his store of gold is derived not merely from gloating alone but also, and more excitingly, from stimulating others to desire it, to hope to inherit it from him, and then frustrating them with the gratuitous cruelty which has been noted as one of the features of the aggressive side of this Freudian type. The practical jokes in Jonson have usually this sadistic character, and the people who perpetrate them are usually trying either to get something for themselves or to keep someone else from getting something. The many kinds of frauds and sharpers—from pickpockets to promoters—who figure in Jonson's plays as prominently as the practical jokers are occupied with similar aims; and Subtle and Face, in *The Alchemist,* lurk closeted, like Volpone, in a somber house, where they are hoarding their cleverness, too, and plotting their victims' undoing.

I am not qualified to "analyze" Jonson in the light of this Freudian conception, and I have no interest in trying to fit him into any formulation of it. I am not even sure that the relation between the workings of the alimentary tract and the other phenomena of personality is, as Freud assumes, a relation of cause and effect; but I am sure that Freud has here really seized upon a nexus of human traits that are involved with one another and has isolated a recognizable type, and it seems to me to leap to the eyes that Jonson belongs to this type. I shall fill in the rest of my picture with the special characteristics of Jonson, which are consistent with the textbook description and which in some cases strikingly illustrate it.

Ben Jonson's enjoyment of tavern life and his great reputation for wit have created, among those who do not read him, an entirely erroneous impression of high spirits and joviality; but his portraits show rather the face of a man who habitually worries, who is sensitive and holds himself aloof, not yielding himself to intimate fellowship. In many of his plays there figures an unsociable and embittered personage who sometimes represents virtue and censors the other characters, but is in other cases presented by Jonson as a thoroughly disagreeable person and the butt of deserved persecution. Such, in the second of these categories, are Macilente in *Every Man Out of His Humour,* Morose in *The Silent Woman,* Surly in *The Alchemist,* and Wasp in *Bartholomew Fair.* The most conspicuous of these is Morose, and Jonson's treatment of him is particularly significant. The dramatist, on a visit to the country, had encountered a local character who gave him an idea for a play. This was a man who had a morbid aversion to noise. Now, Jonson seems never to have inquired the reason, never to have tried to imagine what the life of such a man would be really like; nor could he ever have been conscious of what it was in himself that impelled him to feel so vivid an interest in him. According to his usual custom, he simply put him on the stage as a "humour," an eccentric with an irrational horror of any kind of sound except that of his own voice, who lives in a room with a double wall and the windows "close shut and caulked" in a street too narrow for traffic, and who, declaring that "all discourses but mine own" seem to him "harsh, impertinent, and irksome," makes his servants communicate with him by signs. And the only way that Jonson can find to exploit the possibilities of this neurotic is to make him the agonized victim of a group of ferocious young men, who hunt him in his burrow like a badger, and trick him into marrying a "silent woman," who, immediately after the ceremony—while her sponsors raise a hideous racket —opens fire on him with a frenzy of chatter, and turns out in the end to be a boy in disguise. But Morose himself is cruel through meanness: he has merited the worst he can suffer. He has wanted to disinherit his nephew, and has consigned him, in a venomous outburst, to the direst humiliation and poverty. Through Morose and through the characters like him, Ben Jonson is tormenting himself for what is negative and recessive in his nature. In *Volpone,* the withholder is punished only after he has had his fling at the delight of tormenting others. Miserliness, unsociability, a self-sufficient and systematic spite—these are among Jonson's dominant themes: all the impulses that grasp and deny. In the final scene of *Cynthia's Revels,* the last play of Jonson's first period, he makes Cynthia rhetorically demand:

> When hath Diana, like an envious wretch,
> That glitters only to his soothed self,
> Denying to the world the precious use
> Of hoarded wealth, withheld her friendly aid?

Yet Cynthia is Diana, and Diana is a virgin queen, who has herself forbidden love to her court; and the attitude which she is here repudiating is to supply almost all the subjects for the rest of Jonson's plays, among them all of his best. In these four lines, you have the whole thing in the words that come to his pen: envy, denial, hoarding, withholding. The first of these is very important. (Envy then meant hatred and spite as well as jealousy of what others have, but I am dealing with it here in its modern sense, which is usually the sense of Jonson.) In several of the earlier plays, it has been one of the chief motivations. In those you have had, on the one hand, the worthy and accomplished scholar—Horace of *The Poetaster,* Crites of *Cynthia's Revels*—who is envied by lesser men; and, on the other hand, the poor and exacerbated wit—Macilente in *Every Man Out of His Humour*—who envies lesser men. But both are aspects of the same personality; both are identified with Jonson himself. Whether the injury done the superior man consists of being slandered by fools or by the fools' being better than he, it is the only fulfillment of the play that he is granted his just revenge, and he scores off his victims with a cruelty almost equal to that of Volpone frustrating his mercenary friends.

With this, there is no love in Jonson's plays to set against these negative values. The references to seduction, frequent though they are, in both his plays and his personal poems, suggest nothing but the coldest of appetites, and often show more gratification at the idea of cuckolding a husband than at that of enjoying a woman. In the plays, two sexual types recur, neither of whom finds any satisfaction in sex. Jonson said of his wife, from whom he separated, that she had been "a shrew, yet honest"; and the only women in his plays that have even a semblance of life are shrews of the most pitiless breed. The typical wife in Jonson is always ready to doublecross her husband, and she does not want to allow him a moment of self-confidence or tranquillity: whatever the man does must be wrong; yet she may cherish at the same time an illusion that there waits for her somewhere a lover who can give her what she desires and deserves, and the appearance of a tenth-rate courtier may be enough to turn her head. The recurrent male type is a man who is insanely jealous of his wife but, paradoxically, is willing to prostitute her. The rival of the obsessive jealousy is always an obsessive greed either for money, as in the case of Corvino of *Volpone,* or, as in the case of Fitzdottrel of *The Devil Is an Ass,* for some other material advantage which the husband will enjoy by himself: Fitzdottrel likes to dress up and be seen on public occasions, but he never takes his wife with him. We may suspect, reading Jonson today, a connection between the impotence of these husbands to spend any real love on their wives and their fears that they are going to lose them. We may reflect that the self-centered husband might produce the shrewish wife, or that, living with a shrewish wife, a man might grow more self-centered, if he did not, as usually happens with the unfortunate husbands of Jonson's plays, become totally demoralized. But Jonson had nothing of Shakespeare's grasp of organic human character or situation. It is interesting to contrast these bitches with the heroine of *The Taming of the Shrew.* Katharina's bad temper with men is accompanied by a deep conviction that no man can really want to marry her: it is a defiant assertion of self-respect. And so the jealousy of Othello (if not of Leontes) is explained by his consciousness, as a Moor in Venice, living among cleverer people who feel his color as a bar to close fellowship, of being at a disadvantage with the race to which his wife belongs. Whereas Jonson's two depressing stock figures do not afford very much insight into the causes of the traits they exemplify. Turning up again and again with a monotony of which Shakespeare was incapable, they obviously represent phenomena which Jonson has known at first hand and on which he cannot help dwelling: two more aspects of that negative soul that he is impelled to caricature. Yet sometimes, with his special experience, he can make them reveal themselves—as in the self-torturing Proustian soliloquies of Kitely in *Every Man In His Humour*—in a way that strips off the skin to show, not what is in the depths, but what is just below the surface.

Jonson's positive ideal of womanhood may be summed up in the well-known lyric that begins, "Have you seen but a bright lily grow,/ Before rude hands have touched it?," and ends "O so white! O so soft! O so sweet is she!" It is something quite remote and unreal which he is unable—when he tries, which is seldom, as in the Celia of *Volpone*—to bring to life in his plays, and, though the poems inspired by it are neat and agreeable enough, they have no human tenderness in them, let alone human passion. The touches in Jonson's poetry that come closest to lyric feeling are invariably evocations of coldness: "Like melting snow upon a craggy hill . . . Since nature's pride is now a withered daffodil," or "Except Love's fires the virtue have/ To fright the frost out of the grave," (from a poem in which the same stanza begins with the incredibly prosaic couplet: "As in a ruin, we it call/ One thing to be blown up or fall . . ."). And we may cite from the masque called *The Vision of Delight* the lines that remained in the memory of Joyce's Stephen Dedalus: "I was not wearier where I lay/ By frozen Tithon's side tonight . . ."; as well as the passage from the prose *Discoveries* which Saintsbury selected for praise: "What a deal of cold business doth a man misspend the better part of life in!—in scattering compliments, tendering visits, gathering and venting news, following feasts and plays, making a little winter-love in a dark corner." At the end of *Cynthia's Revels,* Cupid tries to shoot Cynthia's courtiers and make them fall in love with one another, but he finds that his bow is powerless: they have been drinking from the fount of Self-Love, in which Narcissus admired himself, and they are impervious to his shafts. When Diana is told of his presence, she sends him packing at once. Few lovers are united by Jonson. Is there indeed a case in all his work? And in Jonson's latest plays, the heroines undergo a transformation that makes Cynthia seem relatively human. The Lady Pecunia of *The Staple of News,* surrounded by her female retinue, Mortgage, Statute, Band, and Wax, is simply a figure in a financial allegory; and so is Mistress Steel, the Magnetic Lady. Both are heiresses, kept close by guardians and sought by baffled suitors. The feminine principle here has been turned by the instinct for hoarding into something metallic, unyielding. The woman has lost all her womanhood: she is literally the hoarded coin. This evidently appeared to Ben Jonson a perfectly natural pleasantry, but it is quite enough to account for the failure, in his time, of these pieces, and for the distaste that we feel for them today.

To these stock characters of Jonson's theater should be added another that evidently derives from the playwright's social situation as well as from his psychology of hoarding. Ben Jonson, from his own account, was the son of a Scotch gentleman who had possessed some little fortune, but who had been thrown into prison, presumably for his Protestant leanings, in the reign of Bloody Mary, and had had his property confiscated. He died before Ben was born, and Ben's mother married a master bricklayer. Young Ben went to Westminster school, under the patronage of one of the masters, whose attention had been attracted by the boy's ex-

ceptional abilities, and may have started in at Cambridge on a scholarship; but he was obliged, apparently through poverty, to give up his
studies there, and was set to learn the bricklayer's trade, which he
loathed and from which he escaped by enlisting to fight in Flanders.
Now, one of Jonson's favorite clowns, who varies little from play to
play, is a young heir who is an utter numbskull and who, just having
come into his money, begins throwing it away by the handful and soon
finds himself fleeced by sharpers. This figure, too, in a different way from
the envied or the envious man, is obviously the creation of Jonson's own
envy, stimulated, no doubt, from two sources—first, the grievance of the
man of good birth unjustly deprived of his patrimony, and, second, the
sulky resentment of the man who can only withhold against the man who
can freely lavish.

Jonson's hardships and uncertainty in his earlier years—when he can
never have known anything but poverty—must have spurred him to
desperate efforts to ballast and buttress himself. (For, as I have said, I do
not necessarily accept the view of Freud that the training of the excretatory functions must precede the development of other traits which exhibit resistance through hoarding, though it seems certain that, in personalities like Jonson's, these various traits are related.) He had acquired
classical learning where he could not acquire money; and it was to remain for him a reservoir of strength, a basis of social position, to which
he was to go on adding all his life. But his habit of saving and holding
back—did his Scotch ancestry figure here, too?—had an unfortunate
effect on his work, as well as on his personal relations, in that it made
it very difficult for him fully to exploit his talents. It is not that the
audiences of Jonson's day, the readers who have come to him since, have
been unwilling to give themselves to his talents, but that his talents,
authentic though they were, have not given themselves to us—or rather,
that they were able to give themselves for only a limited period and then
only at the expense of much effort. Ben Jonson, at his best, writes bril-
liantly; he has a genuine dramatic imagination. But it is hard for him
to pump up his powers to work that will display their capacities. His
addiction to wine—"drink," Drummond said, "is one of the elements in
which he liveth"—was, I believe, bound up with the problem of getting
himself to the point of high-pressure creative activity. He explained the
strength of *Volpone* on the basis of its having been written at the time
when he had just received a gift of ten dozen of sack; asserted that a
passage in *Catiline* had suffered from having been composed when he
was drinking watered wine; and apologized for the weakness of his later
plays on the ground that he and his "boys"—by which he meant his
drinking companions—had been getting bad wine at their tavern. This
shows that he drank while he was writing; and it is possible that liquor,
though effective in helping him to keep up his high vein, may also have

been to blame for the badness of some of his work. There are at times a peculiar coarseness in the texture of Jonson's writing, a strained falseness in his comic ideas, which, intolerable to a sober mind, may very well have seemed inspired to a constipated writer well primed with sack. What Jonson was aiming at—from *Cynthia's Revels,* say—was a majesty and splendor of art which should rival the classics he venerated and the work of his more dashing contemporaries, with their rhetoric, color, and spirit. But it is hard to be noble and grand with material so negative, so sour, as that which Jonson's experience had given him. To write in blank verse that is also poetry of the imbecile ambitions and the sordid swindles which furnish the whole subject of *The Alchemist* was a feat that even Ben Jonson was never to achieve but once. When he attempts a Roman tragedy, as in *Catiline* or *Sejanus,* his Romans are mostly the envious rogues, the merciless prigs, and the treacherous sluts with whom we are familiar in his comedies, and they make a more unpleasant impression for not being humorously treated. When Jonson attempts Renaissance splendor, he always gives it an element of the factitious as well as an element of the vulgar, which, as Mr. Levin says, have the effect of making it look ridiculous. The dreams of Sir Epicure Mammon bring a kind of hard glow to the writing, but his banquets and his beds and his mirrors are imaginary like the gold that is to buy them: they never get on to the stage as does the "alchemist's" fusty lair. And with *Volpone,* the great difficulty is that the mean motivations of the characters have no intimate connection with the background, the house of a rich Venetian. Volpone is simply another of Jonson's hateful and stingy men, who behaves as if he were envious of others, without being provided by Jonson with any real reason for envy. The magnificence of Jonson's grandees, like the purity of his women, is a value that is always unreal and that can never make a satisfactory counterweight to a poverty and a squalor that are actual and vividly rendered. One has to go to the later French naturalists who were influenced by both Flaubert and Zola to find anything comparable to the poetry which Jonson was able to extract from all the cheap and dirty aspects of London: the "poor spoonful of dead wine, with flies in't"; the gingerbread made of "stale bread, rotten eggs, musty ginger and dead honey"; the rogue out of luck,

> at Pie Corner,
> Taking your meal of steam in, from cooks' stalls.
> Where, like the father of hunger, you did walk
> Piteously costive, with your pinched horn-nose,
> And your complexion of the Roman wash
> Stuck full of black and melancholic worms,
> Like powder-corns shot at th' artillery-yard;

the theater pick-ups, "lean playhouse poultry," as described by fat Ursula of the pig-roasting booth, "that has the bony rump sticking out like the ace of spades or the point of a partizan, that every rib of 'em is like the tooth of a saw; or will so grate 'em [their customers] with their hips and shoulders as—take 'em altogether—they were as good lie with a hurdle." It is the peculiar beauty of *The Alchemist* that the visions of splendor here are all, frankly, complete illusions created out of sordid materials by rogues in the minds of dupes. The poor stupid whore Doll has to impersonate the Queen of Faery and a great lady in romantic circumstances. A more humane writer might have extracted some pathos from this; but Jonson does get an esthetic effect that is quite close to the Flaubertian chagrin.

But, in *Volpone,* where real gold is involved, we are never allowed to see it. The German adaptation of this play made by Stefan Zweig and done here by the Theater Guild, which has also been used as a basis for the current French film, is an improvement on Jonson's original in one very important respect. It shows us what we want to see, what, subconsciously, we have come to demand: the spending, the liberation of Volpone's withheld gold—when Mosca, to everyone's relief, finally flings it about the stage in fistfuls. But Ben Jonson cannot squander his gold, his gold which he has never possessed; he can only squander excrement. Karl Abraham, one of the psychologists quoted in the book referred to above, "cites, in proof of the close association between sadistic and anal impulses instances in his experiences with neurotics when an explosive bowel evacuation has been a substitute for a discharge of anger or rage, or has accompanied it." Certainly Jonson seems to explode in this fashion. The directness with which he gives way to the impulse is probably another cause of his chronic unpopularity. The climax of *The Poetaster* is the administering of emetic pills, the effects of which take, in this case, the form of a poetic joke. The comic high point of *The Alchemist* comes with the locking of one of the characters in a privy, where he will be overcome by the smell. This whole malodorous side of Jonson was given its fullest and most literal expression in the poem called *The Famous Voyage* which was too much for even Gifford and Swinburne, in which he recounts a nocturnal expedition made by two London blades in a wherry through the roofed-over tunnel of Fleet Ditch, which was the sewer for the public privies above it. A hardly less literal letting-go is the whole play of *Bartholomew Fair,* which followed the more pretentious work (from *Sejanus* through *Catiline*) that we have just been discussing. It is Ben Jonson's least strained and inhibited play, and one of his most successful. He drops verse for colloquial prose; he forgets about classical precedents. He dumps out upon his central group of characters, for the most part pusillanimous examples of the lower middle class, puritan parsons and petty officials, with, of course, a young spendthrift from the country, what must have been a lifetime's accumulation of the bill-ingsgate and gutter practices of the pickpockets, booth-keepers, peddlers, pimps, ballad-singers, and professional brawlers of the Elizabethan under-world. This comedy, novel in its day, anticipates both Hogarth and Dickens; but Jonson's impulse to degrade his objects is something not shared by either. Hogarth and Dickens both, for all their appetite for rank vulgarity, are better-humored and more fastidious. The flood of abusive language let loose by the infuriated Pig-Woman, well-written and funny though it is, is outpouring for outpouring's sake: it effects no dramatic move and has in itself no rhetorical development; and the even more filthy travesty of Marlowe's *Hero and Leander* in terms of bankside muck has an ugliness which makes one suspect that Jonson took an ugly delight in defiling a beautiful poem which he could not hope to rival. Yet we cannot but succumb—in certain scenes, at least—to the humor of *Bartholomew Fair*. The tumult of Ursula's booth and her de-votion to her roasting pigs, the monumental pocket-picking episode that moves to its foreseen conclusion almost with the inevitability of tragedy —these somehow create more sympathy (always for the characters outside the law) than anything else in Jonson's plays.

And Ben Jonson is somehow a great man of letters, if he is not often a great artist. His very failure to make the best of his gifts had the result of his leaving a body of work full of hints—unrealized ambitions, un-developed beginnings—which later writers were able to exploit in a way that it was hardly possible for them to do with the work of Shakespeare, which *was* realized, consummate, complete. The most astonishing variety of writers owe quite different kinds of debts to Jonson. It is as if they had found means to deliver, in viable forms of art, the genius that Jon-son had had to withhold. Gifford was certainly right in supposing that Milton owed something to such passages as the opening of *Volpone*, in which the hoarder invokes his gold. The whole comedy of Congreve and Wycherley seems to have grown out of the cynical men-about-town, with their bravura-pieces of wit, in *The Silent Woman;* and Swift must have picked up from Jonson, not only the title of *A Tale of a Tub,* but also the style and tone of his series of poems to Stella, which are so much like certain of those in Jonson's series, *A Celebration of Charis,* as well as his general vein of morosely humorous realism, exemplified in "The Lady's Dressing Room" and "A Description of a City Shower." The comedy of humours eventually led to the one-idea characters of Peacock, which led, later, to those of Aldous Huxley; and it must have contributed to the novels of Dickens, who loved to act Bobadill in *Every Man In His Humour.* Though Tennyson was under the impression that he himself had invented the stanza-form that he made famous in *In Memoriam,* it had already been used by Jonson in his *Elegy* (XXII of *Underwoods*), the tone of which is quite close to Tennyson in his elegiac vein, and in the second of the choruses to *Catiline*, which suggests such weightier use of the meter as one finds in the dedication to Queen Victoria or in the dedication of *Demeter* to Lord Dufferin. And there are touches in Lewis Carroll that seem reminiscent of Jonson: "I passed by the garden and marked with one eye/ How the Owl and the Panther were sharing the pie," recalls a long nonsense speech in *The Vision of Delight:* "Yet would I take the stars to be cruel/ If the crab and the rope-maker ever fight duel," etc.; and Sir Politic Would-be of *Volpone*, with his succession of ridiculous inventions, of which he likes to boast, "Mine own device," is a forerunner of the White Knight. In the first decades of our own century, that very first-rate comic writer, Ronald Firbank, with how little direct contact one cannot tell, represents a very late development of Ben Jonson's typical methods—eviscerated personalities and monstrous motivations labeled with bizarre names—which, though it shows perhaps a certain decadence, keeps also a good deal of vigor. And James Joyce, who told his friend Frank Budgen that Ben Jonson was one of the only four writers that he had ever read completely through, seems to have had in common with Jonson some of the traits of his psychological type, and may be said to have followed his example—failing, sometimes, from faults like Jonson's—rather, perhaps, than to have exploited to better effect any special aspect of Jonson's work. Joyce, too, hoarded words and learning and attempted to impress his reader by unloading his accumulations; he, too, has his coprophilic side and his husbands who acquiesce, at the same time that they torture themselves, in the sleepings-abroad of their wives; he, too, is defiant and arrogant, self-consciously resistant to pressures, and holds himself apart and aloof.

It would be interesting, from this point of view, to compare Ben Jonson at length with Gogol as well as with Joyce. Undoubtedly Gogol is a case even more narrowly developed than Jonson of the type in question here. He, too, likes to store up words—his note-books were full of the jargons of special trades and milieux; and he voids them in long dense sentences that agglutinate as massive paragraphs. His characters, in *Dead Souls*, are themselves almost always collectors, and they sometimes collect sheer rubbish—like Manilov, who saves all his old pipe-ashes. Gogol loves to write about eating, he has little sensual interest in women. His comedy *The Inspector General*, farcical, at once gross and inhuman, has something in common with Jonson's comedies; and, like Jonson, he is powerless to lift himself—in the unfinished later instalments of *Dead Souls*—out of the satirical comedy of roguery into a sterner and less turbid medium. The virtuous judge and the altruistic landowner of the second part of *Dead Souls* are as obviously maniacs as the misers and boors of the first part—as the senators, conspirators, and emperors of Jonson's Roman plays are just as much "compulsive" one-track minds as the characters of his comedy of "humours." So Joyce, with greater genius and wider range than either Jonson or Gogol, cannot seem to function comfortably and freely except when he has given himself, as in his two most ambitious books, the latitude of a comic frame: his protagonists are comic figures, humiliated, persecuted, rueful, and their epics are systematic ironies, in which their heroic pretensions never wholly emerge from the mud. Gogol and Joyce, too, both share with Jonson his ideal of feminine sweetness and purity—seen only in wistful glimpses—that floats somewhere above and divorced from the smelly and dirty earth. With this motif Gogol succeeds least well: the lovely face fleetingly seen in the coach by Chichikov of *Dead Souls,* the maidenly pensionnaire who strikes him dumb at the ball; Jonson, a little better in the lyrics mentioned above; Joyce, with triumphant success in the vision of the wading girl that makes the climax of *A Portrait of the Artist.*

Later years did not mellow Jonson. When he visited Drummond at forty-five, with most of his best work behind him, he was still running down his contemporaries and asserting his own merits as peevishly as in the days when he had written *The Poetaster;* and at a supper given for him by his younger admirers the year before his death, he painfully embarrassed his friends by inordinately praising himself and vilifying his fellow poets. He could never afford to be generous, because he had never achieved what he wanted; and one suspects that, even in the case of such a lesser contemporary as Marston, Jonson's hateful hostility toward him had in it an element of envy of that touch of sublimity and magic which Marston was able to manage and which was quite beyond Jonson's reach. To Drummond he even grumbled about Shakespeare; and his reference to *The Tempest* in *Bartholomew Fair* betrays how much it must have irked him to see his friend, a much older man, find suddenly a new field for his genius in a form so close to that of the masque, in which Jonson had worked for years without ever striking more than an occasional spark from his pedantic made-to-order prettiness. It is therefore all the more a proof of the deep devotion he cherished for the art that they both practiced that he should have put on record so roundly his high opinion of Shakespeare—and not only of Shakespeare, but also of Donne. In his elegy on Shakespeare especially, in estimating him above all their contemporaries and setting him beside the greatest of the ancients, he does justice to all that is noblest in his own aspiring nature, which had to drag so much dead weight, all that is soundest and most acute in his own cramped but virile intellect. The one thing he really loved was literature, and, having served it as well as he could, no touchiness of personal pride could keep him from honoring one who had been fitted to serve it better precisely by the qualification, among others, of possessing, as Jonson said, "an open and free nature," so that he "flowed with that facility that sometimes it was necessary he should be stopped."

Introduction to
Every Man In His Humour

by Arthur Sale

Date and Text

Every Man In His Humour was first acted in 1598 by the Chamberlain's men, the company to which Shakespeare belonged: according to the list of actors in the Folio text, Shakespeare acted in the play, apparently taking the part of old Knowell. The play appeared in Quarto in 1601, and in the Folio of Jonson's works in 1616. There is so great a difference between the two texts that one might almost call them different plays.[1] But there is none of the mystery that surrounds the relationship between the Quarto and Folio texts of many plays of the Shakespeare canon; the Folio text is plainly a careful revision of the Quarto, and the only mystery is—when was the revision carried out? The most natural conclusion is that Jonson rewrote the play when preparing for the press the edition of his *Works* which appeared in 1616. The maturity of style points to a late date and the changes and omissions nearly all point to an enlarged knowledge of dramatic technique and a more assured genius. The care expended on the revision is consonant with the care devoted to the publication of his *Works,* which extends down even to the actual printing—a very rare thing for a dramatist of that age.

This evidence is all circumstantial, but Percy Simpson has been able, with sufficient plausibility, to assign a likely date—1612, when, probably, Jonson first set about the great operation of preparing a definitive edition of his works, amid the jeers of those who thought it characteristic of Ben's arrogance that he should dare to include *plays* under the honorable title of *Works*. However chary one may be of fixing an actual date, it is at least sufficiently clear that the revised version belongs to the

"Introduction to *Every Man In His Humour*." From *Every Man In His Humour,* ed. Arthur Sale, Second Edition, pp. x-xviii. Copyright 1949 by University Tutorial Press Limited. Reprinted by permission of the publisher. The excerpt reproduced here omits a few pages of biographical preface, and several concluding paragraphs.

[1] The *Everyman* reprint of Jonson's plays has both texts.

period of Jonson's greatest plays, and if the play . . . is not among these
plays in respect of greatness, it is not the reviser's fault, but the inherent
limitations in situation and range of the 'prentice play.

To compare the two texts would be at first an interesting, then a
laborious, and finally a nightmare task. The conclusions are evident
from the first and are rarely challengeable; . . . in general the revised
version is superior to the original. The latter is of a similar quality to
Jonson's next play, *Every Man Out of His Humour,* though it is better in plot and situations than that pot-boiling attempt to exploit the
Humours vogue stimulated, if not initiated by *Every Man In His
Humour.* Nevertheless, although detailed comparisons would be, in the
last resort, academic, a number of well-chosen ones would form the
material for useful exercises in literary evaluation. For comparative
studies in dramatic technique such exercises would be valuable as well
as useful; but for calling attention to the underrated excellence of Jonson's mature *verse,* they are of less value, partly because the most typical
humour of the play lends itself best to prose, and partly because the
revised verse is, naturally, still within the magnetic field of the early
verse.

Position in the Jonson Canon

The play continues to be the best known (if only by name) of Jonson's plays. There are several reasons for this odd persistence of acclama-
tion, none of which has any real connection with the merits of the play
—which one would expect to be the only valid test of popularity. These
reasons are part and parcel of that fatal process by which, as Mr. T. S.
Eliot acutely points out in his study of Jonson in *The Sacred Wood,*
Jonson has remained great in name and unread in fact—a victim of his
own massive reputation.

Jonson liked to blow his own trumpet. It is possible that this was less
a form of exhibitionism than a showman's device for raising interest in
his little act. Another dramatist, Mr. G. B. Shaw, has exploited the device
far more systematically and persistently than did Jonson, and with, if
anything, greater effect. At all events, an unknown and unsuccessful
dramatist writes a play in which certain catchy conceptions floating
through the inconstant air of the public consciousness are regularized
and given a local habitation and a name. The play is successful and the
astute author makes haste to have his name prominently and exclusively
fixed to these notions: he writes another play in which he defines these
Humours, contemptuously rejecting all imitations, and says, in effect,
"Patent applied for." Further, he employs a character-spectator and his
"feed" to point out the dramatic beauties of the various Humoured char-

acters, and the wonderful way in which a classical theory of comedy is adapted to the English stage.

In the last sentence we may have a clue to the inordinate attention *Every Man In His Humour* has received. Jonson makes his name *via* the Humours. He also has a classical theory of comedy, which the critics and editors far too easily assume to be the same as his humours theory. *E.M.I.H.H.*, having the advantage of illustrating both theories, is especially convenient for the literary historian. As a result, everyone begins his or her study of Jonson, almost inevitably, with this play, whereas, it might be fitter, in the interest of a just perspective, to read it last—of the important plays at least.[2] Hence the falsely significant position it has acquired in the Jonson canon.

Constituents

In Jonson, everything is subdued unto the quality of the play. The play's the thing. This is vague enough to be true of all good drama, but it is true of Jonson in a special way. Nothing in the play has any reality *apart from its position in the play*. To use an analogy which is exact enough up to a point, the play is a completed jigsaw puzzle, each bit of which is coherent only in its relation to the whole. Here, as in so many other ways, the contrast with Shakespeare is inevitable and illuminating. Each part of a Shakespeare play may have a separate dynamic of its own, which may, or may not, have its proper relationship with the whole. The conception of Falstaff is an obvious example. Whether one feels he is a sort of genial cancer into whose mighty bulk most of the lifeblood of the play is drained, or whether one takes him as a separate and equal organism to the rest of the play, representing another, contrasting, set of values to those of the main plot—it will be agreed that he gives at least the illusion of being able to exist apart from the circumstances and conditions of the plays in which he appears. But one is not likely to feel this of any of Jonson's deliberately flat pieces. In his eyes it would be a breach of decorum—that decorum which is the real conditioning factor of his dramatic theory, whereas the Humours, by comparison, are only the advertisement bills. Jonson maintains this decorum (crippling or not, as you please) more strictly than any of those who were influenced by some aspects of his works. Massinger's best comedy is in the Jonsonian tradition, and owes its characteristic excellence to that tradition, but Overreach is on the way to having that third dimension which Shake-

---

[2] "*E.M.I.H.H.* is the first mature work of Jonson and every student of Jonson must study it, but it is not the play in which Jonson found his genius: it is the last of his plays to be read first." (T. S. Eliot)

speare has and which Jonson rejects, even in such dominating figures as
Sir Epicure Mammon or Volpone.

It is not, then (if we can trust the jigsaw analogy far enough), very
profitable to discuss such supposedly-separate elements of a play as *character* and *plot* in isolation from the play itself. It is true that the pieces
have to be put together in a *certain order* (which is not true of a jigsaw
puzzle, and so the analogy fails at this point), in order to assemble the
whole, but it is not true that this order has any significance apart from
its being the key to the construction. In Shakespeare the players act upon
one another; motives are working, explicitly or behind the scenes; the
plot develops accordingly. In our play, Brainworm *is* the plot; he is the
key to the right ordering of the pieces of the puzzle, but it is useless to
talk of *motive* in connection with him; the plot is one of the Humours
in action: the Humour, by finally overreaching itself, is put out of
action. Which is exactly the dramatist's purpose for the play as a whole.
But it is absurd to talk of Brainworm's motive apart from his Humour.
His Humour *is* the one and only motive. And this applies to the whole
play. How, then, can we hope to give a full account of plot and of character, separate from each other? Kitely's jealousy, for example, although
ultimately based on observations of its operations in real life, is purely
conditioned by the play's total demands. However intensely manifested,
it is not a *study* of jealousy, so much as a *use* of it as an ingredient in
the recipe of the play. As such, Kitely is unlike Othello, and like Ford.
It is significant that the latter appears in a play (*The Merry Wives of
Windsor*) which is prevailingly farce. Jonson's method is akin to that of
farce.

But where farce (in the interests of mirth) consistently sacrifices even
such stock and ready-made characterizing as it possesses, to the situation,
Jonson would condemn such a breach of dramatic *decorum;* the situation in Jonson *reveals* character, and is specially contrived to this end.
In this sense, farce is opposite to the Jonsonian method. And whereas the
aim of farce is solely to awaken laughter, such irresponsibility is repug-
nant to Jonson. There is a good deal more in even an early comedy like
E.M.I.H.H. than there is in a farce, dramatic craftsmanship and other
technical features being equal. What this something extra is, is not too
easy to analyze. It is usually said to be Jonson's realism and satire. Jonson, it is said, is a dissector rather than a creator, and it used even to be
said that his "critical spirit" was ultimately a cause of the decadence of
this period of drama.

Realism and satire are both present in Jonson's comedies, but there
is no difficulty in showing that the former at least is merely incidental.
Except in *Bartholomew Fair*, there is no faithful picture of real life as
there is in, say, Dekker's *Shoemaker's Holiday,* or in *The Roaring Girl.*
In our play, the realism consists largely of local touches and references,
mostly added in the revised version. The original setting was Italian,

names as well. The model is too much that of Roman comedy to allow
realism as an end in itself.

As for satire, there is, in any case, very little overt satire in *E.M.I.H.H.*,
but such satire of *contemporary* men and manners and institutions—satire such as Pope practiced it—as is to be found in Jonsonian comedy, is
not integral to his *greatest* masterpieces. Some of his "dotage" plays consist almost entirely of attack on the false standards of capitalism, and of
such of its enterprises as the press, company-floating, etc. But within the
limits of *E.M.I.H.H., Volpone, The Alchemist, The Silent Woman, Bartholomew Fair,* such contemporary satire is detachable. It is no doubt of
these plays that Mr. Eliot was thinking when he wrote: "But satire like
Jonson's is great in the end not by hitting off its object, but by creating
it; the satire is merely the means which leads to an aesthetic result, the
impulse which projects a new world into a new orbit."

Whether or not this last is true of all great satirists, it at least calls
attention to the *uniqueness* of Jonson's comic world, and corrects the
usual view that his plays are heavy transcripts of contemporary life,
chopped into an arbitrary shape by a rigid application of the classical
unities, of which the sole end is rather pedantic ridicule. Such a reputation has effectually killed him as a dramatist transcending the limits of
space and time and having that element of "permanent modernity"
which is necessary for his plays to be still acted as living theater and not
as museum pieces to illustrate the history of drama.

In the other sense of satire, the Swiftian sense whereby man himself
is castigated, independent of his local ties, Jonson cannot be seriously
considered a satirist. His morality in the large sense reveals itself mainly
in an unsentimental sympathy for, and delight in, roguery, provided it
be unhypocritical and frank. This may indeed be implicitly a satire on
the hypocrisy of respectability, but it makes Jonson a thoroughly un-
orthodox moralist; it is the morality of the enemies, not of the pillars,
of society. Brainworm is a faint dawning of this Villon strain. . . .

Pattern

If, as has been maintained, it is of little use to consider plot and
"character" (*type* would be more appropriate) separately for the purpose
of literary criticism, one has to fall back on considering what one ven-
tures to call the total *pattern* of the play, traced by the various constituents. Jonson is often called heavy-handed and costive. In the matter of
pattern these attacks will not hold. Dryden's analysis of *The Silent
Woman* in the *Essay of Dramatic Poesy* is one way of demonstrating the
trimness and sound structure of Jonson's watertight vessel of comedy. It
is the way of the classical comedy, and Jonson would have paid at least

lipservice to it. But although it establishes the shapeliness of the skeleton, it does not trace the shapely lines of the finished boat. The workman may have been "heavy-handed" and may have taken an unconscionable long time over the building, but the launched vessel does not look the worse for having had a good riveter and a careful attention to detail.

That this *pattern* is rigid may be admitted, but the association of heaviness is misleading; iron is rigid and heavy, but pressed into girders and used with glass it forms the lightest structure known, as architects of the Crystal Palace and the big railway stations first realized. It is a perfect and easily realized whole, however complicated its parts, whereas to the Elizabethan manor, one wing the more or one storey the less seems to matter little in terms of symmetry and of stresses and strains. But here the metaphor breaks down, and we must resort to another, for Jonson's structure is also *independent of the ground;* it is a separate world. It has the perfect structure, the surface tension and iridescence, of a large bubble, but a bubble so constructed that by the laws of its own dynamic it must explode the second it becomes a whole. Jonson's plays blow themselves out of existence; their resolution is necessarily their end. This is true of his 'prentice bubble-blowing in *E.M.I.H.H.* The characters are *in* their Humour and then *out,* and there is nothing more to be said. The purpose for which the parts were assembled is achieved, and not a wrack is left behind. In this play, it is true, the dynamic is more feeble, and the progress rarely deviates from the horizontal; Brainworm's worming is along the ground. But the conception is there.

To conclude, then: although these things are tangible only in the guise of metaphors, which are bound to be partly misleading, it should be evident that though the much-vaunted Humours, and the debt to classical comedy both in structural theory and in aim, do together to some extent determine the *shape* and *limits* of *E.M.I.H.H.*, they tell us little about the dynamic of the play, or of the effect it produces. In the latter respect they may be positively misleading. In particular, the Humours have too much and too unprofitably attracted the attention of the more recent critics.[3] Gifford hardly mentions them. He claims originality for Jonson almost entirely because of his reforms in aim and plot, based on his study of Latin and Greek comedy and of centuries of criticism of these. But the critics have continued to confuse Humours, which belong to *method,* with his supposed didacticism, which belongs to the *ends.* of comedy. This confusion is not so important in the Humours plays themselves as in plays like *The Alchemist,* in which the Humours method of presenting character is absent. In any case, the stock characters of Roman comedy and of the Italian *improvvisatori* (the *Commedia dell'Arte*) are sufficiently close to Jonson's method to serve

[3] A notable exception is H. Levin's introduction to the Nonesuch Jonson.

as models. Besides these he had the galvanized abstractions of the Morality plays in his own country to help him; the influence on him of the Morality tradition, which was still strong in his youth, among the people at least, has been underrated in favor of the catchword "Humours." In some of his last plays he goes straight back to the Morality for his characters (*e.g.*, the goddess Pecunia in *The Staple of News*) and for his didactic attitude. There seems, then, no reason to believe Jonson was not sensitive to this tradition when he was closer to it in time and touch. If it could be demonstrated that Jonson had made an important contribution to comedy with his Humours, one could understand the usual insistence on them, even though they do not account for much in the practice of his middle period of drama. But when did satiric comedy ever cease to isolate the follies of mankind, for ridicule and castigation? Jonson attempted the illusion of novelty by giving them a topical name and a topical dress.

Introduction to
Every Man Out of His Humour

by C. H. Herford

I

The title of *Every Man Out of His Humour* appears to announce it
as a companion piece to its immediate predecessor;—a sister comedy with
an inverted motive, somewhat as *Love's Labors Won* may have been a
converse to *Love's Labors Lost,* or as Fletcher's *The Tamer Tamed*
turned the tables upon *The Taming of the Shrew.* It is clear, however,
that the relation between the two Humour plays is not of this kind at all.
Every Man Out of His Humour is neither a counterpart nor a contrast,
neither a companion piece nor a sequel, to *Every Man In His Humour.*
It is a second handling of the same theme, with a more direct satiric
purpose and a more uncompromising and defiant originality of method.
Jonson had won his spurs; and less than the success of his first great
comedy would have sufficed to remove any restraint imposed by regard
for the stage tradition upon his unfledged genius. Whether the earlier
play was already introduced to its first audience with the haughty
declarations of the Prologue is, as has been said, very doubtful. It is
certain that, however sharply *Every Man In His Humour* traversed
certain romantic proclivities of the stage, it powerfully appealed to the
engrained realism of the Elizabethan audience. It did not give them all
that they wanted; but it gave them, with a vigor and brilliance paralleled
as yet only in the contemporary glory of Falstaff's Eastcheap, what they
wanted most. It was put forward, explicitly or not, as a model or a
standard play, towards which it was desirable the Elizabethan practice
should gravitate; and Elizabethan practice did in fact so gravitate. No
such claim can ever have been advanced or entertained in regard to *Every*

"Introduction to *Every Man Out of His Humour.*" From *Ben Jonson: The Man and
His Work* by C. H. Herford and Percy Simpson, I, 375-398. Copyright 1925 by The
Clarendon Press, Oxford. Reprinted by permission of The Clarendon Press, Oxford.
Roughly two pages of prefatory comment concerning the dating and printing of the
play are here omitted, and the subsections renumbered accordingly.

Man Out of His Humour. Jonson himself, entirely confident as he was of its merits, well knew that they did not lie in conformity to any school of drama, new or old. The play was "strange, and of a particular kind by it selfe"; to be approved possibly by the humanists of the Inns of Court, but "how it will answere the generall expectation, I know not." If he claims that it is "like *Vetus Comoedia*," the likeness lies in its vigorous independence of tradition, and he puts into the mouth of Cordatus a sketch of the history of ancient comedy in which the entire development of the genre is exhibited as a series of innovations in dramatic method. In Aristophanes "this kind of *Poeme* appeared absolute, and fully perfected"; nevertheless, his successors, Menander, Plautus, and the rest, had wholly changed its character.[1] If classical comedy was thus built upon the defiance of precedent, "I see not then, but we should enjoy the same licence, or free power, to illustrate and heighten our invention as they did; and not bee tyed to those strict and regular formes, which the nicenesse of a few (who are nothing but forme) would thrust upon us." This, far more than the peremptory classicism of the Prologue to *Every Man In His Humour* expresses the inner mind of Jonson. It is the spirit which years later speaks ("albeit by adoption") in the sinewy prose of the *Discoveries* under those notable rubrics *"Natura non effoeta"* and *"Non nimium credendum antiquitati."*—"Truth lyes open to all; it is no mans *severall"*; "For to all the observations of the *Ancients,* wee have our owne experience." [2] This haughty confidence in innovation can never have been altogether strange to Jonson: in the present play we see it for the first time let loose without reserve upon the traditional structure and method of the comic drama.

Close and continuous as was Jonson's connection with the drama, immense as were his services to it, drama as then or at any previous time practiced was not an instrument perfectly fitted to serve his aims in literature. He did not approach the stage "as wishing to delight," but with the imperious bent of a critical and scornful nature, to inveigh, to instruct, to eradicate, to amend. His natural gift for drama was moreover probably matched by his gift of analytic and epigrammatic description. To reduce these powerful conflicting faculties to the service of the drama is commonly a slow and difficult process. The exuberant poet of *Brand* and *Peer Gynt* had sternly to transform his whole artistic method before he achieved the terrible reticence of *Ghosts*. But Ibsen's dramatic instinct was from the outset surer and stronger than Jonson's; he thought in drama where Jonson thought in epigram and invective; his social satire never crushes or starves his action, hardly ever overlays or retards it.

---

[1] *Vetus Comoedia* in this passage necessarily means Greek and Roman Comedy. But there was no inconsistency, as Baskervill, *English Elements in Jonson's Early Comedy* (Austin, 1911), p. 212, suggests, in his use of the phrase "Comoedia Vetus in England" to Drummond (*Conv.* xvii. 410) for the ancient native drama.

[2] *Discoveries,* Folio, p. 89.

The most directly polemical aim does not relax his grip upon plot, or the grip of his plot upon us. In the masterpieces of his maturity Jonson was to find a dramatic expression no less potent for the Juvenal that chafed within him. But at the present stage that consummation was still remote, and the impatient Juvenal has forged for himself a satire roughly accommodated indeed to the forms of the traditional drama, but fundamentally inspired and controlled by the purpose of "stripping the ragged follies of the time, naked, as at their birth." His description of the play as a "Comical Satire" emphasizes this purpose, and justifies us in regarding the play, with Baskervill, as a deliberate extension to the theater of the literary fashion of satire set going by Lodge, Davies, Marston, and Hall in the later nineties. At the same time, Jonson was convinced that he had both provided satire with fresh and potent weapons and in effect struck out a fresh and potent type of play. And the result must always have extraordinary interest as a dramatic experiment. Few dramatists have so boldly refashioned the instrument they found to fit it to say what they wanted. Jonson knew the hazards of the experiment, but had no misgivings as to its merit:

> Onely vouchsafe me your attentions,
> And I will give you musicke worth your eares,

while,

> if we faile,
> We must impute it to this onely chance,
> *Arte* hath an enemy cal'd *Ignorance*.[3]

II

The effect of this satiric aim upon the drama is apparent in every point of dramatic plan. It affects the plot-structure, the choice of characters, the dramatic business, the presentment of the entire piece.

Jonson declared in the Induction that he would

> to these courteous eyes oppose a mirrour,
> As large as is the stage, whereon we act:
> Where they shall see the times deformitie
> Anatomiz'd in every nerve, and sinnew.

[3] Introduction, ll. 62-3, 214-16.

The figure is that used by Hamlet to express the aim of drama in general; but Jonson's application of it betrays too clearly the havoc wrought upon his plays by his fierce dissection of his material. He, like Shakespeare, holds up "a mirror" before his audience; but what their "courteous eyes" see in it is not breathing nature, the very age and body of the time, his form and pressure, but a collection of pathological specimens, labeled and classified. He did not start, as the master of those who know and of those who criticize had laid it down that "drama" ought to start, with action, or the imitation of a piece of life; but with a set of persons singled out for their representative obliquities. The "Humours" of the personages in *Every Man In His Humour* are mostly the amusing foibles of estimable men; even the gulls are ridiculed in a gayer temper than their counterparts here; harmless women like Bridget give place to foolish pretenders like Saviolina; and the Jonsonian Falstaff, Clement, who distributes reward and punishment at the close, is attenuated into the lean and bitter Macilente. Yet Jonson claimed complacently, through the mouth of Cordatus, to be restoring the comedy founded upon *imitatio vitae.* He thought he was putting a comedy of real life—"neere, and familiarly allied to the time"—in the place of the comedy of fantastic intrigue, "cross wooing" with a clown for serving man (iii.vi). But what he "imitated" in life was above all its heterogeneous sequence, its motley kaleidoscopic disarray. Few Elizabethan plays ministered so richly to the Elizabethan appetite for profusion of material as this work of the doughty advocate of classic art. It was assuredly no desire to conciliate that here overpowered the classical instinct for order and unity. It was simply that Jonson gave the rein to the impulses of a temperament censorious and aggressive in unsurpassed degree; a temperament in which the critical severity which discovers misdoers everywhere was combined with the militancy which relishes the battle the more the greater the numbers of the foe, and the rigor which suffers no fault to go without its meed of punishment. That a play so inartistic in composition should be the deliberate production of the most self-conscious artist among the Elizabethans strikingly illustrates the complexity of the forces which actually molded and shaped his work. The man of letters remained supreme, imposing the form of literature on everything he wrote. It was a bold, and for a writer so deeply imbued with classical ideals of art a noteworthy, experiment; one, however, of which he himself finally recognized the futility, and which even a generous criticism, admitting to the full the power and brilliance of the writing, is forced to class with the literature which we admire but hardly enjoy.

Jonson was, in effect, applying his dramatic instrument in a fashion familiar enough in medieval and sixteenth century satire, and not unknown to the Greeks. For nearly a hundred years before him *The Ship of Fools,* in Barclay's version, had supplied a homely picturesque figure for the damnatory formula of a satirist as stern as Jonson: *"stultorum plena sunt omnia."* Sebastian Brandt, like Jonson had seriously attempted to "anatomize the time's deformity" in his catalogue of fools, and his ship's crew comprehends in effect representatives of all that he thought noxious in the German society of his time. That Jonson knew the analogous collection by Theophrastus of the "fools" of Athens, we have already seen. Neither Brandt nor Theophrastus, however, appears to have had any influence upon Jonson's choice of representative "humours." His anatomy of society reflects, even more than theirs, the bias of the anatomist's own character, time, and place. Brandt's fools are, above all, people who offend the prudential instincts of a sober, timid, German scholar of the later fifteenth century. Theophrastus' types are, above all, people who offend an Athenian's nice sense of social tact and good breeding. To Jonson, a powerful and militant nature, careless of conventions, and holding his own in all societies, like his great namesake, by force of mind and character little aided by nice observance of proprieties, the most offensive kind of "humour" sprang rather from lack of character than from lack of manners. His "humorists" are not, in general, the men of blunt, discourteous self-assertion, but those who, like the Thackerayan "snob," are lost in some mean or fatuous admiration;—fools of fashion, like Fastidious Brisk, the twin fops Clove and Orange, Puntarvolo, whose foppery, like Jaques' melancholy, is a subtle concoction of his own brain; and in yet more desperate case the rustic Sogliardo, who will have the name of a gentleman, though "he buys it," and Fungoso, Brisk's luckless ape. Or they are infatuated lovers, like Deliro who dotes on Fallace, and Fallace who dotes on Brisk. Saviolina is the dupe of her intellectual vanity, and Sordido of his faith in almanacs. Shabbiest and shadiest of pretenders, but clever enough to play his game for awhile and by no means the worst drawn, is Shift, the professor of "skeldring and odling," an inferior variant of Bobadill. His name was used again in Epigram XII. The mean or fatuous ambitions loomed larger to Jonson's critical eye. Of the failings of the critical temper itself, on the other hand, this most critical of Elizabethan intellects was perhaps but imperfectly aware. But he was acutely alive to, and deeply resented, the infirmities which simulate the severity of criticism—the uncritical malignity of the ribald and the envious man. The "scurrilous, and prophane Jester" that "with absurd *simile's* will transforme any person into deformity" was as abhorrent to Jonson as the unprincipled railer habitually is to the convinced satirist. Macilente, the "man well parted, a sufficient Scholler, and travail'd," approaches Jonson on another side, and more nearly. Jonson was too haughtily self-conscious for envy; but the bitter gibes with which Macilente seeks to correct the blind injustice of Fortune have an unmistakable affinity with those leveled by Jonson's masterful but not malignant criticism. Both men, however Jonson might take sides against them, resembled him to the popular eye. And both, though in the play primarily as victims and objects of the satirist's dramatic exposure, gravitate, as if by natural congeniality, to the satirist's side, and become his agents and executants. The fact, however, that Macilente undoubtedly speaks much of Jonson's mind, and that his voice often elusively resembles the familiar accents of his creator, readily leads to the surmise that the victims of the "comical satire" may be of similarly personal origin or even simply stand for particular persons in Jonson's milieu. Mr. Fleay even postulates this as self-evident; but his actual attempts at identification in detail betray obvious embarrassment, and do not seem to have been convincing even to himself.

III

Jonson was, it is true, if we may trust his own dates, already the object of literary attacks. For three years, he wrote in the "Apologetic Dialogue" to the *Poetaster* in 1601,

> They did provoke me with their petulant stiles
> On every stage.

And, if again we may trust him, he had forborne to retort until "at last, unwilling," he resolved to try what shame could do, and wrote *Poetaster*. It is tolerably certain that his forbearance had not been completely maintained so long; but the statement justifies a presumption against a purely personal interpretation of the intervening plays, only to be overborne by strong evidence. Marston and Dekker, the poets who bore the brunt of *Poetaster,* cannot be shown to have attacked Jonson before the date of *Every Man Out of His Humour*; and Marston had even, in *Histriomastix,* introduced a portrait of Jonson with evidently complimentary intention, an intention for which Jonson was probably far from grateful, but which he can hardly have met by pillorying his admirer.[4] And there is no character in the play who can be plausibly "identified" with either. Critics who take for granted that they must be in the play somewhere discover them, respectively, now in Brisk and Carlo, now in Clove and Orange. The only ground for connecting Marston with Brisk is that Hedon and Crispinus, in the two following plays, where they clearly point to Marston, are generically akin to Brisk, while Clove's affected speech includes various words used by Marston. But Small has shown that the Marston traits of Crispinus are almost entirely those which he does not share with Brisk, and that of Clove's affected words only six out of thirty-nine occur in Marston too. With Dekker-Buffone-

---

[4] Cf. F. G. Fleay, *A Biographical Chronicle of the English Drama, 1559-1642* (London, 1891), ii. 71.

Orange, the case is still more hopeless. The whole assumption does imperfect justice to the serious and even lofty aims of Jonson in this second
Humour play. With whatever success, his aim was to expose the "time's
deformity," the characteristic vices and follies of the day, not to ridicule
individuals. Living examples of these humours have assuredly been encountered by Jonson in plenty; Fastidious Brisk was to be met at every
fashionable ordinary and on the stage of every theater; and features
caught from particular individuals and noted on particular occasions
assuredly mingled with others drawn from his vast reading to furnish
forth the prodigious wealth of characteristic traits by which the several
"humorists" with such unflagging pertinacity exhibit themselves. In this
sense a particular dandy or simpleton may be said to be glanced at, if we
choose; but he is only an insignificant part of the object at which it is
leveled. In general the portrayal is much more liable to the charge of
being too generic than of being too individual; artificial and unreal
invention is a peril much more in question than a too photographic
realism; how stiff and "made-up," for instance, is the figure of Sogliardo
set beside his counterpart in the previous play, Master Stephen! In two
or three cases it seems possible to connect incidents in the play with real
or traditional events of Jonson's time; but we must beware of assuming
that because he borrowed the incidents he also identified the persons.
Thus Brisk's duel with Luculento so closely resembles that of Emulo with
Sir Owen in *Patient Grissel* that both are plausibly regarded as founded
upon an actual duel for which Mr. Fleay has confidently provided com-
batants and a cause of quarrel.[5] Aubrey has, again, preserved the tradition of a calumnious bully, Charles Chester, whom Sir W. Ralegh "once
beat in a tavern and sealed up his mouth, i.e. his upper and nether beard,
with hard wax," which doubtless suggested the sealing of Buffone's lips
by Puntarvolo (V.vi). So neat a retribution was necessarily rare in actual
life, and overtook, by a happy accident, only a single member of the
Chester-Buffone tribe. But its symbolical appropriateness to the offense
exactly fitted it to serve as comic Nemesis for an offender in whom the
whole tribe was embodied.

IV

Whatever personal elements may be interwoven in the intricate texture of the plot and characters, these must then be regarded as pre-
dominantly typical in intention. Certainly if we regard them as a com-

[5] His speculations are acutely dissected by Small, R. A., *The Stage-Quarrel between
Ben Jonson and the So-called Poetasters* (Breslau, 1899), p. 188.

plete expression of what Jonson took to be the "deformity" of the time, we cannot credit him with a very deep or comprehensive scrutiny. They represent chiefly the foibles incident to jealously emphasized class distinctions, and fierce ambition for place and wealth. Some of the gaps in his picture Jonson was himself subsequently to fill in. *Cynthia's Revels, The Alchemist, Bartholomew Fair,* to go no farther, lay bare "nerves and sinews" of the time's deformity which are either not at all or but very slightly "anatomized" here. Inadequate as it is, however, to the complexity of a great and growing civilization, this collection of "humorists" was yet motley and individual enough for their characteristic activities to resist ready inclusion in any straightforward and coherent plot. The several Humours become so many centers of action among which the interest, such as it is, is scattered. There is no common business in which all the persons or any considerable group of them take part; and the private business on which each is bent is palpably contrived with a view to the one business which absorbs the dramatist—that of exhibiting and "curing" Humours. Besides its effect in thus scattering the interest over a number of detached or slightly connected operations, the satiric aim has affected the quality of much of these detached actions themselves. The whole content of each of these miniature plots is of elementary simplicity. The "humorist" has, normally, but two things to do: to exhibit his humour, and to be tricked, jostled, or persuaded "out" of it. Both processes lead easily to developments of doubtful dramatic value. When Macilente enters explaining that he is possessed with envy, or Sogliardo announcing that he means to be a gentleman at all costs, we are reminded of the "program" speeches of the primitive Elizabethan stage. When Sordido hangs himself on the stage we are reminded of its crude violence.[6] The poisoning of Puntarvolo's dog is a trick worthy of a pre-Shakespearean clown. There is little trace as yet of that predilection for symbolic and allusive incident—the *idolon* of the study—which was soon to be so unsparingly indulged. The Fountain of Self-Love, and the forced eructations of Crispinus, in the following plays, were foreshadowed at most in the stopping of Carlo's mouth, a piece of "symbolism" not too recondite, as we saw, to have been actually carried out. Yet this, like Puntarvolo's farcical dialogue with his own gentlewoman, and the Sordido and Saviolina scenes, already mentioned, from Castiglione, still more the original conversion of Macilente referred to below, has little claim to be an example of *imitatio vitae.* The invention, even when

[6] Both this incident and Sogliardo's scene with Saviolina (V.ii) were suggested, as Bang has shown (*Eng. Stud.* xxxvi. 340 f.), by Castiglione's *Courtier.* Jonson was conscious of the objection and vainly attempted to rebut it by the example of Plautus' Alcesimarchus in the *Cistellaria.* Alcesimarchus puts his sword to his breast in the presence of his mistress, and is restrained from using it: Sordido actually hangs himself. And even had Alcesimarchus carried out his purpose, the legitimacy of a death by the sword on the stage does not warrant that of a death by the halter.

brutally realistic, smells indefinably of the lamp, so rarely suggested in
the fresh homely atmosphere of the earlier play.

The comic "catastrophes" are otherwise of varying degrees of dramatic
merit. No complex or subtle psychology is involved or applied. The
"cure" is usually of the rough practical kind which teaches fools who
cannot be taught otherwise, but teaches them rather caution than wisdom. Sordido's "conversion" by the curses of the rustics who have un-
wittingly cut him down is powerfully conceived, but far too summarily
handled to be psychologically convincing; Sordido, accustomed to trample
with brutal cynicism upon the interests of his neighbors, can hardly have
been so deeply moved at the discovery that they hate him, or have discovered it now for the first time. Two only of the "catastrophes" stand
out, as examples of high comedy, and one of them is worthy of the stage
which within the next two years was to witness the production of *Twelfth
Night* and *Much Ado about Nothing*. The catastrophe of which Deliro
and his wife are the subjects is ingeniously contrived to cure two humours
at the same time; for Fallace's discomfiture is Deliro's disillusion; and if
Fallace's cure is but of the external kind, if she is only taught to be more
cautious in her entertainment of Fastidious Brisk's successor, Deliro is
radically healed of "doting" for ever. Still better both in design and
execution is Saviolina's discomfiture (V.ii), which at the same time ex-
plodes the pretensions of Sogliardo. The plot laid by Macilente and the
rest for her exposure is admirably adjusted to her dominant foible, as it
is to Sogliardo's, and has the air of providing them both with what they
most desire. It may seem that Saviolina is too easily taken in; for a
clown trying to play a gentleman is not in reality at all like a gentleman
trying to play a clown. Sogliardo bungles his French and Italian; the
gentleman would have dropped his French and Italian altogether, and
bungled his dialect. Saviolina betrays her quality as an observer of men
in concluding Sogliardo's social rank from the mere trappings of phrase
which may be donned and doffed like any other suit. It is reserved for
her tormentors to point to the ci-devant farmer's horny palm—an argument which its owner's naïve explanation, "Tut, that was with holding
the plough," immediately clinches beyond appeal.

V

Two of the Humours, Buffone and Macilente, hold a position apart in
so far as they are the principal agents in the "cure" of the rest. Others
have incidental parts in the "surgery." Saviolina, who snubs Fastidious
Brisk, shares to that extent in his ultimate cure, as Brisk himself does in
that of Fungoso, and the Hinds in that of Sordido. But in the main it is
Buffone and Macilente, types of the reviling tongue and the malignant

eye, who, simply in the exercise of these "humours" of their own, discover and expose the humours of the rest. The contrast between these sharp correctors and gay mischief-makers, like Brainworm or Lemot, measures the distance traversed by Jonson in passing from comedy touched with satire to satire under comic forms. The exceptional position thus assigned to these two is highly characteristic. The satirist is too convinced of the need for sharp chastisement of folly to deal hardly with those who chastise it from questionable motives. He might have exhibited them sapping innocent happiness and blasting just reputation; he chooses to employ them in the salutary business of pricking bubbles and dispelling dreams. Hence they figure virtually in a double capacity, as the objects of the dramatist's satire and as his executants, and Macilente, at least, does not escape the ambiguous air which this double function involves. They stand between the common herd of victims, the *numerus infinitus stultorum,* whom they chastise, and the solitary embodiment of indignant virtue and his friends, being allied in dramatic function to both. Hence, though finally cured themselves also, their cure is reserved till the very end, when their surgery upon others is virtually complete. And their "cure" when it comes seems to be the most superficial and external imaginable: a temporary pause is induced in the maladies, with every prospect of their breaking out again in undiminished virulence when Buffone releases his lips from the wax, and when fresh fuel has arrived to replenish the fading fires of Macilente, whose

> humour (like a flame) no longer lasts
> Then it hath stuffe to feed it.

Macilente was played by the same actor as Asper, and speaks the Epilogue significantly in Asper's place. In spite of his hint that "the shift" (to Asper's dress) would have been somewhat long, Macilente and Asper are distinguished rather to the intellect than to the imagination; Macilente's animosity against those more fortunate than himself assumes, as it goes on, more and more the complexion of Asper's intolerance of folly, until at the close we find that the "fuel" for lack of which his "humour" flags is not the prosperity of which his and Carlo's victims have been relieved, but the "folly" of which they have "repented."

In the original text, Jonson had, it is true, provided a kind of explanation for Macilente's abrupt conversion. He comes to the Court bent on maligning whatever he encounters there. But the wonder of the Queen's presence strikes the personification of envy suddenly dumb; then, recovering heart, he addresses her in glowing eulogy, his "humour" completely changed. Dramatically, this is a dangerous approach to the *deus ex machina;* but it at least avoided the blank unreason of Macilente's conversion in the [revised] text.

VI

The intellectual scorn toward which Macilente approximates is the un-
alloyed passion of Asper. In Asper, Jonson for the first, but by no means
for the last, time drew his ideal poet. If Asper bears an unmistakable
resemblance to Jonson himself, it is because Jonson, like other men of
massive personality, on the whole was what he wanted to be, and did,
in literature, what he desired should in literature be done. Through
Asper's lips Jonson utters, with a passionate eloquence, the lofty and
vehement scorn which was one of the driving and shaping forces of his
art, and one of the moods in which he most nearly approached poetry.
As a character, Asper is a notable creation, more human and sympathetic
than any other figure in this drama of eccentrics. In his rugged Jonsonian
fashion, he has something both of the grandeur and of the pathos of
Molière's Alceste. No mere prologue sufficed for an exposition of what
was in effect Jonson's apologia for his own prospective policy and
practice as an artist, and in particular a defense of the present play. He
laid hands, accordingly, on a device which may be best described as a
compromise between the traditional Induction and the classical chorus
or Grex.[7] The preliminary debate of Asper with his friends, and the intervening discussions of the two latter, contain admirable dialogue and not
ineffective byplay. But their dramatic vivacity is subordinate to the
business of exposition and self-defense. The two friends Cordatus and
Mitis serve at first, like Pope's Arbuthnot and Horace's Trebatius, to give
the poet occasion, by their prudent or timid warnings, vigorously to indicate his action and expound the object of his campaign. Then, after
Asper's withdrawal, Cordatus, "a man inly acquainted with the scope
and drift of the Plot," learnedly expounds the doctrine on which it rests,
while the gentle Mitis grows yet more obviously a mouthpiece for the
difficulties likely to be occasioned in the conventional hearer by Jonson's
"strange" and "particular" comic methods. His pertinacity in raising
objections is as remarkable as his facile acquiescence in Cordatus' replies. "You have satisfied me, sir," he rejoins, like Master Stephen, but
without the motive and cure of Master Stephen's embarrassing situation.
It was not for nothing that Jonson refused to "afford character" to a
person whose whole dramatic existence consists in alternate exercise and
surrender of the critical spirit. But Mitis' loss of "character" is only an
extreme instance of the general impoverishment of drama in the interest of rhetoric and satiric quality which marks this play as a whole.

[7] The affinities of Jonson's Inductions to earlier Elizabethan examples in the work of
Peele, Greene, and Nashe, are described by Baskervill, *English Elements*, p. 146f.

The Double Plot in *Volpone*

by Jonas A. Barish

For more than two centuries literary critics have been satisfied to dismiss the subplot of *Volpone* as irrelevant and discordant, because of its lack of overt connection with the main plot. Jonson's most sympathetic admirers have been unable to account for the presence of Sir Politic Would-be, Lady Would-be, and Peregrine any more satisfactorily than by styling them a "makeweight" or a kind of comic relief to offset the "sustained gloom" of the chief action.[1] Without questioning the orthodox opinion that the links of intrigue between the two plots are frail, one may nevertheless protest against a view of drama which criticizes a play exclusively in terms of physical action. What appears peripheral on the level of intrigue may conceal other kinds of relevance. And it is on the thematic level that the presence of the Would-be's can be justified and their peculiar antics related to the major motifs of the play.

John D. Rea, in his edition of *Volpone*, seems to have been the first to notice that Sir Politic Would-be, like the characters of the main plot, has his niche in the common beast fable:[2] he is Sir Pol, the chattering poll parrot, and his wife is a deadlier specimen of the same species. Rea's accurate insistence on the loquaciousness of the parrot, however, must be supplemented by recalling that parrots not only habitually

---

"The Double Plot in *Volpone*," by Jonas A. Barish. From *Modern Philology*, LI (1953), 83-92. Copyright 1953 by the University of Chicago. Reprinted by permission of the University of Chicago Press.

[1] The quoted phrases are from George Saintsbury, *A History of Elizabethan Literature* (New York, 1912), p. 181. For substantially the same view see John Addington Symonds, *Ben Jonson* ("English Worthies" series [New York, 1886]), p. 86; Maurice Castelain, *Ben Jonson* (Paris, 1907), p. 301; G. Gregory Smith, *Ben Jonson* ("English Men of Letters" series [London, 1919]), p. 111; C. H. Herford and Percy Simpson (eds.), *Ben Jonson* (Oxford, 1925-50), II, 64; and Arthur Sale (ed.), *Volpone* (London, 1951), pp. vii, 176. Recent studies of Jonson by Townsend, Sackton, and others intimate some uneasiness about the canonical view of the subplot in *Volpone* but do not seriously challenge it.

[2] (New Haven, 1919), p. xxxiii. The further possibility, advanced by Rea (pp. xxx-xliii) and sharply challenged by the Simpsons (IX, 680-82), that Sir Politic was intended as a caricature of Sir Henry Wotton need not be dealt with here. The identification is by no means certain, and if it were, it would not materially affect the present analysis of Sir Politic, whose role transcends mere personal satire.

chatter, they mimic. This banal but important little item of bird lore offers a thread whereby we may find our way through the complex thematic structure of the play. For Sir Politic and Lady Would-be function to a large extent precisely as mimics. They imitate their environment, and without knowing it they travesty the actions of the main characters. In so doing, they perform the function of burlesque traditional to comic subplots in English drama, and they make possible the added density and complexity of vision to which the device of the burlesque subplot lends itself.

His effort to Italianize himself takes the form, with Sir Politic, of an obsession with plots, secrets of state, and Machiavellian intrigue. His wife, on the other hand, apes the local styles in dress and cosmetics, reads the Italian poets, and tries to rival the lascivious Venetians in their own game of seduction.

Further, and more specifically, however, Sir Politic and Lady Would-be caricature the actors of the main plot. Sir Pol figures as a comic distortion of Volpone. As his name implies, he is the would-be politician, the speculator *manqué*, the unsuccessful enterpriser. Volpone, by contrast, is the real politician, the successful enterpriser, whose every stratagem succeeds almost beyond expectation. Sir Pol, like Volpone, is infatuated with his own ingenuity, and like Volpone he nurses his get-rich-quick schemes; but none of these ever progresses beyond the talking stage. While Volpone continues to load his coffers with the treasures that pour in from his dupes, Sir Pol continues to haggle over vegetables in the market and to annotate the purchase of toothpicks.

Lady Would-be, for her part, joins the dizzy game of legacy-hunting. Her antics caricature the more sinister gestures of Corvino, Voltore, and Corbaccio. She is jealous, like Corvino, as meaninglessly and perversely erudite as Voltore, and like Corbaccio, she makes compromising proposals to Mosca which leave her at the mercy of his blackmail. But, like her husband, Lady Would-be is incapable of doing anything to the purpose, and when she plays into Mosca's hands in the fourth act, she becomes the most egregious of the dupes because she is the blindest.

We do not learn of the existence of the Would-be's until the close of the first act,[3] and then only in a scrap of dialogue between Mosca and Volpone. Mosca's panegyric on Celia, following his sarcasms about Lady Would-be, serves to initiate a contrast which prevails throughout the play, between the households of Corvino and Sir Politic. If Corvino's besetting vice is jealousy, that of Sir Pol is uxoriousness, and the contrast

---

[3] For the sake of brevity, this discussion will confine itself as closely as possible to the scenes actually involving the Would-be's. Jonson's sources, which are legion for this play, have been assembled both by Rea and by Herford and Simpson in their editions but will not be considered here. All citations to *Volpone* are from Herford and Simpson, Vol. V.

enlarges itself into a difference between the brutal, obsessive passions of Italy and the milder eccentricities, the acquired follies or humours, of England. The contrast continues to unfold in the opening scene of Act II, where Sir Politic talks to his new acquaintance, Peregrine. Peregrine, it should be mentioned, probably belongs to the beast fable himself, as the pilgrim falcon. A case for this possibility would have to be based on the habits of hawks, commonly trained to hunt other birds. One then might find propriety in the fact of the falcon's hunting the parrot in the play. In Jonson's Epigram LXXXV (Herford and Simpson, VIII, 55), the hawk is described as a bird sacred to Apollo, since it pursues the truth, strikes at ignorance, and makes the fool its quarry. All these activities are performed by Peregrine vis-à-vis Sir Politic.

In the initial scene between them, three chief ideas are developed, all of cardinal importance to the play and all interrelated. The first is the notion of monstrosity. Monstrosity has already made its spectacular appearance in the person of Androgyno and in the passage on Volpone's misbegotten offspring. We are, thereby, already familiar with the moral abnormality of Venice and its inhabitants. The present passage, with its reports of strange marvels sighted in England—a lion whelping in the Tower, a whale discovered in the Thames, porpoises above the bridge— introduces us to an order of monsters more comic than those to be met with in Venice, but to monsters nonetheless, in the proper sense of the word. Sir Pol's prodigies are distant echoes of the moral earthquake rocking Venice, a looking glass for England whereby that country is warned to heed the lesson of the Italian state lest its own follies turn to vices and destroy it.

The enactment of the interlude in the first act, by placing the soul of the fool in the body of the hermaphrodite, has already established an identification between folly and monstrosity.[4] Appropriately enough, then, having discussed monsters, Peregrine and Sir Pol turn to speak of the death of a famous fool, thus reinforcing the link between the two ideas. Sir Pol's excessive reaction to the event prompts Peregrine to inquire maliciously into a possible parentage between the two, and his companion innocently to deny it. The joke here, that Sir Pol is kin to the dead fool through their mutual folly if not through family, merges into a larger reflection on the ubiquity of folly, picking up that suggestion by ricochet, as it were, from the interlude in Act I. When Peregrine asks, "I hope/You thought him not immortall?" (Act II, scene 1, lines 55-56), the question implies its own Jonsonian answer: Master Stone, the fool, is not immortal, but his folly lives on incarnate in hundreds of fools like Sir Politic, much as the soul of Pythagoras, in the interlude, in-

---

[4] For an analysis of the first interlude and its importance to the play as a whole see Harry Levin, "Jonson's Metempsychosis," *PQ*, XXII (1943), 231-39.

vested the body of one fool after another for thousands of years, only to reach its final and most fitting avatar in the person of Androgyno.

The colloquy concerning the Mamuluchi introduces the third chief motif of the scene, that of mimicry. This passage, where baboons are described in various quasi-human postures,[5] acquires added irony from the fact that it is recited by the parrot, the imitative animal par excellence, and also from the fact that the activities of the baboons, like those of Master Stone, the fool, consist chiefly of spying and intriguing and therefore differ so little from the way Sir Pol himself attempts to imitate the Italians.

The arrival of Volpone disguised as a mountebank produces the expected confrontation between the archknave and the complete gull, the latter hopelessly hypnotized by the eloquence of the former. Volpone commences by disdaining certain imputations that have been cast on him by professional rivals. By way of counterattack, he accuses them of not knowing their trade, of being mere "*ground* Ciarlitani," or spurious mountebanks. If there is any doubt about the application of the passage to Sir Politic, it is settled by that individual's cry of admiration: "Note but his bearing, and contempt of these" (II, 2, 58). Sir Politic thus plays charlatan to Volpone's mountebank as, within the larger frame of the play, he plays parrot to Volpone's fox. But Volpone has brought along his own misshapen child, the dwarf Nano, as an accredited imitator. Nano, who fills the role of Zan Fritada, the zany, is the domesticated mimic, the conscious mimic, as Androgyno is the conscious fool, while Sir Pol remains the unconscious mimic and the unconscious fool.

Volpone, pursuing his attack on imitators, assails them for trying to copy his elixir: "Indeed, very many have assay'd, like apes in imitation of that, which is really and essentially in mee, to make of this oyle" (II, 2, 149-50). What is "really and essentially" in Volpone we know already to be monstrosity, so that to imitate Volpone (as Sir Politic does) is to imitate the unnatural, and therefore, in a sense, to place one's self at two removes from nature. But Volpone believes himself, not without justification, to be inimitable. The wretched practitioners who try to duplicate his ointment end in disaster. "Poore wretches!" he concludes, "I rather pittie their folly, and indiscretion, then their losse of time, and money; for those may be recovered by industrie: but to bee a foole borne, is a disease incurable" (II, 2, 157-59). At this moment all that would be needed to drive home the application of Volpone's *sententia* would be a pause on his part, followed by a significant look from Peregrine to Sir

[5] Rea quotes from Edward Topsel's chapter "Of the Cynocephale, or Baboun" in *The Historie of Fourfooted Beastes* (1607): "It is the error of vulgar people to think that *Baboons* are men, differing only in the face or visage. . . . They will imitate all humane actions, loving wonderfully to wear garments . . . they are as lustful and venerous as Goats, attempting to defile all sorts of women" (Rea, p. 178).

Pol.[6] But the situation conceals a further irony. Volpone's aphorism applies to himself. Before long, he, the archknave, will have proved the greatest fool, and this despite the versatility which enables him to transcend for the moment his own preferences, in order to cater to the prejudices of the public. Paradoxically, in this scene, speaking out of character, Volpone utters truths which reverse the premises of his former behavior. In Act I, gold, the great goddess, served him as sovereign remedy and omnipotent healer. For the saltimbanco Scoto of Mantua, peddling his fraudulent elixir, newer and relatively truer axioms celebrate the treasure of health: "O, health! health! the blessing of the rich! the riches of the poore!" (II, 2, 84-85). But with the application of this facile maxim, error descends again. The new truth proves to be only a distorted half-truth. In place of gold, Volpone offers only his humbug ointment as the "most soveraigne, and approved remedie" (II, 2, 103-4). The real point, and he has made it himself, escapes him: to be a fool born is a disease incurable, and it is this disease to which he himself is destined to succumb.

The "little remembrance" which Volpone now presents to Celia proves to be a cosmetic powder with virtues more miraculous than those of the *oglio* itself. It is the powder "That made venus a goddesse (given her by apollo) that kept her perpetually yong, clear'd her wrincles, firm'd her gummes, fill'd her skin, colour'd her haire; from her, deriv'd to helen, and at the sack of *Troy* (unfortunately) lost: till now, in this our age, it was as happily recover'd, by a studious Antiquarie . . . who sent a moyetie of it, to the court of *France* . . . wherewith the ladies there, now, colour theire haire" (II, 2, 235-43). Thus the history of the powder parallels the metempsychoses of Pythagoras. Like Pythagoras' soul, the powder began its career as a gift from Apollo, and in its transmigrations through the goddess of love, the whore of Sparta, and the court ladies of France, it serves to underline the ancient lineage of vanity as a special case of the folly rehearsed in the interlude.

Mosca's opening soliloquy in Act III shows that this excellent counterfeiter is himself, like his master, obsessed by the notion of imitators. His contempt for ordinary parasites suggests that there is a hierarchy of counterfeits, ranging from those who are deeply and essentially false (like himself) to those who practice falsity out of mere affectation, who are, so to speak, falsely false and therefore, again, at two removes from nature. The shift of scene back to Volpone's house produces still another variation on the theme of mimicry. In order to beguile their master from his boredom, the trio of grotesques stage an impromptu interlude, dominated

[6] A proper staging of the scene would involve, I think, placing Sir Pol fairly close to Volpone, so that the two stare each other in the face, the one collecting with ardor every flower of rhetoric that falls from the other. At this moment, Volpone himself might stop to gaze into the infatuated countenance before him: by now Sir Pol's credulity is as apparent to him as it is to Peregrine.

by Nano, who claims that the dwarf can please a rich man better than
the eunuch or the hermaphrodite. The dwarf, explains Nano, is little,
and pretty:

> Else, why doe men say to a creature of my shape,
> So soone as they see him, it's a pritty little ape?
> And, why a pritty ape? but for pleasing imitation
> Of greater mens action, in a ridiculous fashion
> [III, 3, 11-14].

The first interlude, it may be recalled again, established an identification between folly and the unnatural. The present fragment confirms a
further identity between mimicry and deformity, already hinted at in the
mountebank scene where Nano appeared as the zany, or mimic, to
Volpone's Scoto. At this point one may represent some of the relationships in the play diagrammatically as follows:

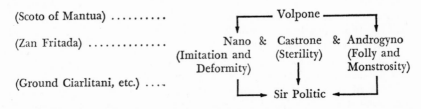

Since Volpone has (presumptively at least) sired both Nano and Androgyno, and since Sir Pol combines the chief attributes of both, one may,
with the aid of the diagram, infer what is already emerging plainly in
context, that mimicry itself is something monstrous and abnormal. It is
unnatural for baboons and apes and parrots to counterfeit human behavior. It is equally unnatural for men to imitate beasts. It argues a perversion of their essential humanity. It is not for nothing, then, that the
chief characters of the play fit into one zoological classification or another.
As men, they duplicate the habits of beasts; as beasts, they brutishly
travesty humanity. They belong to the genus *monster*—half man, half
brute—that order of fabulous creatures whose common denominator is
their unnaturalness, their lack of adherence to whatever category of being
nature has assigned them.

The arrival of Lady Would-be, fuming and fussing over her toilet, and
snapping at her servingwomen, provides still a further object-lesson in
falsity. Here, as so often in Jonson, face physic symbolizes the painted
surface hiding the rotten inside; the cosmetic care of the face signifies
the neglect of the soul. It signifies equally an attachment to appearances,
an incapacity to look beyond the superficies of life or truth. The powder

which Volpone offered to Celia and which Celia did not need, since her beauty was of the platonic sort that revealed the purity of her soul, might with more justice have been given to Lady Would-be, and it is Lady Would-be who deserves the epithet of "lady *vanitie*" (II, 5, 21) with which Corvino, in his jealous tantrum, has stigmatized Celia.

The scene between Lady Would-be and Volpone serves partly as a burlesque of the parallel scenes in Act I between Volpone and the other *captatores*. All the essential ingredients of those scenes reappear, but scrambled and topsy-turvy. Once again Volpone feigns sickness, but this time it is in self-defense against the terrible oratory of Lady Would-be. Once again remedies are prescribed, but these are neither Corbaccio's deadly opiate nor his *aurum palpabile* offered as pump-priming, but the fantastic assortment of old wives' restoratives dredged up from Lady Would-be's infernal memory. She rains down the hailstones of her learning on the helpless Volpone, until the archrogue, anticipating the judgment to be rendered on him in Act V, cries out in despair: "Before I fayned diseases, now I have one" (III, 4, 62). The whole episode is a rich application of the principle of comic justice. If in the final denouement Volpone suffers the penalty of vice, here he reaps the more ludicrous reward of his own folly. Trapped by Lady Would-be's rhetoric, itself a consequence of his own scheming, he is finally driven to pronounce himself cured. But the talking machine grinds on, and only Mosca's happy notion of exciting her jealousy, as he has previously aroused Corvino's, and for the same purpose, succeeds in getting rid of her. As her contribution to Volpone's coffers, she leaves behind a wrought cap of her own making; this forms a suitably ridiculous contrast to the treasures earlier offered by Corvino, Corbaccio, and Voltore.

The same scene serves as introduction and comic distortion of the scene immediately to follow between Volpone and Celia. Celia's unearthly purity is made to seem even more unearthly by its contrast to Lady Would-be's lecherousness, this latter apparent in the lady's addiction to cosmetics, in her slips of the tongue, and in her barely disguised sexual overtures. Lady Would-be's attempted seduction of Volpone having been thwarted, the stage is set for Volpone's attempted seduction of Celia. Volpone commences his wooing with a characteristic boast: "I, before/I would have left my practice, for thy love," he swears, "In varying figures, I would have contended/With the blue PROTEUS, or the horned *floud*" (III, 7, 150-53). Justifiably proud of his powers of disguise, Volpone emphasizes them further by citing a past occasion on which he masqueraded in the ambiguous role of Antinous, Nero's favorite. Embarking on an enumeration of the exotic splendors in store for Celia, he reserves as his final inducement the promise that she will participate, with him, in transmutations without end: "Whil'st we, in changed shapes, act OVIDS tales" (the *Metamorphoses,* of course),

Thou, like EUROPA now, and I like JOVE,
Then I like MARS, and thou like ERYCINE,
So, of the rest, till we have quite run through
And weary'd all the fables of the gods.
Then will I have thee in more moderne formes,
Attired like some sprightly dame of *France*,
Brave *Tuscan* lady, or proud *Spanish* beauty
[III, 7, 221-28].

We have already witnessed, in the first interlude, the metempsychosis of
folly and, in the powder offered to Celia in Act II, the transmigrations
of vanity. Now, as a climax to his eloquence, Volpone rehearses the
metamorphoses of lust. Jonson thus endows his central themes with
vertical depth in time as well as horizontal extension in space. Folly,
vanity, lust, have been, are, will be. At any given moment their practitioners are legion, and often interchangeable.

It is at this point that Celia's refusal crystallizes into a repudiation of
folly, vanity, and lust combined and that her behavior contrasts most
sharply with that of Lady Would-be. The recollection of Lady Would-be
lacquering her face and making indecent advances to Volpone brings
into sharper focus Celia's sudden horror at her own beauty, and her plea
that her face be flayed or smeared with poison, in order to undo the lust
she has aroused. If, for Lady Would-be, the cosmetic art is a necessary
preliminary to sexual conquest, its opposite, the disfigurement of the
face, becomes for Celia the badge of chastity. Where Lady Would-be
strives to adopt Italian vices for her own, Celia's gestures as well as her
name demonstrate her alienation from the moral and spiritual province
of Venice.

Act IV carries us back into the open street, where Sir Pol, ignorant of
the plot developing at Volpone's house, continues babbling of plots in
terms which ordinarily have one meaning for him and another for the
audience. After a patronizing recital of "instructions" to Peregrine on
methods of deportment in Venice, he confides suddenly that his money-
making projects need only the assistance of one trusty henchman in order
to be put into instant execution. Evidently he is hinting that Peregrine
undertake that assignment and thus play Mosca to his Volpone. But
Peregrine contents himself with inquiring into the particulars of the
plots. The most elaborate of these proves to be a way to protect Venice
from the plague by using onions as an index to the state of infection on
ships entering the harbor. This mad scheme, with its echo of Volpone's
claim to have distributed his *oglio* under official patent to all the com-
monwealths of Christendom, serves chiefly to remind us again of the
moral plague prevailing in Venice and of the incomprehension of that
fact on the part of those characters who prattle most about disease and
cure.

The ensuing scene parodies the episode in Act II where Corvino discovers his wife in conversation with the mountebank. Just as Corvino interrupts Volpone while the latter is advertising his medicine, so Lady Would-be bursts in on Sir Politic as the knight is dilating on his schemes and projects. As Corvino babbles jealously of lechers and satyrs, so Lady Would-be jabbers of land sirens, lewd harlots, and fricatrices. Corvino beats away the mountebank. Lady Would-be rails at Peregrine. Both harp on "honor," and both discard that term as soon as it becomes an inconvenience, Corvino when it becomes an obstacle to his plan of inheritance, Lady Would-be when she discovers that Peregrine is no harlot in disguise, but a young gentleman. As for Sir Politic, though he too plays his part in the little impromptu from the *commedia dell'arte,* he remains, unlike Volpone, quite oblivious to the fact. Actually, Sir Pol re-enacts not the role of "Signior FLAMINIO," the lover in disguise—that part, however reluctantly assumed, belongs to Peregrine—but the female role, the "FRANCISCINA," guarded by a jealous "PANTALONE *di besogniosi*" (II, 3, 3-8). The confusion of sexes symbolized in Androgyno, in the indiscriminate journeyings of the soul of Pythagoras, in Volpone's masquerade as Antinous, in Lady Would-be's error, as well as in the reversed masculine-feminine roles of Sir Pol and Lady Would-be, contributes its own kind of abnormality to the deformity of the moral atmosphere chiefly figured by the metamorphoses of beasts into men. And if one regards Sir Politic's uxoriousness as a kind of metaphoric emasculation, one may then equate him with Castrone, as he has already been equated with Nano and Androgyno, to make the pattern of mimicry complete.[7]

The fourth-act trial starts with justice and concludes with a perversion of it. The monsters begotten by Volpone, the prodigies and portents that exercised such a hypnotic effect on Sir Pol, now make a lavish and climactic reappearance in the language of the scene. First they designate their proper objects. But as Voltore begins to exercise his baleful rhetoric, the parlance of unnaturalness, appropriate to the guilty, begins to turn against the innocent. Corbaccio disavows his son for "the meere portent of nature"; he is "an utter stranger" to his loins, a "Monster of men, swine, goate, wolfe, parricide" (IV, 5, 108-12). Finally Lady Would-be arrives, the eternal parrot, to give testimony which virtually clinches the case against Celia:

> Out, thou *chameleon* harlot; now, thine eies
> Vie teares with the *hyaena*
>
> [IV, 6, 2-3].

[7] Actually, Florio's *Worlde of Wordes* (1598) defines *Castrone* not only as "a gelded man," but as "a noddie, a meacocke, a cuckold, a ninnie, a gull" (quoted in Rea, p. 144). Any of these will serve as accurate epithets for Sir Pol, with the possible exception of "cuckold," and if that designation does not fit it is not owing to any lack of effort on Lady Would-be's part.

The beast characters in the play display an unerring faculty for describing the innocent as beasts. Corvino has already called Celia a crocodile, referring to that animal's notorious ability to imitate human tears, and Lady Would-be, though she has her unnatural natural history somewhat confused, invokes another creature famous for its powers of mimicry, the hyena, as well as the even more versatile chameleon.

The juxtaposition of the hyena and the chameleon reminds one that there is a point at which the ideas of metamorphosis and mimicry coalesce. The chameleon, shifting its colors to blend itself with its environment, indulges in a highly developed form of protective mimicry. Volpone carries the principle a step further. He goes through his restless series of transformations not as a shield but in order to prey on his own kind, to satisfy something in his unnatural nature which demands incessant changing of shape and form. But knavery and credulity, mimicry and metamorphosis, alike reflect aspects of one basic folly: the folly of becoming, or trying to become, what one is not, the cardinal sin of losing one's nature. Only Bonario and Celia, of all the creatures in the play, never ape others, never change their shapes, never act contrary to their essential natures. And in the unnatural state of Venice it is chiefly they, the unchanging ones, who are attacked as hyenas and chameleons.

Volpone, in short, may be read as a comic restatement of a theme familiar in Shakespeare's plays of the same period, the theme of disorder. Order figures here not as social balance or political hierarchy, but as a principle of differentiation in nature whereby each species, each sex, maintains its separate identity. With the loss of clear-cut divisions between man and beast, between beast and beast, between male and female, all creatures become monsters. The basic structure of nature is violated. The astronomical portents discussed earlier by Sir Pol and Peregrine in connection with animal prodigies reflect the upheaval of the cosmos itself following the degeneracy of man.

But by this time, justice has become as monstrous as its participants, and the *avocatori* close the session piously intoning their horror at the unnaturalness of Celia and Bonario. Volpone's last and greatest hoax is destined to set the balance of nature right again. It starts, however, with one more act of unnaturalness. Volpone, a monster, who therefore occupies no fixed place in the order of created beings, feigns death and thus symbolically demonstrates his lack of status. One by one the inheritors file in for the legacy, only to find that they have been duped by Mosca.

The first to receive her dismissal is Lady Would-be. Having made overtures to both Mosca and Volpone, she is in a position to be summarily blackmailed. "Goe home," advises Mosca, "and use the poore SIR POL, your knight, well;/For feare I tell some riddles: go, be melancholique" (V, 3, 44-45). Thus the learned lady who knew so many bizarre ways of curing Volpone's melancholy now has the opportunity to treat herself for the same ailment, and so do her colleagues. The value of this scene consists partly in its inflicting comic justice on the legacy-hunters before the *avocatori* render their sterner legal judgments, just as Volpone has already, in Lady Would-be, met a comic foretaste of the retribution which overtakes him at the *Scrutineo*. But since the parrot, for all its shrillness, remains less venal than the crow or vulture, the untrussing of Lady Would-be goes no further. In the realm of the severer truths, vice and folly may appear as different aspects of a similar spiritual malaise. In the realm of poetic justice, however, a distinction continues to be practiced. Vice, which is criminal and attacks others, must suffer public correction, whereas folly, a disease essentially self-destructive, may be dealt with in private and without the assistance of constituted authority. For Lady Would-be it is sufficient that, awakened to some sense of her own folly, she vows to quit Venice and take to sea "for physick."

And so with her preposterous knight, Sir Politic, whom we now encounter for the last time, the victim of a private plot which performs the same service of mortification for him that the final trial scene does for Volpone. The *mercatori* enlisted by Peregrine perform the office of the *avocatori* who pronounce sentence on Volpone, and the divulging of the pathetic notebook, with its scraps from playbooks, becomes the burlesque substitute for the exposure of Volpone's will, in bringing on the disaster. Peregrine, echoing Voltore's suggestion that Volpone be tested on the strappado, warns Sir Pol that his persecutors will put him to the rack. Whereupon the knight remembers an "engine" he has designed against just such emergencies, a tortoise shell. And to the disgust of three hundred years of literary critics he climbs into the ungainly object, playing possum after the fashion of his model, Volpone, who has feigned death in the foregoing scene. The arrival of the merchants brings on the catastrophe:

> MER. 1: What
> Are you, sir? PER: I' am a merchant, that came heere
> To looke upon this tortoyse. MER. 3: How? MER. 1: St. MARKE!
> What beast is this? PER: It is a fish. MER. 2: Come out, here.
> PER: Nay, you may strike him, sir, and tread upon him:
> Hee'll beare a cart
>
> [V, 4, 62-67].

Eventually, by stamping and poking, they goad Sir Politic out of his exoskeleton. The scene thus rephrases in a vein of broadest tomfoolery the essential question of the play: "What kind of creatures are these?" Throughout the action one has seen beasts aping men and men imitating beasts on the moral and psychological levels. Here the theme of mimicry reaches its literal climax in an episode of farce, where the most imitative of the characters puts on the physical integument of an animal and the hired pranksters stand about debating its probable zoological classifica-

tion. The final unshelling of the tortoise, a parallel to the uncasing of
the fox in the last scene, arouses further comment from the merchants:

> MER. 1: 'Twere a rare motion, to be seene, in *Fleet-street!*
> MER. 2: I, i'the terme. MER. 1: Or *Smithfield*, in the faire
>   [V, 4, 77-78].

Sir Politic, thus, so inquisitive about prodigies, has finally become one
himself, a specimen fit to be housed among the freaks of Smithfield or
amid the half-natural, half-artificial curiosities of Fleet Street. With the
knowledge that he is destined to become a victim of the kind of curiosity
he himself has exhibited, his disillusionment is complete and his chastisement effected. He and Lady Would-be, the only survivors, in this play,
of Jonson's earlier humour characters, are now "out of their humour,"
purged of their imitative folly by the strong medicine of ridicule.

Public punishment, however, awaits the actors of the main plot. Jonson
is not sporting here with human follies like those of the Would-be's, but
dealing grimly with inhuman crimes. The names of fabulous monsters,
basilisks and chimeras, continue to echo in our ears as the catastrophe
approaches, fastening themselves at last onto their proper objects, the
conspirators in the game of *captatio*. Voltore's spurious fit spells out in
concrete theatrical terms his unnatural status and the lesson pointed by
the *avocatori:* "These possesse wealth, as sicke men possesse fevers,/
Which, trulyer, may be said to possesse them" (V, 12, 101-2). The delivery
of Volpone's substance to the *Incurabili* places a final and proper valua-
tion on the medicinal powers of gold. The imprisonment of Volpone is
specifically designed to give him the opportunity to acquire in reality
the diseases he has mimicked and the leisure to ponder the accuracy of
his own text: to be a fool born is a disease incurable. Voltore and Corbaccio are henceforth to be secluded from their fellow-men like the unnatural specimens they are, while Corvino's animality is to be the object of a public display more devastating than Sir Politic's brief masquerade as a tortoise.

Thus on successive levels of low comedy and high justice, the monsters
of folly and the monsters of vice suffer purgation, exposed as the sort of
misshapen marvels they themselves have chattered about so freely. The
relative harmlessness of Sir Pol's downfall serves to differentiate his folly
from the viciousness of the Venetians, but the many parallels between
his catastrophe and theirs warn us that his kind of folly is sufficiently
virulent after all, is closely related to graver sins, and, if it persists in
imitating them, must ultimately fall under the same condemnation.

If these observations are accurate, it should be clear in what sense the
subplot of the Would-be's is relevant to the total structure of *Volpone.*
Starting from a contrast between Italian vice and English folly, Jonson
personifies the latter in two brainless English travelers, makes their folly

consist chiefly in mimicry of Italian vice, and Italian vice itself, in its purest form, consist of the more comprehensive form of mimicry we have termed "metamorphosis," thus bringing the two aspects of evil together into the same moral universe and under a common moral judgment; with the use of the beast fable he binds the two together dramatically, and by the distribution of poetic justice he preserves the distinction between them. Each of the episodes involving the Would-be's, including the much despised incident of the tortoise, thus serves a definite dramatic purpose, and one may conclude, then, that the subplot adds a fresh dimension and a profounder insight without which *Volpone,* though it might be a neater play, would also be a poorer and a thinner one.

Comic Plots: *The Alchemist*

by Paul Goodman

Let us take comedy . . . as a relation, a "deflatable accidental connection," among the parts. Consider a farce: again and again the intrigue
is reversed, and the intentions of the agents come to naught; yet we do
not feel pity or fear, but we laugh. We do not feel it tragically because
the actions are "of no account," the agents are "not seriously involved"
or are "completely worthless anyway," and they do not win our sympathy;
we do not suffer. So Aristotle (in *Poetics* v) puts the laughable in the
class of the deformed whether of behavior (ἄισχος, disgraceful, ugly) or
thought (ἁμάρτημα, error). Yet not every deformity is laughable, for
Oedipus is certainly in error and, by Greek standards, Philoctetes' wound
would be disgraceful; but only such cases as are "painless and harmless"
(ἀνώδυνον καὶ οὐ φθαρτικόν). Kant, similarly, says that laughter is an expectation that comes to "absolutely naught"; he must mean while
we ourselves remain secure in our faculties; what is comically destroyed
is not like us. (So, for Kant, comedy is the direct contrary of the sublime,
where it is our intellectual faculties that break down.)

Psychologically, in this comedy of Aristotle and Kant, the positive feeling is malicious pleasure in the destruction and the flooding release from
the strain of attending to an improbable or trivial connection and contemptuously dismissing it. But we may also find an underlying ground
of laughter in what is left after the destruction and the dismissal; this
is pointed to in the theories of comedy of, for instance, Bergson and
Freud. For Bergson the complicated and mechanical are destroyed; the
simple vitality explosively asserts itself. For Freud it is the inhibited
more infantile drives that return—laughter is a kind of freeing from
embarrassment. Thus, pervasively under the deflatable accidental connections of comedy there is an abiding simpler attitude: infantile animality, lubricity, malice, etc.; and at the end there is often a philosophical (abiding) thought springing from the same source—for example,
"Good food is better than battles" (*The Acharnians*). Most popularly
the ending of comic plays is a wedding, but this usually means that a

nondeflatable romantic strand has been a part of the plot, and the whole is not pure comedy but a mixed genre, arousing sympathy and apprehension as well as laughter.

There are two special difficulties, which did not arise for serious plays, in writing out the structure of a comedy. . . . In a serious plot, where everything converges to the same meaning, it does not much matter if we notice small details of acting, inflection, timing; but it is of course just these things that set off the loudest laughter in comedy, when the tiniest touch deflates the biggest balloon. Thus our criticism may quite accurately lay bare the rough structure of what is happening, yet leave the reader in the dark as to why it is funny, for that must be seen and heard in detail performed by a good comedian. Samuel Johnson pointed this out by saying that tragedies may be read in books but that comedies must be experienced on the stage. The second difficulty of exposition comes from the fact that the pervasive underlying drives I have mentioned, that are the energy of loud laughter, cannot be too directly presented, for that would freeze the embarrassment: they exist allusively in the play and dormantly in the audience.

As the chief example for this chapter, I have chosen *The Alchemist,* because among English plays Ben Jonson's are the purest comic actions, as pure deflation, and *The Alchemist* is the most fully worked out, so we can touch on the most points. (Further, a structural analysis of a comedy by Jonson brings out with striking clarity the peculiar delight of this poet, unfunny but very glorious.) . . .

Doubleness of Comic Characters

In the last chapter we started from "seriousness" as an essential relation between the character and his action; let us now explore the relation between a base character and his action. This is "comic" when the intrigue can be reversed or even be deflated (come to nothing), and still the character is not destroyed; yet the intrigue is the intrigue *of* the character in the sense that in part it follows from him and follows from a part of him. This is what I mean by an "accidental" connection. It will be seen at once that a character of comedy has two aspects: that which is destroyed and that which survives in, let us say, "normalcy." Most of the possibilities of this comic relation occur in *The Alchemist.*

1. The character may be composed simply of a comic trait necessary for the intrigue and of the normal trait of being a man, as when a man persists in a single illusion and then awakes from it. When a play is made mainly of such characters, we have a comedy of situation, and we sympathize with the persons in their return to normalcy. In broader kinds of farce such a character is a straight man, brought into the

comedy by his accidental connection with the broader comedians and afterward of no further interest.

2. On the contrary, the disposition to comic intrigues, whether as a butt or as an initiator, may be strongly developed, so that, even after the deflation, the mask survives as a name of ridicule. We think of the mask and not the normal man. These are the humours, and the Jonsonian comedy is mainly comedy of humours, as here the simpleton Abel, Sir Epicure Mammon, the stormy Kastril, the materialistic Puritan.

3. Or not only the comic but also the normal may be strongly developed, as when the deflation of the intrigue purges the normal man of an error or humour. So Surly comes to recognize in himself that "same foolish vice of honesty." Honesty and the need to expose rogues, these are of course humours among the Jonsonian Lovewits and Truewits. For Jonson the flawless normal man is urbane; he knows his way around. But we can see how this same combination of the comic and normal may easily verge on the tragic, as in *Le Misanthrope,* where the disposition to a comic intrigue is really a tragic flaw for a man who is not urbanely normal but serious.

4. On the contrary again, what seems to be a merely comical disposition, such as gluttony, knavery, deviltry, may be so apt for any eventuality that it survives every deflation and proves in the end to be a lively way of normal life. Let us call these traits Wits, like Face, Falstaff (at the end of the first part of *Henry IV*), Figaro, Scapin, or Schweik. In relation to these witty knaves, the other characters are dupes and butts.

5. Or it may be the normal or even heroic part of the character that is most developed and that, in detachment, permits or enjoys or profits by the comedy, like Lovewit or Prince Hal or even Theseus in *A Midsummer Night's Dream.* This is the Urbane.

6. A completely deflatable trait is a Buffoon. Mostly this would occur in passing.

Buffoonery and the Underlying Drives

Comic traits are base because they generate superficial or accidental relations that in the end do not make any difference. But they are not completely absurd, because they generate determinate probable intrigues. A character completely absurd could enter at any time, and from him anything could be expected; he would be the object merely of indifference or contempt.

Yet, since the comic intrigue is combined of the accidental relations of accidental relations, when the combination reaches the utmost limits of accidentality, all the comic characters and their actions tend to become ad libitum, at sea. There is a pervasive buffoonery. Consider Kastril, for example: at the climax he might do or say anything.[1]

What is it, at such a moment, that makes the comedy most delicious and not merely contemptible, since it is apparently so devoid of sense? Obviously it is the emergence of the more elementary but *by no means formless* underlying drives, wanton destructiveness and animal lubricity. Compared with the intricacy of the plot, this underlying part is a dim background, everywhere suggested in the incidents, gestures, language, innuendo, but never given a plot. But, when the plot itself turns to chaos, this part abides and makes sense. A comedy where all "human values" are absolutely deflated proves to be a fertility ritual of the highest human value.

So we shall see that the normalcy that survives the explosion of the comedy, as a resolution, is not the normalcy of everyday but is a lively normalcy, man in a wanton mood. The comic and normal parts of the comic characters are integrally related for this lively function.

Comic Intrigue

Expansion. The combination of incidents probably from the wits, dupes, and humours is, as a whole, the comic intrigue. And it is immediately evident that such an intrigue, unlike the serious plot, is more than the acting-out of the characters, for some comic events befall the characters not as they choose or as is in their disposition but simply because, with quite other ends in view, they have entered the situation. Since the situation is accidentally related to some, it can be accidentally related to others, and, by a compounding of accidents, characters who originally have nothing to do with one another are thrown together. Thus, Surly comes disguised as the amorous Don; Dol, the appropriate bawd, is occupied elsewhere; the Don must have some woman, and Dame Pliant, who has come on other business, happens to be the only other woman; so Surly is thrown with Dame Pliant. Here indeed we have a case not merely of comic probability but of comic necessity (for it depends on the exhaustion of the possibilities), yet it is absurd. In extreme cases mere juxtaposition is a sufficient generator of comic incidents, as in the famous tradition of multi-occupied closets.

Such an intrigue is naturally divergent and expansive, freely introducing new complications, whereas the tragic plot converges to remove just the complexity that it has. Thus one might diagram the action of *The Alchemist* as a kind of expanding balloon. In general, as the strands of

---

[1] Compare this moment of general buffoonery with the "tragic recklessness" of the complex protagonist. . . .

action are more numerous, the unity among them all becomes more accidental to each—the characters become more distracted, the pace more dizzy, the probability more heady and tenuous. (This explains why melodrama, the climactic coming-together of many serious plots—the attack of the Indians, the attempt on the heroine, the coming of the soldiers from the post—is likely to become uproariously funny.)

Probability and Reversal. The strands of a comic action may cross by normal probability, as when a character plans to do something and does it. Or by a comic probability: the characters are thrown into new, unmeant, and still more accidental situations that they have to cope with. Then the comedy is heightened if these new situations surprisingly provoke new traits of characters that have a comic compatibility with the previous traits and intentions. Thus, disappointed at the explosion of the stone, Sir Epicure is provoked to the remorseful outcry, "O my voluptuous mind! I am justly punished" (IV, 5).

This is a comic reversal. But we must make an important distinction. The new situation may be one of continuing comedy or of the return to normalcy (deflation to absolutely naught). Unlike the reversals of tragedy, comic reversals are not brought on by discoveries; rather, they compound the errors. Tragic reversals are apprehensive and fearful, but these heighten daring and bewilderment, or the daring to be bewildered.

In this context we may make a further distinction of the characters in plays like *The Alchemist*. The humours and dupes are subject to continual comic reversals; but the Alchemist himself is the agent of reversals. He knows what is going on; therefore, he is not reversed; he is, however, exposed in the general deflation to normalcy. But Face and Lovewit, the witty and the urbane, are not subject to the deflation either.

Obviously it is the hallmark of Jonsonian comedy to fill out this whole line: humours, knaves, wits, and the urbane. Jonson gives us a hierarchy of malicious intelligence. In *The Alchemist* the hierarchy is kept neat, and the effect is pleasant throughout; Lovewit, the urbane, is not involved in the comedy as an agent, and so he may pleasantly profit from the spoils set free by laughter, namely, sex and an heiress. But perhaps *Volpone* is more profoundly Jonsonian: the Fox is both onlooker and agent; he lusts in the malicious intelligence itself, not in the profits: "Oh more than if I had enjoyed the wench: the pleasure of all womankind's not like it." This is cruel.

(Correspondingly, in Jonson's comedies the underlying suggestiveness is rarely very warm. There is plenty of lubricity but little pornographic excitement. A typical verse: "For she must milk his epididymus." We have the remarkable case of great comedy that is not funny; we are not invited to let go to belly laughter.)

License and Deflation. Ordinarily we expect normal thoughts and feelings to be effective causes, for mistakes and misunderstandings to right themselves, etc. Thus, special comic conditions are prerequisite for comic probability, the compounding of accidents and errors. In a sense every humour provides such conditions. Mammon wills to believe anything that will make him rich, Dame Pliant wants any husband, and the gull wants to be gulled. (And, philosophically considered, no special conditions are required for comic complication; the ordinary illusions of people are obviously self-compounding. To a disinterested view, life is at least as comic and serious as it is "normal.")

Often, however, the poet provides a special comic license to compound errors, in a special place and for a limited time. One is licensed to be mad on St. John's Day or to play tricks on April Fools'. Wine and the party spirit give a license for dirty jokes. In *The Alchemist* the master of the house is away, and this gives a license; the comic complication depends on the erroneous belief that he will be gone for a fortnight. Then we may simply define for plays like *The Alchemist*: Normalcy is the part of the play after the revoking of the comic license (return of Lovewit at the end of Act IV). The reversal to normalcy is the deflation. (Revoking the license is, of course, analogous to discovery and the deflation to the tragic reversal.)

Many comedies are not deflated to normalcy. *The Clouds,* for example, ends with the establishment of the Cloud-Cuckoo Utopia; what need for a deflation? *The Acharnians* is not deflated for the opposite reason; the proposition of the end is witty and true. Comedies that can end undeflated have a peculiar heady glory (and socially are more aphrodisiac).

On the other hand, sentimental comedies, those in which we sympathize with the romantic couple (socially, a vicarious outlet), require the removal of the comic conditions, the revoking of license, in order that the lovers may be no longer anxious. In such cases there is often a comic miracle to clear up the difficulties. This may be a windfall, like the inheritance that falls to Léandre in *Le Médecin malgré lui* and nullifies the old man's objection to the marriage (for his humour is stubborn; he could not be made urbane). A windfall is the removal of comic conditions that are not deflatable; and there are likely to be such stubborn conditions in sentimental comedies because the sympathetic (noncomic) lovers are not likely to be involved for only comic reasons—they would avoid merely comic complication and go off by themselves. The structure, the gratuitous probability, of such windfalls is analogous to the *deus ex machina*: the comic complication has come to a threatening impasse, but the lovers are deserving of better than deflation, etc.

The formal comic license issued and revoked by Jonson is characteristic of his art: he is the controlling comic master who will neither allow a sympathetic plot strand nor, on the other hand, let the comic malice release a libido that carries everything before it.

The Beginning

We may now speak of the beginning, the middle, and the ending.

The beginning is the comic license and the agents who generate the intrigue, not subject to comic reversals but subject to revoking of the license. In *The Alchemist,* Act I, scene 1, could be regarded as a sufficient beginning: the trio who generate the intrigue, the dupes they practice on, the likelihood of a later disruption within the trio because of their quarrels and rivalry (making probable the deflation), and the possible return of the master of the house (revoking the license). The rest follows from this.

But comedy is expansive, and it may be said also that each new humour introduces new comic conditions. Thus in a comedy of this type the effect depends not on a distinction between the beginning and the middle but rather on the continual expansion of the possibilities of accident. This is different from tragedies like *Oedipus,* where each new entrance (*e.g.,* the Messenger from Corinth) eliminates an alternative in the converging plot strands.

The Middle

In the middle the intrigue is enlarged (1) by the introduction of new humours (start of Acts II and III) and (2) by the combination of the previous combinations. The new humours are introduced with a certain probability from what has preceded, as Tribulation enters because he has lead roofing to sell to Sir Epicure for projection; yet each humour has peculiarities that serve as starting places for new trails.

But what principle, then, determines the magnitude of a play so enlarged? For the principle of tragedy, "just what is necessary to produce the reversal," has no place here. Why should not the balloon expand indefinitely, introducing ever new humours and their complications? This question may be answered by two related considerations drawn from the limits of the comic intrigue in itself and from the relation of the intrigue to normalcy.

First, the compounding of accidents cannot be indefinitely comic; after a while it reaches the random or trivial. This occurs when the potentiality of the humours to operate in new reversals has been exhausted. If new humours are introduced with which the previous humours can no longer react, we would no longer have one play. Thus, the plight of Surly when the bellicose Kastril turns on him as the cheat is near the limit; it is only because Kastril has been developed as such a buffoon that this climax of buffoonery is sensible. And that Ananias should now turn on the Spanish fiend with his ruff of pride and his idolatrous breeches is simply wondrous. The next moment would be absurd, but Jonson, of course, allows no next moment. (We might think of a sequence of expansion somewhat as follows: the comic, the buffoon, the absurd, the trivial.)

Second, the probable return of normalcy sets a limit to the comic expansion. But this is integrally probable from what is happening to the intrigue; for we must remember that all the characters have a normal component, and, as the intrigue becomes too tenuous and absurd, the characters must return to normalcy, for otherwise they would be destroyed completely: they would be madmen and not characters of comedy. Thus, we must expect Surly to call the police; but the police and the crowd have not been handled at all, so they need not now be dupes. Another aspect of this is that the comic expansion begins to touch themes that by convention are only normal; thus Jonson cannot allow the chastity of Dame Pliant to be actually comic but only to threaten to be so; so in the comic crisis at the end of Act IV we are near the deflation. Again, from previous to the expansion, there is the probability of the return of normalcy: Lovewit must return, for the possibility was mentioned in the beginning; the license is for a limited time and place. To give another example, at the beginning of *A Midsummer Night's Dream* we are told that "Four nights will quickly dream away the time [of waiting]"; but these nights pass in due course, and then the dreamlike probability is over. And, as with the limited time, so with the place: when the madness becomes so violent that it overflows among the neighbors, there is a deflation. Thus in *Les Précieuses ridicules* the spectacular motion, noise, and crowding of the dance (scene 12) is a sufficient inflation and makes probable the entry of the irate suitors with their sticks.

The Ending: Comic Feelings

The deflation of the comic intrigue is the beginning of the ending. The humours are destroyed. The incidents of the ending comprise the salvaging of what survives in normalcy.

Let us choose this turning point in the plot to discuss the kinds of laughter. (The kinds of comic laughter fit in the spectrum between the giggling of embarrassment on one extreme and the gurgling of animal satisfaction on the other.)

The deflation of the humours is malicious laughter, energized by released destructiveness and made safe by contempt or indifference. The succession of the normal person to the humours is the belly laughter of the released underlying drives. And the resolution is a kind of happy smiling and chuckling.

We have argued above that the audience identifies not with this or that particular character but with the world of the work as a whole, a space and time and drama. In discussing the feelings of comedy, it is essential to bear this in mind. With tragedy, everything centers in the end in the protagonist, so that what is felt for him is not far from what is felt during the work. But with comedy, no such thing.

Malicious laughter is roused in a titillating or embarrassed way by the forethought of the reversals; it is roused restrainedly by every reversal; and it is aroused unrestrainedly at the deflation or reduction of the comedy to absolutely nought. This is the moment of greatest absurdity: "All goes up in fume." Obviously this laughter is not identification with what is deflated; usually it is explained as a laughter of superiority (identification with the author?), that we are *not* that; it is base, we are superior. But I think the case is simpler; it is that we *are,* we are left, even in the dangerous activity of mocking, destroying, childishly laying about us. No superiority or contempt need be inferred; when it is strongly present, the comedy passes over into satire and invective. The energy of ordinarily suppressed destructiveness bursts out laughing. It is as though the base intrigue that we have been following has become a burden, and we are glad to annihilate it.

But then why have we involved ourselves in it from the beginning? It is because of the suggestion of the more elementary animal drives that accompanies the intrigue of base aims and vices. We do not identify with the characters, knaves, and humours, but we identify with their world, which is after all compact of simple childish wants. At the deflation the comic characters are destroyed; they carry off with them the shame and the base imputation. But the point is that what is left is not nothing, but normal persons, we ourselves—nobody has been hurt. Then comes the loud laughter of the released instincts that have all along been suggested; we have allowed ourselves successfully to be seduced. Toward this end the comic reversals and the absorption in the increasingly absurd are capital, for they surprise and distract us, and we find ourselves out further than we intended to go, or even than we knew. We are astonished to be laughing from our bellies. There is no sense to it; it is never "so funny as all that"; but that's just the point.

Jonson's Comic Feelings

Jonson is extremely malicious (and satiric), but he is weak in deep laughter. There is not enough suggestiveness. He presents gluttony but little gusto, and lechery but almost no pornography; only the scatological part is strongly felt, and this expresses itself not so much in excretion as in hostility. (Compare the good nature of a really dirty comedy like *Ubu*.)

On the other hand, Jonson, especially in *The Alchemist*, is glorious in the smiling and chuckling of the resolution, the satisfaction of the cat that has lapped up the cream. We are left with a normalcy that is lively indeed. For other poets liveliness means mainly a wedding, and Jonson nods in this direction by assigning the pretty rich girl to Lovewit: it is the prize of urbanity; there is no romantic nonsense. But what he is mainly concerned with is that poetic justice be given to intelligence and skill, and he works this out in the nicest detail.

Face gets off free. In the beginning, Face and Subtle seemed almost formally identical; but, as the intrigue progresses, we find Face infinitely various, while Subtle is handled more and more as an expert in one line; therefore, Subtle is deflatable, but Face is not. (So in Gogol's "Gamblers" the master-cardsharp is taken by the all-round crooks.) Face is a wit; he can operate in normalcy, where normalcy belongs to a Lovewit, not a Surly who has the vice of honesty. Subtle is not punished, for he was so skillful. The surprising adequacy to normal conditions of what seemed to be a deflatable trait (knavery) is glorious. Glory is the survival, and reward, of a comic trait in the resolution. Glory is the discovery that a deflatable talent is a wit.

I have said that the officers and the crowd are not handled as dupes. Yet surely there is a sense in which they, and a fortiori the normal Sir Epicure and Surly, are made ridiculous by Lovewit and Face. But this is the comic world of everyday, not of accident. Herein one may get "Happiness . . . though with some small strain of his own candour" (V, 5, l. 483). We may take this as the comic thought of the resolution; it is a philosophical truth. (Note that the poet has to apologize for it, for it is not quite the morality of the audience.)

Characters as Aspects of the Plot

In a rough way the characters are introduced as foils: the intrigue is expanded by the interplay of contraries. Dapper and Drugger are dupes, the simpleton and the fool; they make no long speeches. Sir Epicure and Tribulation, the contrary vices, are heroic humours; they make long speeches; and, in the mutual dealing between lust and puritanism, each is secretly subject to the vice of the other. The foil between the friends, Sir Epicure and Surly, expresses an important structural moment, the humorous-normal; it is a probability within the intrigue for the ultimate deflation. Surly and Lovewit, again, are foils in that both aspire for the normal prize, the rich marriage; here the lively-normal or urbane has succession over the humorous-normal. Lastly, Face and the Alchemist are foils. Subtle is the comic genius who gives his name to this particular intrigue, but Face is a wit who can survive for any Jonsonian sequel. Thus Face and Lovewit, the witty and the urbane, are universal characters, not involved in a particular intrigue; and this is expressed by having these two appear together before the curtain (V, 5, ll. 484 *ad fin.*). They can address the audience directly, since they are no longer "in" the play.

The humours are "unsympathetic"; that is, they are completely deflatable without reconstitution. Thus the comedy of humours tends to be a little cruel; and where the humour is involved with a person's happiness and station, as in *Volpone* or in *Le Misanthrope, L'Avare,* and *Tartuffe,* we pass easily from comedy to tragic satire, from the heroic humour to the tragic flaw. The comic talents, the knaves or shrewd fools, on the other hand, are in a certain sense "like the audience"; they have a cleverness that anyone might wish for himself. Thus their deflation calls for such reconstitution as is possible in normalcy. (We might say this formally as follows: The fact that these talents survive so many comic reversals creates a presumption of permanence also in the deflation, which is the last reversal; whereas the fact that the humours are always being reversed implies that they will be reversed out of existence.)

Spectacle

Spectacular disguises and hiding places imply a comic intrigue, accidental connections. In serious plays the disguises are for the most part natural, deep-going traits, as that Orestes does not recognize Iphigenia because of the lapse of time. And hiding places are not serious, because it is not the local place of the actor but his character and thought that must save or destroy him. A disguise on the scene, for instance Surly as the Don, presents us with two traits at once; it is the foretaste of a comic reversal. And, in general, the ability to assume different disguises is a comic talent; it sets intrigues in motion. To be named "Face" is to be a universal wit and to survive. In the setting of *The Alchemist* there are many rooms, from each one of which threatens to emerge a fatal secret, and, of course, Dapper is waiting in the privy.

Further, the spectacle of many persons engaged in heterogeneous occupations is comic; it promises accidental connections. So the Don is pleasure-bound, the Alchemist busy with his retorts, Dol as the Queen of Faerie is waving her wand, Face has his medals, and the carriers are bringing on the leaden roofs of the churches of the elect. Out of this potpourri the disguised actors frequently make asides and out-of-character grimaces, which may be in some other character or "real" and out of the play, normalcy. But the "reality" of the actor is itself comic in the ideality of the theater.

By means of spectacle there are quick reversals and deflations, unmaskings. To be hit with a soft pie is a quick reversal of superficial dignity. When the intrigue is thickly starred with such spectacular reversals, not much prepared, we have the effect of slapstick.

On the other hand, a very effective expression of normalcy is the presence of the normal crowd as opposed to the comic company, for the anonymous crowd is not a humour. Bergson remarks on this well when he says that monstrosities develop in private and are destroyed by publicity. The crowd is active and vociferous but homogeneous and anonymous; it is lively and normal. The crowded comic company is active, vociferous, and heterogeneous. And, following the convention of Roman comedy, we see in *The Alchemist* the contrast of Inside the House, where there is comic license, and Outside, normalcy pounding at the door.

The Time, nearly continuous with the drama, is exhilaratingly crowded. The relation between continuous time and the comedy of juxtaposition is obvious, for where there are many actions, and all of them must be carried on at once, accidental relations are inevitable. Jonson makes good use also of the neo-classical acts, the entrances and curtains: the end of Act I, scene 1, is the end of the formal beginning; Act II, scene 1, and Act III, scene 1, introduce the major heroic humours; and Act V, scene 1, is the entrance of the normal crowd, lively and noisy enough to avoid a letdown after the climax.

Diction

The dramatic irony of comedy is jokes. In serious plays ironic speech makes even the sparse lines of the plot more fatally simple; but jokes fly off in every direction, and each one is a reversal of thought and a deflation of intention. Slapstick is the multitudinous and unprepared deflation of comic appearance, jokes of comic thought. So the feeling of the whole becomes heady and unpredictable. (But, if once the jokes become predictable, the whole falls like a wet cake.)

In an important class of cases it is pointless to distinguish comic thought from comic diction, namely, where laughter is roused by the deflation of sense to sound, as in puns. Speech is sound significant by convention; the comedian breaks the convention. Puns are usually trivial (*e.g.*, Drugger's "angels" are also coins), but Jonson is a master of the sophisms that turn on form of sentences rather than the composition of meanings, what sounds like sense (*e.g.*, Face on Dapper's birth caul: "How! swear by your fac, and in a thing so known unto the Doctor? how shall he then believe you i' the other matter?"). The matter-of-fact tone, the wild absurdity, the careful logic; it is a kind of fun that is as rich as can be, and yet we are not invited to let go but to keep pent up and finally mellowing within us the philosophic wine of how ridiculous the world is. Then a whole character may be deflated to a sound, as we are assured that Dapper is no "chiaus."

The scientific arguments of a Subtle or a Sganarelle are, of course, the same comedy of sophisms. But Molière on the physicians is not savorous but sharp (it is mere folly); he turns the comedy outward in persistent satire; whereas the learned Jonson savors and dreams of learned men, and it is mere folly.

The reduction of character and plot to sound is very marked in those plays (not *The Alchemist*) that employ elaborate comic rhythms; for example, in *The Acharnians* the cretics of the Chorus are so warlike and striking that the soldiers become singers and chorus boys. Gilbert and Sullivan are English masters in this kind and also in the patter songs of individuals.

In general, when the rhythm is kept subordinate to the thought and action, regular rhythm dignifies and ennobles. A simple smooth rhythm that does not call attention to itself makes the speech serious; iambic rhythm elevates colloquial speech. The tack that Jonson takes, however, is to handle the iambics roughly, to bring the music *down* to colloquial speech, and this is a comic diction. Compare an excited moment in *Oedipus* with one in *The Alchemist*: in the tragedy the verse is climactically cut to hemistichs, but in the comedy to six speeches to a pentameter (*e.g.*, I, 1, l. 107). Naturally the audience cannot hear such a meter, but that too is one of Jonson's learned jokes. Also, the crowded heterogeneous scene fits with broken rhythms.

We must not overlook the long speeches in *The Alchemist*, those that most directly give the heroic humours. They are of the lineage of Horace and Martial and just as good. Thus, the marvelous characteristic rhapsodies of Sir Epicure: "Come on, sir. Now you set your foot on shore . . ." (II, 1, ll. 1ff.); "I will have all my beds blown up, not stuft . . ." (II, 2, ll. 145ff.); "We'll therefore go with all, my girl, and live / In a free state . . ." (IV, 1, ll. 156ff.); or Tribulation's "The children of perdition are oft-times / Made instruments . . ." (III, 1, ll. 15ff.). These, with their compactness of idea and firm march of sound, are truly heroic. They are laughable, not part by part but as wholes; this is epic comedy. At the other extreme the dupes do not express themselves at all, as if speech were too grand for them, but the adaptable Face speaks up for them: " 'Slight, I bring you no cheating Clim-o'-the-Cloughs . . ." (I, 2, ll. 244ff.), or "This is my friend Abel, an honest fellow . . ." (I, 3, ll. 396ff.).

Insults and obscenity belong to comedy, both for their malice and to create the suggestive atmosphere of the deep laughter. In the first seven lines of *The Alchemist* we have farting, shitting, and pissing; and we proceed thence to uncomplimentary personal remarks. (I have previously suggested that the cruel use of the excretory is the characteristic libido of Jonson.)

The so-called speech of low characters and any other emphasis on individual tricks of speech (*e.g.,* the dialect of Lucas in *Le Médecin malgré lui*) may or may not be comic, depending on the structure. If the thought, and especially the sentiment, is strongly developed, as in Wordsworth, then the speech appears as a halting attempt to be serious with inadequate means, and the effect is pathetic; but if, by the emphasis, the character is reduced to the mere eccentric use of words, the effect is comic. The particular Jonsonian mixture of base speech and Marlovian high rhetoric is quite his own. He does not mean it to be bombastic and satiric, and it is not; it is not comic but simply strange, the soaring dreams of a gross animal body (indeed, the daring comparison that comes to mind is *L'Après-midi d'un faune!*). And this gross beauty, again, he involves with a matter-of-fact naturalism and an acutely intelligent appraisal of the types of the town.

Finally, there is a good deal of actual "topical reference": to the actual statute of sorcery, to a real highwayman, a current "Persian" incident, etc. Such random actual reference tends to trivialize tragedy, reducing it to the level of news, "his tragedy has become a *fait divers*"—unless, of course, there is one great unified reference to an important current event, in which case the tragedy becomes a kind of tract for the times. In comedies like *The Alchemist,* however, the references to actuality provide a ballast, a comic normalcy of reality continuous with the normalcy of the humours. Such comedy verges into social satire. (Quite different is the effort to use the topical reference as a joke, like a radio comedian; the laughter is then often embarrassed, for the audience is unwilling to deflate the actual world to nought.)

A Note on Sentimental Comedy

As a form of experiencing—as in the Rorschach analysis of apperception—a comic intrigue is a structure of "wholes" and "small details." As in seeing together two wholes of characters-and-their-intentions some small detail suddenly assumes prominence and compels a reorganization; and the new structure is again reversed by a small detail; and so on, until we become heady and expect anything whatever to occur. Concretely, we have seen, every such comic reversal is grounded in resentment, malice, and lubricity; and in the sudden change these are released with increasing laughter and glory.

Comic experience is universal, yet it is quite extraordinary. It requires, on the one hand, a considerable intellectuality, to make sudden connections through small details rather than through the large parts; thus small children have no comic sense; they take everything seriously and cannot abstract. Yet, on the other hand, it requires a tolerance of the underlying forbidden drives. Comedy is the art of hyperintelligent monkeys, and Jonson was apt for it.

In the average person, however, such a form of experience is likely to rouse anxiety. Comedy in which both the intellectual and the animal elements are strongly developed is rare in literature. Far more common, as pure comedy, are farces, slapsticks, strings of gags, where no large whole is developed and not much of the ordinary world is destroyed. And the most popular kind of whole play is sentimental comedy, a mixture of a comic intrigue with a sympathetic love story; this is the so-called "New Comedy" (*e.g.,* of Terence), a kind of descendant of the Old Comedy tamed and of the tragedy-with-a-happy-ending.

In sentimental comedy the romantic plot persists from the beginning to the end; it is not deflated. The romantic plot is not noncomic in the sense of being merely normal (outside the comic license); the love story excites an independent interest, with feelings of desire, anxiety, fulfillment; it gives the audience something to latch on to. This sympathetic line, with which the audience can identify, is crossed by the malicious and resentful accidents of the comic intrigue—and the whole is an accurate imitation of the insecurities of adolescent sexuality.

Epicene

by Edward B. Partridge

I

Harry Levin claims that Jonson's trick of making his characters say something which frequently has little explicit meaning reaches its logical limit in *Epicene*, "where everything spoken has a high nuisance value and the words themselves become sheer filagree." [1] There is some truth to this claim, though not so much as Levin and Alexander Sackton (who elaborated on it in *Rhetoric as a Dramatic Language in Ben Jonson*) make for it. At first glance the language of *Epicene* seems remarkably direct and unequivocal; much of it, of course, remains so after repeated glances. But to think that "everything spoken" has primarily a nuisance value is likely to make one ignore the subtle allusiveness of much that is spoken.

Allusive language is one of the slier ways of throwing discourse into the parallel engagement of metaphorical language. Allusions suggest another area of experience—a series of concepts or a set of emotions—which can be seen juxtaposed, for a moment, to the rest of the discourse. This juxtaposition of the two worlds—the world of the characters in action and the world suggested by the allusions—creates some of the comic effect of Jonson's plays.

We might begin with the allusions to *epicene*. As a substantive, *epicene* means one who partakes of the characteristics of both sexes. As an adjective, it carries this meaning and, by transference, also means "adapted to both sexes." An example of this meaning, according to the *OED*, is Fuller's use of the word in his *Worthies,* where he described "those Epicoene, and Hermaphrodite Convents wherein Monks and Nuns lived together." Furthermore, *epicene* was sometimes used in the seventeenth century to mean "effeminate," though its use in Jonson's "Epi-

"*Epicene.*" From *The Broken Compass: A Study of the Major Comedies of Ben Jonson* by Edward B. Partridge (New York, 1958). Reprinted by permission of the Columbia University Press.

[1] Levin, ed., *Ben Jonson: Selected Works* (New York, 1938), 30.

gram on the Court Pucell" does not seem to carry this meaning, as the *OED* claims it does. The lines are:

> What though with Tribade lust she force a Muse,
>   And in an Epicoene fury can write newes
> Equall with that, which for the best newes goes,
>   As aërie light, and as like wit as those? [2]

"Epicoene" can not properly mean "effeminate" here: a woman does not do things in an "effeminate" way. It seems rather to carry the meanings already explained and to imply something unnatural. This suggestion of the unnatural is emphasized by both "Tribade" and "force," "Tribade" referring to a woman who practices unnatural vice with other women, and "force" suggesting a sexual assault. Thus, "Epicoene fury" has more a coloring of the masculine or the hermaphroditic than of the effeminate. In short, the main point about all seventeenth century uses of *epicene* is that they suggested the abnormal no man's land (and no woman's land, too) between the normal male and the normal female. This meaning is, I think, central to *The Silent Woman*.

The title, *Epicene*, refers to much more than the central twist of the plot in which Morose's wife turns out to be a boy. Nearly everyone in the play is epicene in some way. Note, for example, Truewit's description of the epicene women who have lately formed a College: "A new foundation, sir, here i' the towne, of ladies, that call themselves the Collegiates, an order betweene courtiers, and country-madames, that live from their husbands; and give entertainment to all the *Wits,* and *Braveries* o' the time, as they call 'hem: crie downe, or up, what they like, or dislike in a braine, or a fashion, with most masculine, or rather *hermaphroditicall* authoritie: . . ." (I. i. 73-80). As Truewit describes these Collegiates, they seem to belong to some intermediate sex between courtiers and women. Though "courtiers" then could be used for both sexes, it is generally used in this play to refer to men. Truewit seems dubious about their exact nature when he tells how they criticize wit and fashion, at first thinking them "masculine"—that is, too bold to be feminine—then amending it to *"hermaphroditicall"* apparently because they look like women but act like men. Though "College" was used loosely for "company," "Collegiates" might have suggested something unfeminine in an age when only men gathered in colleges and, above all, only men criticized authoritatively. Jonson emphasizes the educational sense of the term by alluding to the learning, grammar, honors, and heraldry of their College.

Lady Centaure seems the most clearly epicene of these Collegiates.

[2] Herford and Simpson, VIII, 222.

Characteristically, Jonson suggests her abnormal nature in her name. In the Elizabethan Age "centaur" referred not merely to the fabulous creature with the head, trunk, and arms of a man, joined to the body and legs of a horse, but also, by a figurative extension, to an unnatural hybrid creation or to the intimate union of diverse natures (*OED*). Dekker's use of the word in 1606 reveals this second meaning: "Sixe of these *Centaures* (that are halfe man, halfe beast, and halfe divell)." [3] In classical literature the centaur is typically goatish, mischievous, and lustful; in so far as it has any single sexual nature, it is male (a female centaur is possible, but extremely rare). A centaur and a satyr may really be the same.[4] In this play Lady Centaure looks like a woman, and in part acts like one, but the masculine side of her nature is implied by Haughty's remark that Centaure "has immortaliz'd her selfe, with taming of her wilde male" (IV. iii. 27-28), apparently by forcing her husband to give her the requisites of a fashionable lady.

All of these Ladies appear so far from the feminine—or what is generally considered the feminine—that Morose, on hearing their loud threats to have him blanketed, cries out, "O, mankind generation!" (V. iv. 22). I take *mankind* to mean *masculine* or *mannish*, thus disagreeing with Percy Simpson who says that it comes from *mankeen* and means infuriated.[5] Possibly Jonson plays with both meanings, but the primary meaning seems to me to be *masculine*. In two plays written about the time of *Epicene* Shakespeare used *mankind* to mean *masculine:* see *The Winter's Tale*, II. iii. 86, and *Coriolanus*, IV. ii. 24. Johnson's comment on the *Coriolanus* passage managed to combine both ideas: "A *mankind* woman is a woman with the roughness of a man, and, in an aggravated sense, a woman ferocious, violent, and eager to shed blood." [6] In Beaumont's *The Woman Hater* (1607), III. ii, the woman hater, running away from a lady who pursues and tries to seduce him, asks, "Are women grown so mankind? Must they be wooing?" In all of these passages, as well as in Morose's exclamation, *mankind* is best understood, I think, to mean primarily *masculine* or *mannish*. The mannishness of these women is suggested by other remarks. For instance: after being solicited by Haughty, Centaure, and Mavis in turn, Dauphine says, "I was never so assaulted" (V. ii. 52). Assaulting the opposite sex is generally thought to be a male privilege. Again: note the comment of the Ladies on Dauphine's neatness. Though "judiciall in his clothes," he is "not so superlatively neat as some. . . . That weare purer linnen then our selves, and professe more neatness then the *french hermaphrodite!*" (IV. vi. 26-31).

[3] *The Non-Dramatic Works of Thomas Dekker,* ed. A. B. Grosart (1884), II, 79.
[4] See the chapter on centaurs in John C. Lawson, *Modern Greek Folklore and Ancient Greek Religion* (Cambridge, 1910), 192-253.
[5] Herford and Simpson, X, 45.
[6] See the notes in the Shakespeare Variorum edition of these plays.

Neatness is often thought, not always justifiably, to be more characteristic of women than men. The effeminate man has long been associated with a too careful attention to his face and dress, just as the woman who is careless about her neatness seems less feminine. The Ladies thus unconsciously reveal both their own deviation from the feminine and the deviation of their suitors from the masculine. Epicene adds a remark to this conversation which suggests the inverted sexual customs of their epicene lives. These neat men, according to her, "are the only theeves of our fame: that thinke to take us with that perfume, or with that lace. . . ." Men have managed sometimes to interest women, sometimes even to "take" them, but customarily they have used other means than perfume and lace. True, we ought to remember that men in Jacobean London did wear lace and use perfume in a way that modern men do not. Yet excessive attention to dress was continually satirized by the dramatists, because it was both irrational and unmanly. The more normal way of attracting women—and as comic as the epicene way—is dramatized in the physical conquest of La Foole and Daw by Dauphine, who is, as a result, besieged by the Ladies. Finally, the sterility of these women makes them less feminine. They have "those excellent receits" to keep from bearing children: "How should we maintayne our youth and beautie, else?" (IV. iii. 57-60).

The "most masculine, or rather *hermaphroditicall* authoritie" of these Ladies Collegiate is best shown by the only one of them whom we see with her husband—Mistress Otter. Perhaps because she is only a "pretender" to their learning, she takes their instruction most seriously. Captain Otter is first mentioned as an *"animal amphibium"* because he has had command on land and sea, but we learn from La Foole that his wife "commands all at home." Clerimont then concludes that "she is Captaine OTTER?" (I. iv. 26-30). Just before the third act when we first see the Otters, Truewit prepares us for the comic view of their transposed marital relationship. Captain Otter, Truewit says, "is his wifes Subject, he calls her Princesse, and at such times as these, followes her up and down the house like a page, with his hat off, partly for heate, partly for reverence" (II. vi. 54-57). Modern listeners might not appreciate the full reversal implied in "his wifes Subject," but anyone who lived before women achieved the legal right to own property and the possession of great financial power (which is the power to subjugate man) must have been aware that the usual relation of husband and wife is reversed, so that she is Captain Otter and he is "like a page."

The first scene in Act III carries out this reversal. Captain Otter begs to be heard; Mistress Otter rails at him and asks him, "Do I allow you your halfe-crowne a day, to spend, where you will. . . . Who gives you your maintenance, I pray you? who allowes you your horse-meat and man's meat?" (III. i. 36-40). Clerimont, who witnesses this feminine usurpation of the role of the male, observes, "Alas, what a tyrannie, is this poore fellow married too" (III. ii. 10-11). The ultimate reversal of roles appears in the fourth act scene when, according to the stage direction, Mistress Otter *"falls upon him and beates him."*

But more important than the epicene nature of Mistress Otter is the epicene nature of Epicene herself (or, rather, himself). When first seen, Epicene is quiet enough to please even Morose. Then, as soon as the wedding is over, complaining loudly, she turns on Morose, who laments, "O immodestie! a manifest woman!" Since "manifest" implies a display so evident that no other proof is needed, Morose seems to be saying that a loud, demanding voice is woman's most characteristic feature. (Morose previously praised Epicene for not taking pleasure in her tongue "which is a womans chiefest pleasure" [II. v. 41-42]). A moment later Epicene tells Mute that she will have none of his "unnaturall dumbnesse in my house; in a family where I governe." The marriage is a minute old, and the wife governs. Morose's answer reveals his awareness of their strange marriage and Epicene's peculiar nature: "She is my Regent already! I have married a PENTHESILEA, a SEMIRAMIS, sold my liberty to a distaffe" (III. iv. 54-58). The allusions are revealing. Penthesilea, the daughter of Ares, was the queen of the Amazons who fought in the Trojan war. Semiramis, the wife of Ninus, the mythical founder of the Assyrian empire, ruled for many years after the death of her husband. Like Penthesilea, she was especially renowned in war. Soon after, Morose alludes again to the Amazons, those curiously epicene beings from antiquity, when he cries out, "O *Amazonian* impudence!" (III. v. 41). Her impudence seems Amazonian to others than Morose. Truewit, for instance, describes how all the noise and "her masculine, and lowd commanding, and urging the whole family, makes him thinke he has married a *furie*" (IV. i. 9-11). When Epicene is changed from a demure girl to an Amazon, she takes on a new name. Haughty tells her, "I'll call you MOROSE still now, as I call CENTAURE, and MAVIS" (IV. iii. 14-15). From then until she is revealed to be a boy, she is called by this masculine name. It is only just that, since she has taken over the authoritative power of Morose, she should also take over his name.

Just as Captain Otter becomes epicene as his wife becomes Captain Otter, so Morose loses or is willing to lose his male dominance after Epicene's "masculine, and lowd commanding." The first sign of a change in Morose comes after he has frightened Mistress Otter with a "huge long naked weapon."

> MOR. Would I could redeeme it with the losse of an eye (nephew), a hand, or any other member.
> DAV. Mary, god forbid, sir, that you should geld your selfe, to anger your wife.
> MOR. So. it would rid me of her!   (IV. iv. 8-12)

This willingness to become a eunuch so long as it rids him of his epicene wife prompts him later to plead impotence as a reason for divorce. "I am no man," he tells the Ladies, "utterly unabled in nature, by reason of *frigidity*, to performe the duties, or any the least office of a husband" (V. iv. 44-47). When this ruse of declaring himself "no man" fails, he welcomes even that reflection on virility which the Elizabethans thought the most comic—being a cuckold. "O, let me worship and adore you," he cries to La Foole and Daw after they swear that they have lain with Epicene (V. iv. 120). Castration, impotence, and being a wittol—all suggest that Morose would even lose his own maleness to get rid of a wife who at first seemed feminine but proved epicene.

The epicene natures of the women throw the masculine natures of the men out of line. When one sex changes, the other is likely to change. Otter's nature is dislocated by his wife's masculinity, so that the description of him as *"animal amphibium"* alludes to his divided nature as well as to his amphibious command. Jonson was fond of this sort of word play. In the masque, *Neptune's Triumph*, there is *"Amphibion Archy,"* who is described as the chief "o the *Epicoene* gender, Hees, and Shees." [7] The Broker in *The Staple of News* is called *"Amphibion"* because he is a "creature of two natures" (II. iv. 132). The adjective *amphibion* (or *amphibious*) meant having two modes of existence or being of doubtful nature. Browne's statement—"We are onely that amphibious piece between a corporall and spirituall essence"—is the best known example of this use in the seventeenth century. Otter is an amphibious piece in this play—a being of doubtful nature who looks like a man, but does not act like one.

Another epicene man is La Foole, who is spoken of first as "a precious mannikin" (I. iii. 25)—that is, a little man or a pygmy. When he speaks, he apparently speaks in an effeminate manner—rapidly and all in one breath. Talking also characterizes Sir John Daw whom Truewit calls, "The onely talking sir i' the towne!" (I. ii. 66). As we have seen already, to Morose "womans chiefest pleasure" is her tongue. That the audience is apparently expected to associate women and talking can be inferred from the ironic subtitle—*The Silent Woman*. Who ever heard of a silent woman? Daw's barely sensible poem reflects this same assumption:

> Silence in woman, is like speech in man,
>   Deny't who can.
>
> .   .   .   .   .
>
>   Nor, is't a tale,
> That female vice should be a vertue male,
> Or masculine vice, a female vertue be.
>   (II. iii. 123-128)

[7] Herford and Simpson, VII, 689.

There is little sense to this in itself, but from the context we gather that, though Daw means it one way, we should take it another way. Daw seems to mean that speech is a defect ("vice" = defect) in a woman just as it is a virtue in a man. *"I know to speake,"* he says in the last line of the poem, *"and shee to hold her peace."* Silence, which Daw considers woman's crowning virtue, would then be man's great defect. Daw's distinction between the sexes is so extreme and so unsupported by facts that it is comic to most normal people. The normal Elizabethan feeling about silence and women was probably voiced by Zantippa in Peele's *Old Wives' Tale,* ll. 731-732: "A woman without a tongue is as a soldier without his weapon." The whole play suggests that both a silent woman and a talkative man are, if anything, inversions of the normal. The tendency of Daw and La Foole to gossip maliciously suggests the inversion of their natures which their actions reveal. Their feminine or at least nonmasculine natures are implied also by their lack of courage. One thinks, perhaps erroneously, that men are usually courageous and that women are usually frightened. Helena in *A Midsummer Night's Dream,* III. ii. 302, says, "I am a right maid for my cowardice." Sir Andrew Aguecheek's fear makes him ridiculous, but Viola's fear seems only normal to the spectator, though it makes her ridiculous to the other characters who do not know that she is really a woman. Similarly, when Daw and La Foole prove themselves so frightened that they allow themselves to be publicly humiliated rather than act on their valiant words, we think of them as somewhat less than the men they appear to be. The Ladies Collegiate are loud, demanding, and aggressive. All, like Centaure, try to tame their wild males. All, in short, are Amazons. Of the men only Clerimont, Truewit, and Dauphine are not warped by the Amazonian natures of these epicene women.

Yet even these apparently normal men are somewhat ambiguous, sexually. Truewit's first speech in the play suggests the epicene quality of their sexual experience when he remarks that "betweene his mistris abroad, and his engle at home, Clerimont can melt away his time." Since an "engle" was a young boy kept for erotic purposes, Truewit is explaining how Clerimont enjoys the pleasures of both sexes. There had already been an allusion to the homosexual relationship of the Boy and Clerimont in the latter's fourth speech in this first scene. The sexual ambiguity of the characters in this play is nowhere better suggested than in the Boy's remark that the Lady "puts a perruke o' my head; and askes me an' I will weare her gowne; and I say, no: and then she hits me a blow o' the eare, and calls me innocent, and lets me goe" (I. i. 16-18). She calls him innocent because he (who is unconsciously feminine in his relationship to Clerimont) refuses to be consciously feminine in his relationship to the aggressive Lady. To be sophisticated (as opposed to innocent) apparently means to be quadri-sexual: a man to both men and women, and a woman to both women and men.

II

This interest in beings who have the characteristics of both sexes suggests that the play is fundamentally concerned with deviations from a norm. Like all of Jonson's major comedies, *Epicene* explores the question of decorum—here, the decorum of the sexes and the decorum of society. We recognize that most of the characters are epicene because we still have, even in this age of the emancipated woman, a sense of what is normal for the sexes. We may lack Jonson's strong sense of decorum, perhaps because we can not entirely agree with his concept of what is natural. Jonson clearly anticipated that sense of "nature" which became a central dogma in the neo-classic age: that is, the natural is the normal and the universal. Normally, men are brave and aggressive, and women are passive and reserved—or are supposed to be. A cowardly man and an aggressive woman become, in a comedy, ludicrous. Some of Jonson's rigid sense of the decorum of nature has been lost in an age which, like the present one, looks on deviations from nature as pathological—that is, as pitiful. For example, Morose. To many, the spectacle of indolent men torturing a man highly sensitive to noise is closer to sadism than to pure comedy. The reviewer for *The Times* in 1924 thought that, in the Phoenix Society production of the play, Morose was a "tragic figure" tormented by "bounders." [8] But to previous ages such "comedy of affliction" was a social rather than a medical matter. Morose is comic, rather than psychopathic, because he is selfish and vain. When he says, "all discourses, but mine owne, afflict mee, they seeme harsh, impertinent, and irksome" (II. i. 4-5), we hear the voice of a proud, not a sick man. Or, rather, Morose's affliction is a disease, but a ridiculous disease. Note that Truewit asks Clerimont, "But is the disease so ridiculous in him, as it is made?" (I. i. 148-149). To us no disease seems ridiculous, not even those which are ostensibly the fault of the diseased person—venereal diseases, for instance. But to the seventeenth century many sicknesses were ridiculous. Bedlam was a comedy, and D'Avenant's diseased nose, the source of countless jibes. The laughter, cruel to us but simply toughminded to earlier ages, apparently came from a sense of decorum so rigid that even the deviations of sickness became ludicrous. No healthy, rational man—the terms overlapped for Jonson—should be so sensitive to noise as Morose. He should be "cured," as Truewit suggests in the last line of the play—that is, brought in line with what Truewit thinks is normal. "Cure" is borrowed from medicine, as the whole theory of the comedy of humours is, and both keep something of their medical sense

[8] *The Times,* November 19, 1924, p. 12, col. 3.

even when used as Jonson used them; but they are applied to social rather than physical troubles—to hypocrisy, not heart trouble.

One way to observe how Jonson explores the question of what is natural is to note the allusions to deviations from nature—to prodigies and to the strange, the unnatural, and the monstrous. A prodigy to the Elizabethans was something out of the ordinary course of nature, something either abnormal or monstrous. Because Morose is so ridiculously sensitive to noise, Truewit thinks, "There was never such a prodigie heard of" (I. ii. 3). Morose himself has a contrary view of prodigies. When someone winds a horn outside of his house, he cries out, "What villaine? what prodigie of mankind is that?" (II. i. 38-39). Just as Morose thinks that anyone (except himself) who makes noise is a prodigy, so Truewit thinks complete silence is unnatural. To him the silent Morose and Mute are "fishes! *Pythagoreans* all! This is strange" (II. ii. 3). Pythagoreans were noted for their secrecy as well as for their belief in metempsychosis. Speechless men may look human, but they have the souls of fishes: they are "strange." "Strange" and its equivalents are crucial words to everyone in the play. "Strange sights," according to Truewit, can be seen daily in these times of masques, plays, Puritan preachings, and mad folk (II. ii. 33-36). He then proceeds to tell Morose the "monstrous hazards" that Morose shall run with a wife. Among these hazards is the possibility of marrying a woman who will "antidate" him cuckold by conveying her virginity to a friend. "The like has beene heard of, in nature. 'Tis no devis'd, impossible thing, sir" (II. ii. 145-147).

The relationship between Epicene and Morose appears to others and to themselves as strange, even monstrous. At their first meeting Morose tells her that his behavior, being "rare," may appear strange (II. v. 23). Truewit had previously complimented Epicene on "this rare vertue of your silence" (II. iv. 91). Epicene has another idea about silence which appears when she calls Mute down for his "coacted, unnaturall dumbnesse" (III. iv. 54). Speechlessness apparently seems a deviation from nature to the Ladies Collegiate too because they come to see Epicene, thinking her a prodigy, but they find her normal—that is, loquacious. Her loquacity, so natural to them, later seems only a "monstrous" impertinency to Morose (IV. iv. 36). Just as she seems a monster to him, so he seems a "prodigious creature" to Mavis when he pleads impotence (V. iv. 48). The spectators, who stand outside of this created world, measure its prodigies against their own concept of what is normal and natural, and find, presumably, that most of its strange creatures are comic.

Connected with this question of what is natural is another question, a favorite in the seventeenth century—what is the relation of art and nature? This question is brought up early in the opening scene when Clerimont curses Lady Haughty's "peec'd beautie"—pieced, apparently, from her washings, patchings, paintings, and perfumings. Because her artificial beauty offends him, he writes the famous song, "Still to be neat, still to be drest." In this song Clerimont upholds simplicity and nature because, so he thinks, the artifices of powder and perfume may only conceal what is not sweet and not sound. Such pretenses are *"adulteries"*— that is, adulterations or debasings of what should be natural. The natural to him is simple, careless, and free. To be natural a woman must be unpinned, uncorseted, and unadorned. Truewit declares himself to be "clearly o' the other side": he loves "a good dressing, before any beautie o' the world." "Beautie," one gathers, is only nature; "a good dressing" is art. A well-dressed woman is "like a delicate garden" to Truewit, apparently because nature in her is trimmed, artificially nurtured, and artfully arranged; its delicacy comes deliberately, not naturally. Art, as he uses it, means the technique of revealing what is naturally attractive and of concealing what is naturally ugly; thus, if a woman has "good legs," she should "wear short clothes." Nor should a lover wish to see his lady make herself up any more than one would ask to see gilders overlaying a base metal with a thin covering of gold: one must not discover "how little serves, with the helpe of art, to adorne a great deale." A lover should only approach his lady when she is a "compleat, and finish'd" work of art.

Because clothes are the most common of all artifices by which the natural is concealed, the relation between art and nature is suggested most clearly in allusions to dress. Clerimont seems swayed from his earlier disdain for the artifices of women when he sees Lady Haughty in all her finery. Truewit assures him that "Women ought to repaire the losses, time and yeeres have made i' their features, with dressings" (IV. i. 35-37). In the conversation that follows this observation, art takes on an added dimension: it comes to mean social decorum. Truewit repeats his former point that a woman should artfully conceal her natural limitations. Then the talk slips over into what is socially acceptable when Clerimont ridicules some women whose laughter is rude because it is loud, and Truewit ridicules women whose walk is offensive because it is as huge as that of an ostrich. Characteristically, Truewit says, "I love measure i' the feet"—"measure" meaning moderation as well as rhythm. Decorous behavior, then, is to the whole person what careful dressing is to the body: an artistic way of repairing the defects of an offensive nature. Even the uncourtly Morose shares the courtly conviction that art can serve and rival nature. He tells Epicene that he longs to have his wife be the first in all fashions, have her council of tailors, "and then come foorth, varied like Nature, or oftner then she, and better, by the helpe of Art, her aemulous servant" (II. v. 73-75). On a lower social plane Otter reveals that he too is aware of how women can use the artificial to gild or transform the natural. When he is drunk enough to be brave, he begins to curse his wife for being naturally vile. She makes herself endurable only by the most ingenious artifices. "Every part o' the towne ownes a peece of her," Otter claims. "She takes her selfe asunder still when she goes to bed," and the next day, "is put together againe, like a great *Germane clocke*" (IV. ii. 94-99).

But clothes do not merely artificially conceal nature or repair the losses that the years have made; at times the artistic can take the place of the natural: a person's dress can become the person. Thus, in this play as in other comedies of Jonson, knighthood is thought to be largely a matter of clothes. Clerimont, speaking of Sir John Daw, asks, "Was there ever such a two yards of knighthood, measur'd out by *Time,* to be sold to laughter?" (II. iv. 151-152). In a bitter arraignment of knighthood Morose implies that the artificial can become the natural when he says that knighthood "shall want clothes, and by reason of that, wit, to foole to lawyers" (II. v. 125-126). The most striking reference to the way that dress can change man's nature is Truewit's remark about the disguised Otter and Cut-beard. After he fits them out as a divine and a canon lawyer, he tells Dauphine, "the knaves doe not know themselves, they are so exalted, and alter'd. Preferment changes any man" (V. iii. 3-5). Dress can so alter what a man is thought to be that his own nature is changed accordingly.

Epicene, then, is a comedy about nature, normality, and decorum. Its various scenes explore comically and searchingly a number of questions to which, since it is a play, it does not offer any final answers. What is natural and normal for the sexes? What does society expect of men and women? Are women normally gossipy and men normally courageous? What is the relation between the natural and the artificial in social intercourse? But, though the play offers no final answers, it suggests throughout that the various answers dramatized in the physical and verbal action of the play are comic in so far as they violate certain standards of what is masculine and what is feminine, as well as what is natural and what is artificial in dress, behavior, and beauty—standards which, presumably, the spectators bring to the theater with them.

Comparing Jonson's text with any of the many adaptations of the play may reveal how effective its allusive language is in bringing these standards to the attention of the audience. For instance, George Colman's acting version in 1776. Colman had a good eye for emphasizing the farcical element in the plot, but apparently little feeling for what Jonson's language might suggest. The 1776 acting version is a simpler and, by eighteenth century standards, a more genteel play, but its comedy is thinner and more obvious because Colman (who said in his prologue that Jonson's farce was "somewhat stale") cut out much of the play's allusive language. Though he kept in the speech about the Collegiates who speak with masculine or hermaphroditical authority and Morose's reference to "mankind generation," he generally shifted the emphasis away from the comedy of sexual deviations by cutting out the references to the bisexual boy, the Collegiates' living away from their husbands, and

Morose's castration, impotence, and cuckolding. The result is what is known as a "cleaner" play, but a tamer and less searching one. In the same way the theme of art versus nature is mangled: the song, "Still to be neat," is kept, though transferred to an earlier passage in the play, but Truewit's first act remarks are cut out, along with most of the crucial references to clothes. In short, for all its deceptive likeness to the play that Jonson wrote in his unrefined age, Colman's version is a far less suggestive comedy about nature, artifice, and not particularly epicene people.

Colman's treatment of *Epicene* is typical of most adaptations, and prophetic of many modern readings of it. But unless one is aware of the allusiveness of Jonson's language, which adapters like Colman have mangled and which modern readers often disregard, one can not entirely understand Dryden's comment that there is "more art and acuteness of fancy in [*Epicene*] than in any of Ben Jonson's [plays]." [9]

[9] *The Works of John Dryden,* ed. Scott and Saintsbury (London, 1892), XV, 351.

Unifying Symbols in the Comedy of Ben Jonson

by Ray L. Heffner, Jr.

Critics since the seventeenth century have agreed that Ben Jonson is a master of comic structure, but there has been serious disagreement as to just what kind of structure it is in which he excels. To Dryden, Jonson was pre-eminent among English dramatists because he obeyed the neo-classic rules of unity of time, place, and action. Of the three, unity of action is fundamental, and it is Jonson's plotting that Dryden found most praiseworthy. He preferred *The Silent Woman* above all other plays because he found it an ideal combination of the scope, variety, and naturalness of the English drama with the control and careful organization of the French. And the *examen* of that play in the *Essay of Dramatic Poesy* emphasizes that there is immense variety of character and incident but that the action is "entirely one." [1] Critics in recent years, however, have disputed Dryden's picture of a regular, neo-classic Jonson, especially in the matter of plot structure. Freda L. Townsend, for example, argues persuasively that none of Jonson's great comedies has the unified action characteristic of Terentian comedy and enjoined by neo-classic precept.[2] She compares Jonson's art with that of Ariosto and the baroque painters, and she sees *Bartholomew Fair* rather than *The Silent Woman* as the culmination of his development away from a simply unified comedy toward one which involves the intricate interweaving of as many different interests as possible. T. S. Eliot perhaps best sums up this "modern" view of Jonson's technique when he says that his "immense dramatic constructive skill" is not so much in plot as in "doing without a plot," and adds:

> The plot does not hold the play together; what holds the play together is a unity of inspiration that radiates into plot and personages alike.[3]

"Unifying Symbols in the Comedy of Ben Jonson," by Ray L. Heffner, Jr. From *English Stage Comedy*, ed. W. K. Wimsatt, Jr., *English Institute Essays 1954*, pp. 74-97. Copyright © 1955 by the Columbia University Press. Reprinted by permission of the Columbia University Press.

[1] *Essays of John Dryden*, ed. by W. P. Ker (Oxford, 1926), 1, 83.

[2] *Apologie for Bartholmew Fayre: the Art of Jonson's Comedies* (New York, Modern Language Association, 1947), *passim*, especially pp. 91-97.

[3] "Ben Jonson," *Elizabethan Essays* (London, 1934), p. 77.

The views of Eliot and Miss Townsend seem to me substantially more correct than that of Dryden on this matter. In this paper I shall try to define more precisely the "unity of inspiration" which Eliot and others have found in Jonson's comedy and to describe the dramatic devices by which it is expressed. Briefly, I believe that the essential unity of Jonson's comedy is thematic. In each of his major plays he explores an idea or a cluster of related ideas through a variety of characters and actions. And the central expression of the unifying idea is usually not in a fully developed plot but in a fantastic comic conceit, an extravagant exaggeration of human folly, to which all of the more realistically conceived characters and incidents have reference.

For such an investigation the crucial cases are *The Silent Woman* and *Bartholomew Fair,* Dryden's ideal "regular" comedy and Miss Townsend's ideal "baroque" comedy. If I can show that, despite the very evident differences in superficial structure, a similar kind of thematic unity underlies each of these and that it is expressed in similar symbolic devices, my analysis may have some claim to inclusiveness.

In the case of *The Silent Woman*, I must first undertake to show that it is not, even at the level of action, held together by the "noble intrigue" as Dryden analyzes it. Dryden's spokesman Neander, accepting the definition of unity of action given earlier in the debate by Crites, tries to show that at least one English comedy adheres to the rule. Crites' principles are those derived by Renaissance and neo-classic criticism mainly from the practice of Terence. The emphasis is on the single, clearly defined aim of the action, which should be announced in the *protasis* or beginning of the play, delayed by all sorts of complications and counter-intrigues in the *epitasis* or middle, and finally brought to completion by the *catastrophe* or denouement. Neander discusses *The Silent Woman* as if it follows exactly this formula. "The action of the play is entirely one," he says, "the end or aim of which is the settling of Morose's estate on Dauphine." And he continues:

> You see, till the very last scene, new difficulties arising to obstruct the action of the play; and when the audience is brought into despair that the business can naturally be effected, then, and not before, the discovery is made.[4]

If we consider the play in retrospect, after we have seen or read the last scene, we may agree with Neander that the securing of Morose's estate is the central aim of the whole. Dauphine's sensational revelation of the true sex of Epicene does indeed finally and irrevocably secure for him the estate, and after the play is over we can see that all the intrigues of Truewit and Clerimont, no matter what their intended purpose, have

[4] Ker, *Essays of Dryden,* 1, 88.

aided Dauphine's scheme by exhausting his uncle's patience and thus making the old man desperate enough to sign the settlement. But the fact that the true nature of Dauphine's scheme is concealed until the very end makes a great difference in the kind of unity which can be perceived by the audience during the course of the play. The settling of Morose's estate on Dauphine is not the ostensible aim of the action after Act III, for the audience as well as the other characters have been led to believe that Dauphine's purposes have been fully accomplished by the marriage of Morose and Epicene. No new difficulties arise to obstruct this action in Acts IV and V: we assume it has already been settled and our attention has turned to other matters. Even in the early acts the course of Dauphine's intrigue is remarkably smooth, and little suspense of the kind Dryden describes is generated. By the last scene, far from being brought into despair that the business of the estate can naturally be effected, we have forgotten all about it and are surprised to see it reintroduced.

As the play unfolds, the settling of Morose's estate upon Dauphine is but one among several aims which give rise to action, and it is dominant only in Act II. It is much more accurate to consider *The Silent Woman* as consisting not of a Terentian plot depending upon the delayed completion of a single, well-defined objective but of a number of separable though related actions which are initiated and brought to completion at various points in the play and which are skillfully arranged to overlay and interlock. Each of these actions is essentially a trick played on a dupe or a group of dupes, and each has four fairly well-defined stages: (1) the exposition of background material, including the characterization of the dupe; (2) the planning of the trick by the intriguer; (3) the actual execution of the trick; and (4) the reminiscence of the trick as a source of continued laughter. The general plan is that a different major action occupies the center of attention in each act except the first, which consists of exposition of material for all the actions to follow. Act II is thus centered on Dauphine's scheme to marry his uncle to Epicene, Act III on Truewit's scheme to torment Morose by moving Sir Amorous La Foole's dinner party to Morose's house, Act IV on the double scheme to discredit the foolish knights and make all the Collegiate Ladies fall in love with Dauphine, and Act V on the tormenting of Morose through the mock discussion of marriage annulment by the pretended canon lawyer and divine.

This basic plan is complicated by the introduction of several minor actions, notably the one precipitating the disgrace of Captain Tom Otter, and by the overlapping previously mentioned. At almost every point at least three actions are under simultaneous consideration: one is at the peak of fulfillment, a second has passed its climax but is still producing laughter, and the groundwork for a third is being carefully prepared.

These sundry intrigues are connected in a number of different ways.

The peculiarities of the various dupes which make them fit objects of ridicule are all described in the course of an apparently aimless conversation in Act I, so that the jokes played on them later in the play, though they seem to arise spontaneously out of particular situations, nevertheless are not unexpected. All the tricks are planned by the same group of witty companions, most of them by Truewit, and every character has some part in more than one intrigue. Often one intrigue depends on the completion of another, as the transferring of the banquet on the completion of the marriage. And the final revelation of Epicene's sex, as Miss Townsend points out, has some relevance to all the major actions[5]; it not only accomplishes Morose's divorce and gains the estate for Dauphine, it also shows the foolish knights to be liars and discomfits the Collegiate Ladies, who have had to depend on a despised male for the vindication of their honors.

Such an elaborate intertwining of episodes demonstrates great technical skill in what Renaissance criticism called *disposition* and *economy*.[6] But we are still entitled to ask, is this the only kind of structure the play possesses? Are there no more fundamental relationships among these various characters and actions, of which the mechanical interconnections we have been discussing are but the external evidences? The thematic structure of the play will be clearer if we consider that its real center is not in any of the tricks or schemes but in the ridiculous situation in which Morose finds himself. My argument is not genetic, but a brief look at the probable sources of the play may help to confirm this impression. The sources of the separable parts are extremely varied. Passages of dialogue come from Juvenal and Ovid, many of the characters belong in the series of satiric portraits stretching back through Jonson's early plays and through contemporary nondramatic satire; the aborted duel between the two knights seems to come from *Twelfth Night,* the conflict between Dauphine and his uncle bears some resemblance to *A Trick to Catch the Old One,* and the device of trickery through concealed sex may come from Aretino's comedy *Il Marescalco.*[7] But the center around which all this material is arranged is clearly the comic conceit which Jonson took from a declamation of Libanius—the ludicrous plight of a noise-hating man married by fraud to a noisy woman.

[5] Townsend, *Bartholmew Fayre,* p. 64.

[6] In his *Discoveries* (lines 1815-20 in the Herford and Simpson edition) Jonson speaks slightingly of Terence's skill in these matters, though it was much praised by most Renaissance critics. For the meaning of the terms, see Marvin T. Herrick, *Comic Theory in the Sixteenth Century* ("Illinois Studies in Language and Literature," Vol. xxxiv, Nos. 1-2 [Urbana, 1950]), pp. 94-106.

[7] For these and other sources see C. H. Herford and Percy and Evelyn Simpson, *Ben Jonson* (Oxford, 1925-52), II 72-79 (1925), and the notes in Vol. x (1950); also the edition by Julia Ward Henry ("Yale Studies in English," No. xxxi [New York, 1906]), pp. xxviii-lvi, and O. J. Campbell, "The Relation of *Epicoene* to Aretino's *Il Marescalco,*" *PMLA,* xlvi (1931), 752-62.

Herford and Simpson observe that, "The amusing oration of Libanius offered but slender stuff for drama." [8] This is true enough, in that it contained only a situation and not a complete plot, and the implications of that situation were but little developed. The Morosus of Libanius merely describes the horrors of his noise-ridden existence and pleads with the judges for permission to commit suicide. The oration could not simply be translated to the stage without the addition of much extra material. But it is, nevertheless, an admirable idea for a comedy. For one thing, it epitomizes the eternal battle of the sexes for supremacy, including the hypocrisies of courtship and the wrangling after marriage. And then also, in its opposition of noisy people to noise haters, it suggests another eternal theme, the debate between the active and the quiet life. In constructing a play around the conceit of Libanius, Jonson greatly complicates both these latent themes, through his interpretation of the Morose-Epicene relationship and through the addition of other characters and actions.

Jonson's interpretation of the central situation is summarized in the scene in which Morose interrogates his intended bride (II. v.). There we learn that the old man's hatred of noise is the outward manifestation of two allied character traits. First, he has been at court and has recoiled in horror from all forms of courtliness. He tests his bride-to-be by pointing out to her that if she forbear the use of her tongue she will be unable to trade "pretty girds, scoffes, and daliance" with her admirers; she cannot, like the ladies in court, "affect . . . to seeme learn'd, to seeme judicious, to seeme sharpe, and conceited"; and she will be manifestly unable to "have her counsell of taylors, lineners, lace-women, embroyderers, and sit with 'hem sometimes twise a day, upon *French* intelligences" so as "to be the first and principall in all fashions." The meaning of the play's central symbol of noise is thus considerably developed in this scene; a noisy woman is a woman given over to all the vanity, hypocrisy, and affectation to which her sex and the courtly society of her age are prone. Morose can concentrate his hatred of all these things by hating the inclusive and concrete symbol, noise itself.

The second important aspect of Morose's idiosyncracy is his passion for having his own way in all things. In his first soliloquy he admits that "all discourses, but mine owne, afflict mee" (II. i.). He admires the absolute obedience which oriental potentates command from members of their households; and the silence of his own servants indicates their complete subservience to his will, for they can answer perfectly well by signs so long as their judgments "jump" with his. Epicene thus throws him into ecstasies of happiness when she answers to all his questions, "Judge you, forsooth," and "I leave it to wisdome, and you sir."

Morose's attitude towards his nephew illustrates both these aspects of

---

[8] *Ben Jonson*, II, 76 (1925).

his character. After putting his intended bride successfully through the test, he breaks into a scornful tirade at the notion of Sir Dauphine's knighthood:

> He would be knighted, forsooth, and thought by that meanes to raigne over me, his title must doe it: no kinsman, I will now make you bring mee the tenth lords, and the sixteenth ladies letter, kinsman; and it shall doe you no good kinsman. Your knighthood it selfe shall come on it's knees, and it shall be rejected. (II.v.)

By the coup of his marriage, Morose hopes to express his contempt for all the world of lords, ladies, and courtly society, as well as his complete dominance over all members of his family. The comic irony in his situation is that he inevitably brings all his troubles on himself, because his two desires, to command and to live apart, though so closely related, cannot both be fulfilled on his terms. An ascetic hermit might live apart and rail against the court; a great lord might command absolute obedience from all around him. But Morose will make no sacrifice; he will be the ultimate of both at once. In seeking to extend his circle of dominance beyond his servant and his barber to include a wife, he brings in upon himself the torrent of courtly commotion from which he has fled. In seeking to make his power over his nephew absolute, he loses all. When Dauphine says to him at the end of the play, "Now you may goe in and rest, be as private as you will, sir," his sarcastic words may seem more than a little cruel, but it is the logic of the world that decrees Morose's sentence. He can be "private" only when he gives up all pretense of being an absolute autocrat, and this he has just done by submitting himself humbly to his nephew's will and judgment.

The other material in the play consists largely of a set of mirrors which, by reflecting various aspects of this central situation, extend its significance. The Collegiate Ladies, for example, are embodiments of all the courtly vices and affectations which Morose lumps under the heading of "female noise." The most prominent feature of their composite portrait is, in Morose's words, that they "affect to seem judicious." As Truewit says in the first act,

> [They are] an order betweene courtiers, and country-madames, that live from their husbands; and give entertainment to all the *Wits,* and *Braveries* o' the time, as they call 'hem: crie downe, or up, what they like, or dislike in a braine, or a fashion, with most masculine, or rather *hermaphroditicall* authoritie. (I.i.)

The Collegiates are thus an appropriate part of the flood of noise that pours in upon Morose after the wedding through which he had hoped to assert his masculine dominance and to declare his independence from all courtliness. The ladies' pretense to authority is just as absurd as Morose's.

This is demonstrated in Act IV by the disgrace of the two knights whom they had cried up as wits and braveries, and especially by the ease with which the ladies can be turned from one opinion to its exact opposite, from idolizing the two knights to despising them, from despising Dauphine to being infatuated with him. As Truewit says, his tricks prove that

> all their actions are governed by crude opinion, without reason or cause; they know not why they doe any thing: but as they are inform'd, beleeve, judge, praise, condemne, love, hate, and in aemulation one of another, doe all these things alike. (IV.vi.)

Sir John Daw and Sir Amorous La Foole are the male representatives of the affected courtliness which Morose despises. In contrast to the three ladies, these two have separate identities at the beginning, though they are merged into a composite portrait as the action progresses. Sir John is the "wit" or fool intellectual, Sir Amorous the "bravery" or fool social. Jonson had treated varieties of both in earlier plays, but he fits these into his present scheme by emphasizing in both cases the noisiness of their folly. Sir John is the "onely talking sir i'th' towne" whom Truewit dares not visit for the danger to his ears. His conversation is noise not only because it is verbose but also because it is inopportune and disorderly. He insists upon reading his wretched verses, whether or not the company desires to hear them; he pours out the names of authors in an undisciplined stream. The garrulity of Sir Amorous has similar characteristics though different subject matter. Clerimont emphasizes that this knight's pretentious courtesy respects neither place, person, nor season:

> He will salute a Judge upon the bench, and a Bishop in the pulpit, a Lawyer when hee is pleading at the barre, and a Lady when shee is daunceing in a masque, and put her out. He do's give playes, and suppers, and invites his guests to 'hem, aloud, out of his windore, as they ride by in coaches. (I.iii.)

When Sir Amorous appears on the scene, he does, as Clerimont has predicted, "tell us his pedigree, now; and what meat he has to dinner; and, who are his guests; and, the whole course of his fortunes," all in one breath.

The two knights thus give a wider meaning to the notion of a noisy man in much the same way as the Collegiates and Morose's interrogation of Epicene widen the meaning of a noisy woman. Noise is ungentlemanly boasting about one's poetic and critical powers, about one's family, friends, and hospitality, and, toward the end of the play, about one's sexual powers and conquests. The one gentlemanly attribute to which the two do not conspicuously pretend is courage on the field of battle.

We may therefore be somewhat puzzled when the main trick against them seems to turn on their cowardice, and we sympathize with Mrs. Doll Mavis when she defends her judgment of them by saying, "I commended but their wits, madame, and their braveries. I never look'd toward their valours" (IV.vi.). But what has been exposed in the mock duel is not only cowardice but pliability. Like the ladies who admire them, the knights have no real standards for judging either books or men, but are governed entirely by rumor and fashion. Therefore it is ridiculously easy for Truewit to persuade each knight that the other, whose pacific disposition he should know well, is a raging lion thirsting for his blood. If either knight had been made more on the model of the swaggering *miles gloriosus,* the point about how easy it is to make a fool believe the exact opposite of the obvious truth would have been blunted.

The themes of courtly behavior, the battle between the sexes, and the pretense to authority are intertwined with that of noise versus silence wherever one looks in the play, even in the foolish madrigals of modesty and silence written by Sir John Daw. In the action involving Captain and Mrs. Tom Otter, all these subjects are invested with an atmosphere of comedy lower than that of the rest of the play. For the salient fact about the Otters is that they are of a lower social class than any of the other main characters. Mrs. Otter is a rich China woman struggling for admission to the exclusive Ladies' College; Captain Tom is at home among the bulls and bears but unsure of himself in the company of knights and wits. Here again the citizen-couple who welcome instruction in the courtly follies are familiar figures from Jonson's early comical satire, but the portraits are modified to fit the thematic pattern of this play. The Collegiate Ladies may pretend to a nice discernment in brains and fashions, but Mrs. Otter comprehends fashionable feminism rather differently and expresses her "masculine, or rather *hermaphroditicall* authority" more elementally by pummeling her husband. And Captain Tom's noises are his boisterous but rather pathetic drinking bouts, accompanied by drum and trumpet, by which he hopes to gain a reputation among the gentry and to assert his independence from his wife. This is the comic realm of Maggie and Jiggs, the hen-pecked husband sneaking out to the corner saloon to escape his social-climbing wife, but the relationships between this farcical situation and the central one of Morose and Epicene are clear and are emphasized at every turn. Like the characters in most Elizabethan comic sub-plots, the Otters burlesque the main action while at the same time extending its meaning toward the universal.

As the clumsy, middle class Otters contrast with the more assured aristocrats, so all the pliable pretenders to courtliness contrast with the true gentlemen and scholars, Truewit, Clerimont, and Dauphine. Within this group of intriguers, however, there is a further important contrast. Clerimont is relatively undeveloped as a character, but the differences between Truewit and Dauphine are stressed. Truewit is boisterous and boastful about the jokes he contrives. He must have the widest possible audience; as Dauphine tells him, "This is thy extreme vanitie, now: thou think'st thou wert undone, if every jest thou mak'st were not publish'd" (IV.v.). Dauphine, on the other hand, moves quietly about his purposes and keeps his own counsel. Truewit characteristically invents his fun on the spur of the moment, out of the materials at hand, and is apt to promise to do something (like making all the Collegiates fall in love with Dauphine) before he has the slightest idea how it can be brought about. Dauphine's plans have been months in preparation, and he betrays little hint of his purposes until they actually have been accomplished.

The rivalry of these two for the title of master plotter runs as a subdued motive through all the action. It is most prominent in the first two acts, when Truewit's rash and suddenly conceived scheme to dissuade Morose from marrying almost upsets Dauphine's carefully laid plot. It might seem that the contrast is all in favor of the quiet, modest, but in the end more effective Dauphine. Truewit assumes too readily that he can read the entire situation at first glance, and that he can easily manipulate the stubborn Morose. He becomes almost a comic butt himself when he ridiculously tries to pretend that he has foreseen from the first the really quite unexpected consequence of his action. The denouement especially would seem to prove that Dauphine is the real master at playing chess with characters and humours, and Truewit just the bungling amateur. But Jonson is not writing a treatise after the manner of Plutarch on the virtue of silence and the folly of garrulity. Dauphine and Truewit share the honors in the closing scene, and there is more than a little to be said throughout the play for Truewit's engaging love of good fun for its own sake as against Dauphine's colder, more practical scheming. Instead of arguing a simple thesis, Jonson is investigating another aspect of his central symbol of noise. Just as he holds a brief neither for the noise of courtly affectation nor for Morose's extreme hatred of it, so he argues neither for the noisy wit nor for the quiet wit but is content to explore the differences between them.

The essential movement of *The Silent Woman,* then, is the exploration of themes implicit in the central comic conceit of a noise-hating man married to a noisy woman. Noise and the hatred of noise take on the proportion of symbols as they are given ever-widening meanings by the various particulars of social satire. The play's realism and its fantastic caricature can hardly be disentangled, for they are held together firmly in the same comic structure.

Much the same things can be said of *Bartholomew Fair,* despite its even greater complexity and its different kind of surface plan. In this play, characters, actions, interests are all multiplied. If in *The Silent Woman* there are usually three separable intrigues in motion at the same time, they all have a similar pattern of development and are under the control of no more than three intriguers. But in *Bartholomew Fair* five or six actions seem always to be ripening simultaneously, there are more than a dozen intriguers, and no single pattern of development will fit all the kinds of action which the fair breeds. Jonson, however, adheres to a firm if complicated plan in devising the apparent chaos of his fair, and this play has a thematic structure much like that of *The Silent Woman*. Here again Jonson is not arguing a thesis but is investigating diverse aspects of a central problem; here again the various parts of his play are used to mirror each other; and here again the "unity of inspiration" is best expressed by a character who is a fantastic caricature, in an extremely absurd situation which is reflected by all the more "realistic" figures in the play.

The central theme is the problem of what "warrant" men have or pretend to have for their actions. The problem touches both epistemology and ethics—the questions of how we know what we think we know, and why we behave as we do. Stated thus, it is very broad indeed, but it is brought into focus by several concrete symbols of legal sanction. The Induction, for example, is built on the device of a formal contract between the playwright and the audience, giving the customers license to judge the play, but only within specified limits. The play itself opens with Proctor John Littlewit discussing a marriage license taken out by Bartholomew Cokes and Grace Wellborn, and the possession of this document becomes of central importance not only in gulling the testy "governor" Humphrey Wasp but also in the "romantic" plot involving Grace, the two witty gallants, and Dame Purecraft.

The most important symbol of this basic theme, however, is the "warrant" which the madman Troubleall demands of almost all the characters in the fourth act. This demented former officer of the Court of Pie-Powders, who has neither appeared nor been mentioned earlier in the play, is obsessed with the necessity of documentary sanction for even the slightest action. As the watchman Bristle explains, Troubleall will do nothing unless he has first obtained a scrap of paper with Justice Overdo's name signed to it:

> He will not eate a crust, nor drinke a little, nor make him in his apparell, ready. His wife, Sirreverence, cannot get him make his water, or shift his shirt, without his warrant. (IV.i.)

In Troubleall's absurd humor we have the same kind of grand, extravagant comic conceit as that provided by Morose's hatred of all noise. It is the ultimate extreme, the fantastic caricature of the widespread and not unnatural human craving for clearly defined authority, and it serves as the most significant unifying device in the play. Troubleall intervenes crucially in several of the threads of plot, settling the dispute between

Grace's lovers, freeing Overdo and Busy from the stocks, and enabling Quarlous to cheat Justice Overdo and marry the rich widow Purecraft. But beyond his service as a catalyst of action. Troubleall's main function is, as his name suggests, to trouble everybody as he darts suddenly on and off the stage with his embarrassing question, "Have you a warrant for what you do?" This leads to a re-examination of the motives of all the characters, a new scrutiny of what warrant they really have and what they pretend to have for their beliefs and their deeds.

Neither the outright fools nor the outright knaves are much troubled by the great question. The booby Cokes, who has never sought a reason for anything he did, exclaims scornfully, "As if a man need a warrant to lose any thing with!" And Wasp, who pretends to "judgment and knowledge of matters" but who really is just as much motivated by irrational whim as his foolish pupil, cries out during the game of vapors, "I have no reason, nor I will heare of no reason, nor I will looke for no reason, and he is an Asse, that either knowes any, or lookes for't from me" (IV.iv.). Among the knaves, Edgeworth the cutpurse is jolted for a moment by Troubleall's question, thinking that his villainy has been found out, but he quickly returns to planning his next robbery. Most resolute of all is the pimp Knockem, who immediately sits down and *forges* Troubleall a warrant for whatever he may want. As Cokes is motivated by sheer whim, so the sharpers of the fair are motivated by sheer desire for gain, and neither feels the need for further justification.

The watchmen Haggis and Bristle, however, who are on the fringes of the fair's knavery, are led to reflect that Justice Overdo is "a very parantory person" who can get very angry indeed when he has a mind to, "and when hee is angry, be it right or wrong; hee has the Law on's side, ever" (IV.i.). In other words, "warrant" for the watchmen is contained entirely in the unpredictable personality of the judge whom they serve; they have no concern with the guilt or innocence of those whom they incarcerate, and if there is ethics behind the law, they do not comprehend it.

Justice Overdo himself has a double function in the play. For the watchmen and for Troubleall, his name stands as a symbol for the ultimate authority which requires no rational understanding. But as a character in the action, Overdo has his own "warrants" for his conduct, and they are neither irrational nor hypocritical. His motives—to protect the innocent and reprehend the guilty—are beyond reproach; nor is his reliance for his general ethics upon Stoic philosophy as expounded by the Roman poets in itself anything but admirable. And he has the further laudable desire to base his judicial decisions on exact information; he will trust no spies, foolish constables, or sleepy watchmen, but will visit the fair in disguise, to search out enormities for himself at first hand. But for all this the Justice is completely ineffectual, because he cannot interpret correctly what he sees, and because he fails to differen-

tiate between the minor vanities and major iniquities of the fair. Many
are the yearly enormities of the place, as he says, but he concentrates on
the evils of bottle-ale, tobacco, and puppet shows and fails to see the robbery and seduction going on under his nose. Even when he taxes the
right knaves, it is for the wrong crimes. Through the characterization of
Justice Overdo, Jonson seems to me to add the warning that even the
best of warrants is not in itself sufficient to insure right action; Overdo
is reminded at the end that his first name is Adam and he is but flesh
and blood, subject to error like the rest of us. Even such admirable principles as reverence for the classics and reliance upon the facts of evidence
can, if adhered to blindly, become fetishes almost as ludicrous as Troubleall's trust in a signature.

The application of the theme of warrant to Rabbi Zeal-of-the-Land
Busy, who pretends to find authority for everything he does in the words
of scripture but who really is motivated by the most elemental greed and
gluttony, and whose ingenious discovery of theological reasons for the
consumption of roast pig by the faithful is perhaps the funniest scene in
the entire play, need not be further elaborated. The most interesting
effects of Troubleall's persistent questioning are those upon Dame Purecraft and upon Quarlous. The Puritan widow is seized with a frenzied
desire to reform; the witty gentleman comes close to becoming an outright knave.

For Dame Purecraft, Troubleall's madness seems the only possible
alternative to the life of double dealing she has been leading. She exclaims:

> Mad doe they call him! the world is mad in error, but hee is mad in truth.
> . . . O, that I might be his yoake-fellow, and be mad with him, what a
> many should wee draw to madnesse in truth, with us! (IV.vi.)

"Madness in error" in the specific case of Dame Purecraft means reliance
upon the Puritan interpretation of Biblical authority. In the first scene
of Act IV she had replied confidently to Troubleall's question, "Yes, I
have a warrant out of the word." But now she admits freely that her
adherence to scriptural authority was but subterfuge for wicked self-
seeking, and she wants to exchange her hypocritical Puritanism for the
absolute and ingenuous madness which Troubleall represents. The final
irony is that she gains for a husband not a real madman but a gentle-
man-rogue disguised as a lunatic, Quarlous tricked out for his own selfish
purposes in the clothes of Troubleall. Even the search for pure irration-
ality thus turns out to be futile; Dame Purecraft is yoked with the image
of her former self, and her glorious repentance and conversion have been
in vain.

Quarlous comes to a similar conclusion that the only choice is between
knavery and madness, but he has little hesitation in choosing knavery.

As he stands aside to deliberate Dame Purecraft's proposal, he reasons thus:

> It is money that I want, why should I not marry the money, when 'tis offer'd mee? I have a *License* and all, it is but razing out one name, and putting in another. There's no playing with a man's fortune! I am resolv'd! I were truly mad, an' I would not! (V.ii.)

And so he proceeds not only to marry the rich widow but also to extract money by fraud from Justice Overdo, from his erstwhile friend Winwife, and from Grace, the girl for whom he has so recently declared his love. The warrant which Quarlous abandons is the code of a gentleman, including the chivalric ideals of loyalty to one's friend and undying devotion to one's mistress. But the movement of the play here as elsewhere is toward the discovery of true motives rather than toward change of character, for though Quarlous has loudly protested both love and friendship, he has never really been governed by either.

Quarlous' mode of thinking and of acting approaches more and more closely that of those absolute rogues, the inhabitants of the fair. And Quarlous is just as loud in protesting his difference from the fair people as Humphrey Wasp is in protesting his difference from his foolish pupil. Quarlous resents being greeted familiarly by such rascals as Knockem and Whit, and in a very revealing passage he first lashes out at the cutpurse Edgeworth for treating him like one of "your companions in beastlinesse." He then proceeds to find excuses for having been accessory before and after the fact to a robbery:

> Goe your wayes, talke not to me, the hangman is onely fit to discourse with you. . . . I am sorry I employ'd this fellow; for he thinks me such: *Facinus quos inquinat, aequat*. But, it was for sport. And would I make it serious, the getting of this Licence is nothing to me, without other circumstances concurre. (IV.vi.)

This is a piece of rationalization worthy of the master, Rabbi Busy; and we observe with some amusement that Quarlous immediately starts taking steps to *make* the other circumstances concur through fraud.

The emphasis in *Bartholomew Fair* is thus on the narrow range of motives that actually govern men's actions, in contrast to the wide variety of warrants which they pretend to have. Notable prominence is given to primitive motivations: Busy scents after pork like a hound, both Mrs. Littlewit and Mrs. Overdo are drawn into the clutches of the pimps by the necessity for relieving themselves, and the longing of a pregnant woman is the ostensible reason which sets the whole Littlewit party in motion towards the fair. As the many hypocrisies are revealed, the only distinction which seems to hold up is that between fools and knaves, between Cokes and the rogues who prey on him. The other characters are seen as approaching more and more closely to these extremes, until all search for warrant seems as absurd as Troubleall's, since all authority is either as corrupt as the watchmen or as irrational as Wasp or as blind as Justice Overdo. Whim, animal appetite, and sordid greed have complete sway over men's actions without as well as within the fair; the fair merely provides the heightened conditions under which disguises fall off and the elemental motivations become manifest.

In both the plays we have been considering then, fantastic exaggerations like Morose's hatred of noise and Troubleall's search for a warrant provide the lenses through which the behavior of more realistically conceived characters can be observed and brought into focus. It is chiefly in his grand comic conceits that Jonson's "unity of inspiration" resides, for in them the interplay of realistic satire and fantastic caricature is most highly concentrated, and from them it does truly "radiate into plot and personages alike."

It is this interplay between realism and fantasy which seems to me the very essence of Jonson's comedy. To decry, as Herford and Simpson do, the prominence of the "farcical horror-of-noise-motive" in *The Silent Woman,* and to regret the "deepseated contrarieties in Jonson's own artistic nature, where the bent of a great realist for truth and nature never overcame the satirist's and humorist's weakness for fantastic caricature" [9] is, I believe, seriously to misunderstand Jonson's art. His purpose was always to hold the mirror up to nature, but not simply to present the world of common experience, uncriticized and unstructured. Without the extravagant caricatures which he develops into organizing symbols, Jonson's comedy would lack not only the unity but also the universality of great art.

If Jonson's comedy is of the sort here suggested, then a comparison with Aristophanes may not be amiss. Here again we have a mingling of fantasy and realism, and here again we have a comic structure centered not on a plot but on the exploration of an extravagant conceit. Jonson has almost always been discussed as if he belonged in the tradition of Menander, Plautus, and Terence—of New Comedy. I believe that we might gain more insight into his art if we considered him instead in the quite different tradition of Old Comedy. Perhaps Jonson meant more than we have given him credit for meaning when he said of the comedy he was working to develop that it was not bound by Terentian rules but was "of a particular kind by itself, somewhat like *Vetus Comoedia.*" [10]

[9] *Ben Jonson,* II, 76-78 (1925).
[10] Induction to *Every Man Out of His Humour.*

Catiline and the Nature
of Jonson's Tragic Fable

by Joseph Allen Bryant, Jr.

Although the principal subject of this paper is Ben Jonson's second tragedy, *Catiline His Conspiracy* (1611), a good deal of what I have to say is equally applicable to his earlier and somewhat more ambitious *Sejanus His Fall* (1603).[1] The two plays are alike in many ways. For one thing, neither of them has ever been popular. Even among professed admirers, very few have been willing to praise them as highly as Jonson thought they deserved to be praised, and fewer still have seen any genuine tragedy in them. In fact, most criticism, favorable as well as unfavorable, has centered on such interesting but essentially peripheral matters as Jonson's use of the Senecan ghost and chorus (in *Catiline*), his portrayal of character, his reconstruction of the Roman scene, and, of course, his rhetoric. Discussions of Jonson's plots have scarcely gone beyond the problem of identifying his sources, and almost no one has touched upon the question of whether any real importance attaches to the use he made of those sources. This would not be particularly surprising, perhaps, if we were dealing with some competent journeyman, like Thomas Heywood for example, whose selection and use of sources is a matter of mainly academic interest; but in Jonson we have a playwright who not only aimed at something more than a popularly successful play but also set unusually great store by authenticity of fable—or "truth of argument," as he called it—where tragedy was concerned (*Works*, IV, 350). His manipulation of material, therefore, especially at points where the disagreement of authoritative sources about a major issue forced him to make a choice, becomes a matter of considerable interest. It is certainly of interest to the historian, for it shows the sort of interpretation of history an intelligent and well-informed classical student of the seventeenth century might reasonably hold. My point, however, is that it is

"*Catiline* and the Nature of Jonson's Tragic Fable." From *PMLA* LXIX (1954), 265-277. Reprinted by permission of the Modern Language Association.
[1] Citations from Jonson in my text are to *Ben Jonson*, ed. C. H. Herford and Percy and Evelyn Simpson, 10 vols. (Oxford, 1925-50)—hereafter referred to as *Works*. *Sejanus* and *Catiline* appear in Vols. IV and V, respectively.

also a matter of literary interest. It can be shown, I think, that Jonson's ordering of his fable, rightly understood, gives the clue to why and how he expected these plays to be judged as tragedies rather than merely as serious history plays. In other words, it lets one see the conception of tragic drama that he worked by.

Nevertheless, any adequate criticism of Jonson's tragedies must begin with a consideration of them as history plays; for, as I shall explain later in more detail, the basic and distinctive fact about Jonson's tragic fable is that it depends upon a verifiable historical context. That is, it comes to us as verifiable historiography in dramatic form and consequently derives at least part of its authority from the authority of recorded history. We hardly need Jonson's pronouncement about "truth of argument" to tell us this much about his tragic fable. Ample evidence that he wanted us to accept his plays both as history and as drama lies in the careful documentation that he provided for the quarto of *Sejanus,* which was almost equivalent to an announcement that he wanted his dramatic segment to retain its identification with the larger "true" story from which it had been taken. *Catiline,* of course, is equally capable of such documentation, as subsequent scholarship has shown, though Jonson did not actually provide footnotes for any printed version of the play.[2] Here, too, he drew upon recognized authorities, Plutarch, Dio Cassius, Cicero, and Sallust—sometimes directly and sometimes through the intermediary of a compendium called *Historia Conjurationis Catilinariae,* by the Renaissance scholar Constantius Felicius Durantinus.[3] His principal source, however, was Sallust's *Bellum Catilinae,* from which he took the main outline of his plot, some of his important dialogue, and numerous hints for developing his characters.[4] We can best begin the examination of Jonson's *Catiline* by comparing it with that.

In both works the story concerns Lucius Catilina, a profligate and unscrupulous young nobleman who sought to seize complete control of the government and become a second Sulla; and Jonson's play begins, as does the main portion of Sallust's account, with Catiline's second attempt to snatch the power. In Act I we see the meeting of the conspirators at which Catiline announced his plan, promising Rome itself as a prize to those who would support him and compelling all present to attest their allegiance by drinking a mixture of wine and human blood. In Act II we see how Catiline's conspiracy was doomed when the patriotic Fulvia elected to barter what little virtue she had for such information as the garrulous conspirator Curius was able to give her. Acts III and IV show

---

[2] See the discussion of sources in *Works,* X, 117-119, and *passim* in the notes to the play, pp. 121-161.

[3] See Ellen M. T. Duffy, "Ben Jonson's Debt to Renaissance Scholarship in *Sejanus* and *Catiline,*" *MLR,* XLII (1947), 24-30.

[4] In preparing this paper, I have used the Loeb ed. of Sallust's works, trans. J. C. Rolfe (London, 1920).

us how Cicero, having defeated Catiline for the consulship, used Fulvia's information to frustrate Catiline's attempt to have him assassinated; then how he brought the whole conspiracy into the open, addressing Catiline in the Senate and calling upon him to leave the city; and, finally, how he managed to forestall the attempt of Catiline's adherents to turn the warlike Allobroges against Rome, their nominal ally. The last act shows the complete collapse of the conspiracy; we see there how the conspirators remaining at Rome were apprehended and executed, and we hear how Catiline and the remnant of his two legions met destruction in the desperate stand at Fesulae. For this much of his plot, certainly, Jonson could have cited the authority of Sallust; and, indeed, one can say that he did effectually cite it by the way he allowed most of his characters to develop and by the things he had them say. At any rate, one who knows his Sallust at all well must immediately recognize Sallust's mark on Jonson's play.

Sallust's mark on *Catiline* is evident in still another respect. One way of looking at *Bellum Catilinae* is to regard it as a political sermon on the pitfalls of prosperity and power with the narrative serving as a rather well-developed *exemplum*. The best single statement of theme in it is perhaps the following one from Chapter X:

> . . . when our country had grown great through toil and the practice of justice, when great kings had been vanquished in war, savage tribes and mighty peoples subdued by force of arms, when Carthage, the rival of Rome's sway, had perished root and branch, and all seas and lands were open, then Fortune began to grow cruel and to bring confusion into all our affairs. Those who had found it easy to bear hardship and dangers, anxiety and adversity, found leisure and wealth, desirable under other circumstances, a burden and a curse. Hence the lust for power first, then for money, grew upon them; these were, I may say, the root of all evils. For avarice destroyed honor, integrity, and all other noble qualities; taught in their place insolence, cruelty, to neglect the gods, to set a price on everything. . . . At first these vices grew slowly, from time to time they were punished; finally, when the disease had spread like a deadly plague, the state was changed and a government second to none in equity and excellence became cruel and intolerable.

What we have here is really something more than a statement of theme. It virtually amounts to a statement of Sallust's philosophy of history, according to which everything that man achieves—institutions, cities, states—partakes of the corrupt nature of man's physical body and has "an end as well as a beginning . . . rise and fall, wax and wane" (*Bellum Iugurthinum*, ii.3). Unlike the Greek historian Polybius, from whom he probably derived his cyclic view of history, Sallust regarded the inevitability of decline in man's political structures as the consequence not of some natural order but of man's own willful depravity and his inability

to live by reason.[5] According to his view, reason, virtue, and immortality, in man and in man's commonwealth, are inseparable. "If men had
as great regard for honorable enterprises as they have ardor in pursuing what is foreign to their interests," he wrote in his *Bellum Iugurthinum,* ". . . they would control fate rather than be controlled by it,
and would attain to that height of greatness where from mortals their
glory would make them immortal" (i.5). Yet Sallust was pessimistic
about the ability of mankind, either individually or collectively, to live
for very long by the light of reason, especially if subjected to the temptations of power, luxury, and ease. Rome herself, as he saw it, was responsible for Catiline and would in time produce others like him unless
she saw the error of her ways. For these sentiments Jonson also found
a place in his play. His best statement of them, one which is none the
less Sallustian for having been translated in part from Petronius' *Satyri-
con,* comes in the Chorus to Act I:

> Rome, now, is Mistris of the whole
> World, sea, and land, to either pole;
> And even that fortune will destroy
> The power that made it: she doth joy
> So much in plentie, wealth, and ease,
> As, now, th'excesse is her disease. . . .
>   Hence comes that wild, and vast expence,
> That hath enforc'd *Romes* vertue, thence,
> Which simple poverty first made:
> And, now, ambition doth invade
> Her state, with eating avarice,
> Riot, and every other vice. . . .
> Such ruine of her manners *Rome*
> Doth suffer now, as shee's become
> (Without the gods it soone gaine-say)
> Both her owne spoiler, and owne prey.

In spite of all these similarities, however, Jonson's work in import is
so different from Sallust's that one may easily imagine that Sallust, had
he been able to read the play or see it performed, would have rejected it
utterly. The reason for the difference lies in one group of additions which
Jonson made to the plot as he found it in Sallust. I do not mean here such
essentially minor additions, or elaborations, as the introduction of Sylla's
ghost at the beginning of the play, the detailed representation of what
went on in Fulvia's boudoir, or the inclusion of the blood-drinking scene
in Act I. Of such additions as these Sallust doubtless would have ap-

---

[5] This was the view of most Stoics; see Eduard Zeller, *The Stoics, Epicureans and
Sceptics,* trans. O. J. Reichel (London, 1892), pp. 249ff.

proved, for they support admirably his own interpretation and evaluation of the events in the story.[6] What I have in mind is the additions that
concern the supposed complicity of Julius Caesar in Catiline's plot. In
these Jonson made use of material that he found in the other sources I
have mentioned—particularly in the accounts of Plutarch and Dio,
which Durantinus had accepted and used—together with a few details
from his own fertile imagination. The net product was a plausible version of Catiline's conspiracy, but one considerably different from any that
had gone before it and vastly different from the one that Sallust had
written.

According to Sallust, Caesar was accused of complicity with Catiline
by Quintus Catulus and Gaius Piso, both of whom were bitter enemies
of Caesar (*Bellum Cat.*, xlviii); but the charges of these two were manifestly false and failed to influence Cicero. Caesar's only direct participation in the affair was his address to the Senate, in which he urged that the
conspirators be punished with confiscation of property and imprisonment
rather than with death. Sallust reports this speech in full, as he does the
reply of Marcus Cato, who urged successfully that the guilty ones be
executed (li-lii); but he tries to forestall any adverse criticism of Caesar
that the speeches might suggest, by appending to his report a pair of
character sketches which present the two men as equal in merit. Cato
and Caesar, he declares, are the only two of "towering merit" that Rome
has produced in his lifetime. Cato is the representative of those virtues
by means of which Rome managed to survive a specific peril; Caesar, of
those virtues which enabled her somewhat later to weather a stormy
period of change and emerge a great and enduring power. By contrast,
Cicero, who holds a central position in Jonson's version of the story, is
called merely the "best of consuls" (xliii).

The interpretation of Caesar that one gets from *Catiline His Conspiracy* is, of course, anything but sympathetic. Jonson lets us see Caesar
first in the opening scene of Act III, in which Cicero addresses the people
for the first time as consul. Caesar, standing in the background, makes
such disgruntled remarks that Cato accuses him of being envious. Immediately afterward, he greets the defeated Catiline and by means of
side-whispers makes arrangements to meet him privately. Later, at
Catiline's house, he gives his friend some memorable instruction in the
principles of worldly success. All this, fictitious as it is, can be justified
as legitimate use of what some have called "the historical imagination,"
provided one takes as fact the reported suspicions of such anti-Caesareans
as Plutarch and Dio. Similarly justifiable, but equally fictitious, are

---

[6] Sylla's soliloquy, which opens the play, may be taken as a dramatic representation
of one of Catiline's motives as given in *Bellum Catilinae* v.6; and the scene in Fulvia's
boudoir (all of Act II) is worked up from bare suggestions in *Bellum Catilinae* xxiii-
xxv. Sallust mentions the rumor of a blood-drinking episode (*ibid.*, xxii) but admits
that he has no proof that it ever took place.

Caesar's asides to Crassus during Cicero's first oration against Catiline (most of which Jonson uses)[7]; Caesar's interruption of Cicero to protest what he regards as the vilification of Catiline; and Caesar's greeting to Catiline as the latter makes his fateful entrance into the Senate. Yet these details, all from Act IV, make it impossible to view Caesar's proposal to the Senate in Act V—faithful as it is to Sallust's account—in the light that Sallust put upon it. Instead of being the wise counsel of a man conscious that great states should put aside petty vindictiveness and exercise clemency whenever possible, it has now become the shrewd maneuver of a Machiavellian villain to protect the weapons in his private arsenal and keep them in readiness for another attempt to assassinate the body politic. The conspiracy, we see, is not really Catiline's after all, but Caesar's.

If we were judging Jonson's play as history, we should probably have to say that here he has gone a bit too far. It is true that his portrayal of Caesar as an ambitious, unscrupulous machinator was one that a generation nourished on several editions of North's translation of Plutarch might reasonably accept; yet it was not the only portrait of Caesar then current; nor is it one that historians unanimously incline toward today. Furthermore, even Plutarch had admitted that Caesar's complicity in this affair was only rumored, not proved (*Caesar,* vii); and of Caesar's speech in the Senate, he had said only that it was the action of a brilliant opportunist with political ambitions.[8] Indeed, from what Plutarch and the other anti-Caesareans have to say about Caesar's behavior during Catiline's conspiracy, one can conclude at most that at this point in his career he was still only potentially dangerous to the commonwealth. Jonson, of course, unequivocally represents him as a very real and present danger. This immediately calls to mind the primary criterion by which Jonson expected a tragedy to be judged, "truth of argument," and the fact that for him that criterion seems to have demanded primarily an argument which could be verified, or at least supported by the testimony of reliable witnesses.[9] In Jonson's defense, one can say that as a *dramatist*-historian he was almost bound to represent everything

[7] Jonson also makes considerable use of the 2nd, 3rd, and 4th Catilinarian orations, the *Pro Sulla,* the *Pro Murena,* and the *Pro Caelio.* His borrowings from Cicero, however, are designed mainly to give authority to Cicero's own speeches. For a convenient tabulation of these borrowings, see *Catiline,* ed. Lynn Harold Harris, Yale Studies in Eng., LIII (New Haven, 1916), p. xx.

[8] *Cato the Younger,* xxii. Plutarch makes it clear, however, that even here Caesar had his ultimate goal of absolute rule in mind. North translates the passage as follows: "Caesar being an excellent spoken man, and that rather desired to nourish than to quench any such stirrs or seditions in the Common-wealth, being fit for his purpose long determined of, made an Oration full of sweet pleasant words." *Lives of the Noble Grecians & Romans* (Cambridge, 1676), p. 644.

[9] See my "The Significance of Ben Jonson's First Requirement for Tragedy," *SP,* XLIX (1952), 195-213.

concretely, his own opinion as well as reported fact. Moreover, his opinion about Caesar's part in the conspiracy, concretely represented as it is, does not affect his representation of the main action, for which he has ample authority to back him up. There, even by our own standards, he shows a respect for the business of the historian that is matched by few of his contemporaries, historians as well as dramatists. In fact, it is difficult to see how a dramatist-historian in any age could have done much better. Where reliable sources all declare something to be true, Jonson reports it; where reliable sources disagree, he exercises the historian's prerogative to act as judge; where reliable sources are silent, he exercises the dramatist's prerogative to fill in the gaps as his own judgment and understanding of the facts seem to direct him. The resulting reconstruction of history is, to be sure, a distortion; but it is necessarily so—just as all reconstructions of the past, whether dramatic or nondramatic, are necessarily distortions, contrived compounds of fact, judgment, and imagination. Jonson's large "distortion"—that is, the main action of the play —has the advantage of being one that the average modern reader with a historical consciousness can accept.[10] His lesser distortion about Caesar's part in the conspiracy, a matter upon which no Roman historian would venture to commit himself with any finality, does not have that advantage. It comes as something of a shock and immediately (though, of course, vainly) begs proof. Defending Jonson again, one can say it probably came as a much milder shock to the Jacobeans, who were more accustomed to unflattering characterizations of Caesar than we are. Even Bacon, who has won the praise of modern historians for his scholarly study of Henry VII, was not averse to saying positively of Caesar that he "secretly favored the madnesses of Catiline and his conspirators." [11]

This does not mean that Jonson's expansion of the part of Caesar is without special significance for *Catiline*. On the contrary, it is of very great significance. What it does is to set Caesar and Catiline on the one hand against Cato and Cicero on the other, thus altering the balance of the original narrative and converting a relatively simple story of the discovery and suppression of one man's plot into a study of the complex

[10] He does not, *e.g.*, shuffle events, introduce patent anachronisms, or irresponsibly invent parts of the action to suit his purposes. In fact, Jonson's sequence of events does not differ materially from that in the account by M. Cary, *Cambridge Ancient History* (1932), IX, 491-504.

[11] *Imago Civilis Julii Caesaris*, in *The Works of Francis Bacon*, ed. James Spedding *et al.* (London, 1858-59), VI, 337. The tone of Bacon's portrait is aptly illustrated by the following selection (Spedding's trans., p. 342): "He sought reputation and fame not for themselves, but as instruments of power. By natural impulse therefore, not by any moral guiling, he aspired rather to possess it than to be thought worthy of it: a thing which gave him favor with the people, who had no dignity of their own; but with the nobles and great persons, who wished also to preserve their own dignity, procured him the reputation of covetousness and boldness. Wherein assuredly they were not far from the truth."

struggle between such forces as make for disintegration in a state and those forces which tend to preserve its integrity. The original narrative is still there, of course: Cicero still detects the villainy of Catiline and leads the way to his removal and destruction. But in the context that Jonson gives it, this action is roughly analogous to a sick man's detection and treatment of an annoying symptom while the fatal cancer eats patiently away at a vital organ. Cato, the representative of all those virtues which have made Rome rich and powerful, is the surgeon in the case. It is he who sees the truth writ large in Jonson's choruses, that "the excess is her disease," who descries the genuinely rebellious cell in the body politic and would cut it out before it is too late. But Cato, unfortunately, is a surgeon who receives more praise than attention from his patient, and his diagnosis goes unheeded. Thus the play ends, with Cato's warning lost, Caesar temporarily checked but still free to plan and act, and Cicero naïvely comforted at the destruction of Catiline.

At this point the critical reader, or spectator, may reasonably ask: But where is the tragedy in this curiously incomplete thing that Jonson has made out of Sallust's story? Who in it, for that matter, can be called a tragic hero? or who even a tragic villain? Caesar and Cato appear too little and too late to qualify. Cicero, though he enjoys after Act III the brightest light that Jonson chooses to throw, performs no action that we could call tragic; and Catiline after that act holds only the occasional focus of our attention. To answer such objections as these, we need to return to what I referred to in the beginning as the basic and distinctive fact about Jonson's tragedies, that they require a historical context. The reader cannot begin to understand either *Catiline* or *Sejanus* unless he is willing to bring a knowledge of history with him to the play and look before and after what he finds there. For *Catiline*, this means he must have, in addition to a familiarity with the story of Sallust, a private knowledge of at least Plutarch's treatment of Caesar, and preferably some knowledge of Suetonius' and Dio's as well; that is, he needs to have clearly in mind the character of Caesar as these three portray it and be prepared to see in Caesar, as Sallust does not, the primary threat to the Roman Republic.[12] For *Sejanus*, it means having in mind the first six

[12] Plutarch's recognition that Caesar was a threat to the commonwealth almost from the outset of his career is illustrated by the following observation near the beginning of his *Caesar* (trans. North, ed. cit., p. 592): ". . . he ever kept a good board, and fared well at his Table, and was very liberal besides: the which indeed did advance him forward, and brought him in estimation with the people. His enemies judging that this favour of the common people would soon quail, when he could no longer hold out that charge and expence, suffered him to run on, till by little and little he was grown to be of great strength and power. But in fine, when they had thus given him the bridle to grow to this greatness, and that they could not then pull him back, though indeed in sight it would turn to the destruction of the whole state and Commonwealth of ROME: too late they found, that there is not so little a beginning of any thing, but continuance of time will soon make it strong, when through contempt

books of Tacitus' *Annals* and, once more, corresponding portions from Dio. If the reader brings less than this to Jonson's tragedies, he risks his chances of understanding what they are about. Consider, for example, the significance of Jonson's introducing a full-blown Machiavellian Caesar in the midst of a play ostensibly based on Sallust. It is, to say the least, a rather striking departure from a well-established norm, and Jonson expects us to recognize it as such. Without a knowledge of Sallust, however, we miss the shock completely and fail to notice, as the play proceeds, that the author has not only levelled out whatever tragic potentialities his original narrative had within its own limits but has thrown open the shutters, as it were, to let that original action serve as an illuminating symbol for an action of much greater scope: the whole rise and fall of the Roman Republic. I do not propose to defend Jonson's use of such an allusive technique in a play intended for the public theater. He should have known better. Yet the fact remains that if we disappoint Jonson in his expectations, either through lack of learning or through failure to grasp what he is trying to do, we get from *Catiline* only the moderately interesting melodrama that so many have seen in it; the play remains essentially a conflict of personalities that is terminated abruptly with the death of one of the villains but is never really satisfactorily resolved.

Discussion of Jonson's Roman plays almost inevitably suggests a comparison with those of Shakespeare; yet the resemblances are for the most part superficial. We find a similar respect for order in both, a similar contempt for the fickle mob, and a similar belief in the workings of Providence. Both men, in short, were essentially aristocratic in temperament and essentially religious; but Shakespeare's monarchism and his belief in the divine right of kings set him apart from Jonson, whose inclination toward what might be called classical republicanism is discernible in both of his tragedies, but especially in *Catiline*. Shakespeare was more apt to emphasize rebellion and disorder as overt manifestations of man's innate proclivity to disobedience; Jonson, to emphasize them as symptoms of civil decay, which he interpreted as the result of man's unwillingness to live by reason and to assume responsibility. More significant in a discussion of Jonson's tragic fable, however, is the fact that his plots, in comparison with Shakespeare's, seem incomplete and incon-

there is no impediment to hinder the greatness." Dio's general opinion of Caesar follows the same line; of Caesar's unscrupulousness he writes: ". . . he showed himself perfectly ready to serve and flatter everybody, even ordinary persons, and shrank from no speech or action in order to get possession of the objects for which he strove."—*Roman History*, xxxvii.37, trans. Earnest Cary, Loeb Classical Library (1914), III, 159. Suetonius, of course, goes farther than either Plutarch or Dio toward establishing Caesar's complete lack of scruple, moral or otherwise; see especially *Divus Iulius*, lii, lxxvi. Harris (p. xix) has asserted that Suetonius was Jonson's principal source for the character of Caesar; but Jonson could have found all he needed for that in Plutarch.

156 *Joseph Allen Bryant, Jr.*

clusive. *Coriolanus* gives us a full study of the tragedy of Coriolanus;
Julius Caesar gives us such a study of Brutus; but neither Jonson's
Sejanus nor his *Catiline* gives us a well-rounded tragedy of any single
character. In this connection it is worth noting, I think, that one could
make a play remarkably like *Catiline* out of the first eight scenes of *Julius
Caesar*—that is, a play that would end with Brutus and Antony standing
together, still not declared enemies, at the scene of Caesar's murder.
Possibly Jonson had something like this in mind when he complained
that Shakespeare's version could have stood considerably more "blot-
ting." Perhaps he had in mind a play that would show Brutus, like
Cicero, taking desperate steps to rid the commonwealth of an obvious
danger and succeeding in his effort, all the while neglecting to appreciate
the far greater danger at his right hand. In any case, such a *Julius Caesar*
could show us next to nothing of Shakespeare's tragic hero: we should
not see the consequences of Brutus' blindness; we should not see his
fall. In fact, Brutus would never really command the focus of our attention. The figure in our eye would almost certainly be, as in *Catiline*, the
commonwealth itself—the commonwealth which lapsed so far into decay
that even its would-be saviors were necessarily afflicted to some extent
with the blindness of degeneracy. But, again, that figure would be in our
eye *only* if we were prepared to see it, prepared to bring to the play a
context that would both give meaning to and derive meaning from the
dramatized segment.

Shakespeare, of course, never wrote anything remotely like this. Even
in his plays dealing with English history, the focus of interest is always
on human personalities and human conflicts; and the state as a metaphysical entity, if it appears at all, appears only intermittently, as the
ground for action and not as a leading participant in the action. For
example, no one on seeing *Richard II* would doubt for a moment that
what happens there is symptomatic of conditions in that "sea-walled
garden" of which both Gaunt and the unhappy Gardener speak. One
can, if one wishes, read the play as a political sermon, or rather as an
exemplum for one. Yet for all that, *Richard II* remains a self-contained
play about Richard and Bolingbroke; it requires no sequel and very little
commentary to make it intelligible. When Shakespeare came to write
tragedy, he continued to make his work intelligible in terms of the represented action alone. All his tragedies deal with historical subjects, but
history does not contribute very much to our understanding of them; nor
do they, in turn, contribute very much to our understanding of the
historical events with which they deal. They provoke commentary, to be
sure, but they require no context; for the commonwealth in Shakespearean tragedy is indifferently Rome, England, or Denmark. What
holds our attention is always the complete representation of a single
action of a single tragic protagonist—a Hamlet, a Lear, a Macbeth, or
a Coriolanus—and as such Shakespearean tragedy is self-sufficient.

To appreciate Jonsonian tragedy, on the other hand, we have to begin by recognizing the fact that the representation of the Roman scene in it is as accurate as contemporary historical scholarship could provide. We have to be keenly aware that here no seventeenth century clock could possibly strike the hour and no English watch walk the streets at night. The scene we see is literally Rome, and the event portrayed is one that actually took place there at a definite point in time. In short, it is important to recognize that Jonson's Roman plays superimpose their claim to tragic stature upon a solid initial appeal to history; and, whatever else they may be, they fall within the limits of a definition of the history play that is strict enough to exclude everything that Shakespeare ever wrote. For Shakespeare, history was only a means to an end, a source of material from which he could fashion a fable to reveal something of that true substance which is only faintly and imperfectly reflected in mundane affairs. For Jonson, history was an end in itself; it was man's best source of truth outside the realm of supernatural revelation. In fact, Jonson's attitude toward history does not differ materially from that held by many of his Puritan foes, who placed secular history next to sacred as a guide to the ways of Providence. Had they been dramatists, they, too, would probably have declared it the dramatist's function first of all to respect the facts transmitted to him and to reveal his chosen segment of history accurately, both in outline and in detail.

Fidelity to history, however, does not alone make a tragedy; and Jonson's Roman plays, if they are to be called tragedies, must justify their title by some other means. They do that, I think, by virtue of the context to which the plays, as history, implicitly allude. As we have already seen, Jonson's practice in both *Catiline* and *Sejanus* indicates that he recognized a second function for the dramatist-historian: if it was his function to cast his light upon the segment of history, it was also his function to reveal with the penumbra of that light the broad movement, the larger action, from which the chosen segment should draw its full significance. And in both of Jonson's Roman plays that larger action turns out to be a tragic action, with the state itself taking the role of tragic protagonist. Jonson, of course, was not the first to see that states as well as men may grow prideful in the prosperity that humility, work, and simple virtues bring them to; nor was he the first to see that civil pride is a state of blindness and goes before a fall; but it may be said, I believe, that he was the first to make drama serve as a medium for presenting the tragedy of a whole state; such a tragedy, certainly, could not be presented entire within the limits of a five-act play without sacrificing the concreteness and particularity that are the essence of the dramatic. Jonson's method was to select for representation recognizable segments of tragic patterns that he found in the verified history of the Roman commonwealth. What he gives us in *Sejanus,* as I have shown elsewhere,[13]

---

[13] "The Nature of the Conflict in Jonson's *Sejanus*," *Vanderbilt Studies in the Humanities,* I (1951), 197-219.

is a representation of that part of the pattern of civil tragedy in which the virtuous element of the commonwealth, in this case the remnant of all that is essentially Rome, has been reduced to inactivity and near impotence as a consequence of its own complacence and blindness.[14] The activity in the play is largely confined to that of the evil forces which Rome has blindly let grow until they have all but destroyed her. Yet this spectacle, sorry as it is, is not altogether depressing; for we see by it that evil, freed of restraint, becomes in time its own punisher and destroyer; and we also see, in the last scene, that something of the Old Rome still remains, that she has at last learned humility and patience, and that she may contemplate at least the distant future with some hope. The activity of Jonson's *Catiline* presents a different, yet equally recognizable, selection from the pattern of tragedy. Here we have the picture of a state at the peak of its prosperity and power and pride, capable of detecting a symptom but incapable of interpreting the significance of that symptom, confidently and blindly taking the first step toward disaster. One might almost say it is a detailed picture of the climax of the tragic pattern. Jonson has achieved this picture—and, one should add, achieved it without sacrificing verisimilitude—partly by striking a balance among those characters with tragic possibilities in order to let the figure of *res publica* stand clear as a protagonist in its own right, and partly (though less importantly) by underscoring that figure as tragic protagonist in his choruses. Catiline the symptom, Caesar the disease, Cicero the will of the state, Cato its all but submerged conscience—all these are elements in a body politic that is outwardly flourishing but spiritually doomed. In Jonson's image of that body politic we see at once the source of its greatness and the disintegration that lies ahead, both amply confirmed by the verifiable context to which the play implicitly alludes. In no other play, not even in *Sejanus,* is the tragedy of a whole state indicated so movingly, so subtly, and yet with such terrifying clarity. In short, *Catiline His Conspiracy* is a remarkable dramatic accomplishment, one effected with amazing economy and with no violence to fact save the anachronistic representation of Caesar's character. And even in this Jonson has done nothing more reprehensible than to sketch in qualities which most seventeenth century readers would have been willing to admit Caesar possessed, at least *in potentia,* at the time of the Catilinarian conspiracy.

I have already suggested that Jonson was at fault for writing plays that ask too much of his audience. Some may argue, too, that his understanding of tragedy was at fault: that in pushing back the limits of tragedy he wrote plays which were really the measure of his limitations. Yet it is futile, I think, to argue about what Jonson might have done; and, in any case, that is beside the point. Most people would agree that

---

[14] Cf. Shakespeare's representation of this point of low ebb among the forces for good in *King Lear,* IV.

Shakespearean tragedy is infinitely preferable to the Jonsonian variety. The point is that Jonson did not try to write Shakespearean tragedy. What he did try to write, whether he should have tried to write it or not, represents an extension rather than a restriction of the scope of tragedy. We have, as a result, two early examples of that extension which, in the dramas and novels of the twentieth century, was later to become commonplace. Within this broader field, of his own choosing and partly of his own creation, Jonson's achievement bears comparison with that of any other artist, early or late. This much, at any rate, cannot safely be disputed.

The Jonsonian Masque
as a Literary Form

by Dolora Cunningham

Jonson's masques have generally been considered as fanciful mixtures of spectacular and dramatic elements, characterized by a heavy display of learning and, for modern democratic taste, a troublesome flattery of the king. They have seldom been accorded the dignity of serious literary efforts; and yet if one looks twice at the author's own comments upon his work, one is struck by the unusually wide discrepancy between what Jonson thought he was doing and what critics have told us he was doing.[1]

A masque, as Jonson himself conceived it, is a form of dramatic entertainment in which the logical working out of a central idea or device provides the action. The particular kind of action proper to the form resides in the symbolic representation of contrasted conditions, usually of order or virtue as opposed to disorder or depravity. It consists of "one entire body or figure," as Jonson puts it, comprising distinct members, each expressed for itself, yet harmonized by the device so that the whole is complete in itself. The nature of the device is explained by language at times dramatic and at times narrative, and the whole is further illustrated by music, spectacle, and symbolic characters in a sequence of dances. Each member is brought in separately, for its own sake, in the parts of the work, but each contributes to the illustration of the whole. Each has meaning in terms of the device, which turns on a sudden change —involving discovery of the masquers, transformation of the entire scene, and recognition of the virtues embodied in the king—and arouses wonder and respect in the spectators. By these means, a masque accomplishes its purpose of honoring magnificence, in the ethical sense, and of inciting in the beholders a conscious moral imitation of the virtues embodied in kingship.

"The Jonsonian Masque as a Literary Form." From *ELH, A Journal of English Literary History,* XXII (1955), 108-124. Reprinted by permission of the Johns Hopkins Press.

[1] For a summary of the criticism, see *Ben Jonson,* ed. C. H. Herford, Percy Simpson, and Evelyn M. Simpson (Oxford: The Clarendon Press, 1925), Vol. II, pp. 249ff. The two basic books on the English masque are Rudolf Brotanek, *Die Englischchen Maskenspiele* (Leipzig, 1902) and Paul Reyher, *Les Masques anglais* (Paris, 1909).

This definition has been derived from Jonson's remarks about his aims and methods in writing masques and, of course, is modeled on Aristotle's famous definition of tragedy. The relevance of the formal definition to Jonson's masques can, perhaps, be clarified by calling to mind the three broad principles on which he based his whole theory and practice of the masque: the principle of decorum, the principle of hierarchical unity, and the principle of profit conjoined with pleasure—all familiar in various ways to students of Renaissance literature.

Although the notion of decorum is variously complicated, there are certain obvious applications which bear directly upon a proper understanding of Jonson's intentions. Most important of these, perhaps, is the stern precept that the device, the central idea of the masque, must express what is proper to the occasion:

> The nature and propertie of these Devices being, to present alwaies some one entire bodie, or figure, . . . where also is to be noted, that the *Symboles* used, are not, neither ought to be, simply *Hieroglyphickes, Emblemes,* or *Impreses,* but a mixed character, partaking somewhat of all, and peculiarly apted to these more magnificent Inventions: wherein, the garments and ensignes deliver the nature of the person, and the word the present office. Neither was it becomming, or could it stand with the dignitie of these shewes (. . .) to require a Truch-man, . . . but so to be presented, as upon the view, they might, without cloud, or obscuritie, declare themselves to the sharpe and learned,[2]

Again in his notes to *The Masque of Queens,* Jonson explains:

> To whome they all did reverence, and she spake, uttring, by way of question, the end wherefore they came: which, if it had bene done eyther before, or other-wise, it had not bene so naturall. For, to have made themselves their owne decipherers, and each one to have told, upon their entrance, *what they were, and whether they would,* had bene a most piteous hearing, and utterly unworthy any quality of a *Poeme* [ll. 98ff].

Decorum, then, motivates both the selection of the central idea and the manner of working it out, determining also the kind of dialogue and action and the type of decoration to be used. The device together with its illustrative parts must be appropriate to the dignity of poetry in itself and to the dignity of the royal audience whose honor is the primary concern of every court masque.

Since the masque, as Jonson practiced it, is a form having its own purposes and conventions, to impose the techniques of the regular drama would be improper. It is true, however, that Jonson introduced the

---

[2] *The Entertainment at Fenchurch,* ll. 247ff. In all references to Jonson's masques, including his prefaces and commentaries, I shall refer to lines only; all of the references are to Volume VII of the Herford and Simpson *Ben Jonson* (Oxford, 1941).

materials of comedy into several anti-masques and that the established order of progression in his masques is from disorder to order as in comedy. But he did not confuse the two forms. We know from his prefaces and commentaries and from the masques themselves that he kept certain distinctions clearly in mind. He used comic materials and characters in the anti-masque, for example, to give variety and to act as foils to the noble persons who performed the main masque. In *Oberon, The Faery Prince,* where the Satyrs of the anti-masque are opposed to the Fairies of the main masque, the connection lies in their being opposites, as in the *Masque of Queens* Ignorance is the opposite of Fame. In *Oberon,* Silenus strengthens the connection by intervening in both anti-masque and masque: as "prefect" of the Satyrs, he rebukes their goings-on, and after they have been silenced, he speaks the praise to the state which marks the beginning of the solemn main masque (ll. 335-57).

Love Restored is the first of Jonson's masques where the comic actions and dialogue, which originally introduced the grotesque dance, have taken over entirely; it is also the first in which the characters of the anti-masque speak in prose, as though Jonson would emphasize the contrast between what is proper to these undignified personages and what is proper to the persons of high estate who perform the main masque and speak in verse. Although the grotesque dance was not to be entirely excluded from future anti-masques, in other respects the anti-masque did become much like a scene of prose comedy.

In *Mercury Vindicated from the Alchemists at Court,* Jonson adapts to the masque material he had already used in comedy. In *The Alchemist,* he had satirized the alchemists' pretensions to make gold and had mocked the illusions of their dupes; here he satirizes, primarily, the imperfect, mutilated creatures of the alchemists' laboratories, who are contrasted with the excellences of nature. To handle this varied material, which paralleled the various types of extravagant people often found in his comedies, the formal device of the double anti-masque dance was at hand. This made it possible for Jonson to present separate grotesque dances, first, the "troupe of threadbare Alchymists" and, then, their "imperfect creatures, with helmes of lymbecks on their heads." His contempt for the two is conceived and presented within the convention of the masque, and what in *The Alchemist* was material for comedy is here found to be as aptly material for a masque.

Jonson's originality in developing the anti-masque is, nevertheless, guided by the three principles which he explained in the preface to *The Masque of Queens*: contrast, continuity, and variety. The anti-masque is not a masque but a spectacle of strangeness; it is not magnificent, where the main masque is by definition magnificent, but it is strictly accordant with the device of the main masque. Its main function is to provide a purposeful variety within a given masque and the variety of novelty with respect to past entertainments:

I was carefull to decline not only from others, but mine owne stepps in that kind, since the last yeare I had an *Anti-Masque* of Boyes: and therefore, now, devis'd that twelve Women, in the habite of Haggs, or Witches . . . , should fill that part (ll. 14-19).

In *Oberon* he will have Satyrs; in *Love Freed,* a brood of Follies; in *Mercury Vindicated,* alchemists and their creatures. By adapting the comic induction to the purpose of anti-masque, he avails himself of new materials to support the demand for variety.

If we think, as many of us apparently do, that the comic induction endangered the masque and that by comparison the main masque is a colorless rudiment,[3] it is because we cannot see the latter. Literature bulks larger in the first part, and we have thereby a clearer picture of the induction, whether comical or otherwise, than we have of the ceremonious main masque. We must reconstruct its movements from Jonson's descriptions, which were written for precisely this purpose. But such necessity does not justify our taking a part for the whole in order to condemn the author for writing comedy instead of masque or masque instead of comedy. Where in a comedy can we find the equivalent of the main masque, which concludes with the unique dance participated in by the audience? The simple fact that the induction is more vivid to us does not prove that it was so to Jonson's audience, and, indeed, most of the contemporary references are largely devoted to the dancing and beauty of the main masque.[4] It does, however, seem to support Jonson's point that literature is the formative principle and soul of masque and alone can give it life.

In a comedy, moreover, there is not necessarily a pattern whereby one set of characters representing the violation of accepted standards is followed by another set representing their observance. In a masque it is not enough that fools and monsters be vanquished or held up to scorn; they must be both vanquished and supplanted by the representatives of virtue and order.

For the characters in Jonson's masques are symbolic rather than dramatic. They are means of illustrating the general device, so that any change in character is dependent upon transformation, as, for example, in *Lethe,* where the lovers only think they have died for love when they have simply lost their wits. The Fates insist that they are not dead, that Love, though he often subdues other states, cannot subdue the Fates. Mercury bids the lovers to drink of Lethe's stream that they may forget Love's name, and then to rise up and shake off the shadows which made them mistake themselves for dead (ll. 118-21). Or, a change of character might depend upon a complete change of setting and persons, as in

[3] Herford and Simpson, Vol. II, p. 297.
[4] See, for example, Bacon's remarks on "Masques and Triumphs" in *A Harmony of Lord Bacon's Essays,* ed. Edward Arber (London, 1871).

Pleasure Reconciled to Virtue, where legitimate Pleasure must banish Comus before it can be reconciled with Virtue; and in the second anti-masque Virtue must defeat the degenerate Pigmies before the princes can profit from the reconciliation. In other words, the forces of chaos must be defeated before the representatives of order can be displayed to complete the contrast. The lesson seems to be that before we can have a sane and ordered society, we must get rid of the enemies of reason and virtue. Although such an undertaking necessarily implies conflict, it is here different from ordinary dramatic conflict.

The hierarchical structure which Jonson sought in the masque is concisely defined in his notes to the *Entertainment at Fenchurch*:

> The nature and propertie of these Devices being, to present alwaies some one entire bodie, or figure, consisting of distinct members, and each of these expressing it selfe, in the owne active spheare, yet all, with that generall harmonie so connexed, and disposed, as no one little part can be missing to the illustration of the whole (ll. 247ff.).

The various formal elements should be carefully arranged around the central device, for the whole must have the unity of a work of art and uphold in all its various parts the current and fall of a single device. The function of spectacle, for example, is to make known whom a person represents and the function of speech to explain his place in the whole scheme. The parts do not blend into each other to form an organic unity; each part exists rather for its own value and expresses itself in its own sphere but is so disposed and connected as to make a clearly defined contribution to the illustration of the whole.

Although carefully distinguished from the main masque, the anti-masque is always in accordance with the idea which controls both. Jonson makes sure of the anti-masque in *Lethe,* for example, by having the same persons assume the roles of frantic lovers and intelligent lovers. This identity of persons quite naturally makes for continuity between the two main parts, but more than this, it involves progression of character, which is something quite different from modern notions of character development. Mercury and the Fates discover, through dialogue, the condition of the lovers and are responsible for their transformation. The conflict between Mercury and Cupid and their reconciliation are responsible for the final restoration of the lovers to a condition of balanced humanity, and this change in condition is motivated by definable external causes. In the process of restoration, all of the diverse arts are used, each of them contributing something to the ultimate end. The anti-masque dance expresses the way the lovers had lived in love and is, as Mercury states, the means of shaking off the shadows they had moved in before drinking from Lethe's stream. Their transformation is brought about through the joint efforts of poetry and dancing and not by a sudden change of costume or scene. Their return to an harmonious exercise of their human faculties is encouraged by the Chorus, so that the music expresses their conversion from disorder to harmony as it introduces the ordered dances of the main masque. When Cupid appears to praise the refined motions of the first dance, his speech is expressive of the dance, which in turn is expressive of the lovers' changed condition and therefore of the idea on which the entire invention turns.[5]

A corollary of hierarchical unity is Jonson's law that no one element is to infringe on the duties proper to another. This corollary is derived by the principle of decorum, and maintains that spectacle should not try to do the work of poetry, or poetry of spectacle, for this is to violate order and destroy the unity of the masque. In the preface to the *Masque of Blackness,* Jonson explains:

> The honor, and splendor of these *spectacles* was such in the performance, as could those houres have lasted, this of mine, now, had been a most unprofitable worke. But (when it is the fate, even of the greatest, and most absolute births, to need, and borrow a life of posteritie) little had beene done to the studie of *magnificence* in these, if presently with the rage of the people, who (as a part of greatnesse) are priviledged by custome, to deface their *carkasses,* the *spirits* had also perished (ll. 1-10).

The dignity of poetry must be given due recognition; the literary part must not be forced to yield place to other elements, particularly the spectacle of Inigo Jones; the poet must not be the mere servant of the carpenter and scene-painter. For these things are mortal and fade away, and literature alone can keep the masque alive. The description of the spectacle and the explanation of the various devices are important, also, because they make it possible for posterity to reconstruct the actual performance, to reproduce those elements of scenery, dance, and music which make a direct appeal to the senses and are in large measure responsible for the desired effect of magnificence.

But Jonson was very jealous of the dignity of poetry and, if it were to have anything to do with the masque, it must have a higher role than that of mere reporting. Conversely, the masque form, to be worthy of poetry, must be stabilized and improved. This improvement, Jonson firmly believed, could be realized only through the contribution of the poet, who would furnish the soul of the form:

> It is a noble and just advantage, that the things subjected to *understanding* have of those which are objected to *sense,* that the one sort are but

[5] Jonson's comment on the dance in *Hymenaei* (ll. 310-15) supports the interpretation: *"Here, they daunced forth a moste neate and curious measure, full of* Subtilty *and* Device; *which was so excellently performed, as it seemed to take away that* Spirit *from the* Invention, *which the* Invention *gave to it: and left it doubtfull, whether the* Formes *flow'd more perfectly from the* Authors *braine, or their feete."*

momentarie, and meerely taking; the other impressing, and lasting: Else
the glorie of all these *solemnities* had perish'd like a blaze, and gone out, in
the *beholders* eyes. So short-liv'd are the *bodies* of all things, in comparison
of their *soules* . . . This it is hath made the most royall *Princes,* and
greatest *persons* (who are commonly the *personaters* of these *actions*) not
onely studious of riches, and magnificence in the outward celebration, or
shew; (which rightly becomes them) but curious after the most high, and
heartie *inventions,* to furnish the inward parts: (and those grounded upon
antiquitie, and solide *learnings*) which, though their *voyce* be taught to
sound to present occasions, their *sense,* or doth, or should always lay hold
on more remov'd *mysteries.*[6]

The theory of literature set forth here rests upon the familiar Christian
dualism—of physical and spiritual, transitory and eternal—which is
reflected in the two levels of literal and symbolical meaning which should
be present in a masque. For Jonson clearly regarded the masque as a
literary form in much the same way as he regarded tragedy as a literary
form. He carefully distinguished the various elements and specific purposes of the traditional masque and attempted to make each of these
cooperate in a final unified structure, the central hinge of which is the
idea having its basis in a philosophical-ethical concept. Consequently,
the particular nature of the device must be such that the shift of scene
in the spectacle would have meaning in terms of the device and that it
would be capable of being illustrated by a sufficient number of symbolic
figures who could reasonably be supposed to enter into a sequence of
dances. All of this is to contribute to a certain definable effect: respect
for magnificence, which is the ethical virtue especially appropriate to
royalty.

It was by way of magnificence that Jonson's masques achieved the
traditional goal of profit conjoined with pleasure. In his preface to the
Masque of Queens, Jonson explains:

For which reason, I chose the Argument, . . . : observing that rule of the
best *Artist,* to suffer no object of delight to passe without his mixture of
profit, and example (ll. 5-9).

And again in the preface to *Love's Triumph*:

Whereas all Repraesentations especially those of this nature in court,
publique Spectacles, eyther have bene, or ought to be the mirrors of mans
life, whose ends, for the excellence of their exhibiters . . . ought alwayes
to carry a mixture of profit, with them, no lesse then delight; Wee, . . .
resolved on this following argument (ll. 1-15).

[6] *Hymenaei,* ll. 1-20.

The invention should exhibit moral truth and be grounded solidly on learning, by which Jonson meant largely, though not wholly, the learning of antiquity. It is fairly obvious, for example, that his conception of magnificence owed a good deal to Aristotle's definition of the virtue:

> The magnificent man is like an artist; for he can see what is fitting and spend large sums tastefully. For . . . a state of character is determined by its activities and its objects. Now the expenses of the magnificent man are large and fitting. Such, therefore, are also his results; for thus there will be a great expenditure and one that is fitting to its result. . . . And the magnificent man will spend such sums for honor's sake; for this is common to the virtues . . . . And he will consider how the result can be made most beautiful and most becoming rather than for how much it can be produced and how it can be produced most cheaply. It is necessary, then, that the magnificent man be also liberal. . . . The most valuable possession is that which is worth most, . . . but the most valuable work of art is that which is great and beautiful (for the contemplation of such a work inspires admiration, and so does magnificence); and a work has an excellence—vis. magnificence—which involves magnitude. Magnificence is an attribute of expenditures of the kind which we call honourable, *e.g.*, those connected with the gods . . . and all those that are proper objects of public-spirited ambition (*Ethics.* 1122a19-1122a20).

The effect of contemplating magnificence is admiration, which in turn, according to Jonson's directives, should give rise to such activities as understanding, respect, and moral imitation. The masque is intended to arouse in the spectators respect for the king and the traditional virtues of kingship, respect for and faith in the established social order. Since the aspect of kingship most often honored is magnificence, the means of honoring royalty must, according to the principle of decorum, be magnificent; they must be proper to their end. The masque, in order to praise this virtue adequately and gain the desired end, must be magnificent in all its parts. Jonson tells us explicitly, in his preface to the *Masque of Blackness,* that the end proposed for the whole is magnificence:

> But (when it is the fate, even of the greatest, and most absolute births, to need, and borrow a life of posterite) little had bene done to the studie of *magnificence* in these, if presently . . . the *spirits* had also perished (ll. 3-9).

And in *Love Restored* the contrast on which the device turns is actually between niggardliness and magnificence, between the meanness of mind represented by Plutus and the largeness of mind symbolized by Love and his followers. But all of the various mean characters in Jonson's anti-masques are made to contribute, by contrast with the nobles of the main masque, to the magnificent purpose of the whole.

Since James I was pre-eminently the man of high birth, great expenditure on public occasions was becoming to him.[7] To spend lavishly for the production of a masque was virtuous in these circumstances, and such expenditure, both in its activities and its objects, met all of Aristotle's requirements for magnificence. By definition an attribute of royalty, magnificence is expressed and honored in the Jonsonian masque so as to achieve the specific effects of admiration and respect, which, though clearly related, are nevertheless distinct.

Admiration is, of course, a technical term in Renaissance ethics and literary criticism. The complex history of the term with special reference to tragedy has been traced by Professor J. V. Cunningham, who summarizes the traditional notion of wonder as an end of poetry:

> Wonder in Shakespeare is the effect of tragic incident and tragic style, as well as of the marvellous turn in events. But this does not exhaust the complexity of the notion of wonder; one more strand at least remains to be unravelled. For the notion derives not only from the tradition of literary criticism, as the proper effect of marvellous events, and the tradition of rhetoric, as the proper effect of marvellous eloquence, but it derives also from the tradition of philosophy, in which wonder is the primary cause of learning.[8]

Speaking in the role of spectator, Jonson describes the effect of *Hymenaei*:

> Such was the exquisit performance, as (beside the *pompe, splendor,* or what we may call *apparelling* of such *Presentments*) that alone (had all else beene absent) was of power to surprize with delight, and steale away the *spectators* from themselves. Nor was there wanting whatsoever might give to the *furniture,* or *complement;* eyther in *riches,* or strangenesse of the *habites,* delicacie of *daunces,* magnificence of the *scene,* or divine rapture of *musique* (ll. 568-76).

Surprise, delight, and self-forgetfulness are all effects proper to wonder, which, Jonson characteristically emphasizes, depends not so much upon splendor in "the apparelling" as upon grace in the execution, effective speech, and harmony of all the parts.

Although Jonson was not the only writer of masques who aimed at wonder, his means of securing it helps us to distinguish the Jonsonian masque from the work of others who, in general, depended largely upon spectacle. Campion, for example, relied upon fantastic transformations and music, and in his *Lords Maske,* Prometheus, the patron of mankind, is asked to

---

[7] *The Masque of Queens,* according to E. K. Chambers' account, cost the Exchequer three thousand pounds: *The Elizabethan Stage* (Oxford, 1923), Vol. I, p. 384.

[8] *Woe or Wonder: The Emotional Effect of Shakespearean Tragedy* (University of Denver Press, 1951), p. 96.

> . . . fill the lookers eyes
> With admiration of thy fire and light,
> And from thy hand let wonders fly tonight.[9]

Prometheus promises that the stars, which he has stolen from heaven to contribute to "this night's honor," will be transformed into human figures—that is, he will "let wonders fly"—and that he will have Orpheus apply his music, "for it well helps to induce a Courtly miracle." Where Campion used music to achieve these spectacular miracles, Jonson, although placing considerable faith in the unifying force of a central device, insisted that each element must contribute to the over-all effect.

Directives to the spectators, as in Elizabethan drama generally, are to be found throughout Jonson's masques. In the *Masque of Blackness*, Oceanus' amazement at the appearance of the Ethiopian river is the cue to the audience:

> My ceaseless current, now, amazed stands!
> To see thy labour, through so many lands (ll. 115-16).

They are to be amazed at Niger's presence and their amazement is to be an incitement to knowledge; as they wonder at the sight and how it came about, so Jonson fulfills his general purpose of letting no object of delight pass without its due mixture of profit.

Hymen's first speech in *Hymenaei* is preceded by "some signs of admiration" which lead him to question the cause of "the more than usuall light" inspiring his admiration. After Reason has banished "The foure untemp'red Humors," they retire "amazed" while Hymen orders the ceremonies of the main masque. Toward the end, as the champions of Truth and Opinion prepare for battle, "a striking light seem'd to fill all the hall," and an angel appears to exhort the hearers:

> Princes, attend a tale of height, and wonder.
> TRUTH is descended in a second thunder (ll. 880-81).

In *Oberon* the dance of the lesser Fairies is preceded by a Song which embodies an explicit list of wonder's causes and effects:

> Seeke you majestie, to strike?
> Bid the world produce his [James'] like.
> Seeke you glorie, to amaze?
>   Here, let all eyes stand at gaze.
> Seeke you wisedome, to inspire?
>   Touch, then, at no others fire.

[9] *Campion's Works*, ed. P. Vivian (Oxford, 1909), ll. 30-32.

> Seeke you knowledge, to direct?
>   Trust to his, without suspect.
> Seeke you pietie, to lead?
>   In his foot-steps, only, tread.
> Every virtue of a king,
> And of all, in him, we sing.   (ll. 370-81)

The magnificence of King James strikes and amazes all eyes, and this wonder, in turn, incites the spectators to contemplate the other kingly virtues of wisdom, knowledge, and piety, by which they are to be inspired, directed, and led.

This relationship between wonder and its virtues is further clarified in *The Vision of Delight*, where Wonder speaks to describe the beauties of the main masque and Phant'sie's reply proposes pleasure and knowledge as the two effects proper to wonder:

> How better then they are, are all things made
> By Wonder! But a while refresh thine eye,
> Ile put thee to thy oftner, what, and why?   (ll. 167-69)

After the masquers are discovered as the glories of the spring, Wonder again inquires into the causes of so much glory: "Whose power is this? What God?" And Phant'sie gives the promised explanation:

> Behold a King
> Whose presence maketh this perpetuall *Spring*,
> The glories of which Spring grow in that Bower,
> And are the marks and beauties of his power   (ll. 200-04)

In this recognition scene, the masquers are directed by the Choir to express their homage in a dance; their knowledge of the source of wonder, that is, leads to an expression of respect. Nothing could be more explicit than this personification of the effect which Jonson sought for the masque.

The proper response of the audience is, moreover, governed by the all-pervasive principle of decorum. In *Oberon*, after a song in which James is called "the wonder . . . of tongues, of eares, of eyes," the Sylvane rebukes the Satyres of the anti-masque (ll. 310-22); although their antics have been delightful, they are not properly respectful and must give way, because they are incapable of experiencing the respect which the main masque should arouse in them. The Sylvane goes on to say that Oberon with his knights have come to "give the honor of their being" to the king, and Silenus, the moderator of the Satyres, replies:

And may they well. For this indeed is hee,
My boyes, whom you must quake at, when you see . . . .
He is the matter of vertue, and plac'd high.
His meditations, to his height, are even.   (ll. 336-42)

Jonson obviously took great care to remind his audience that the wonderful was to lead them not merely to a fatuous delight but to knowledge and respect. In the closing songs of *News from the New World,* he speaks complimentarily but precisely:

How ere the brightnesse may amaze,
    Move you, and stand not still at gaze,
        As dazeled with the light;
But with your motions fill the place,
And let their fulnesse win you[r] Grace,
        Till you collect your sight.
So while the warmth you doe confesse,
And temper of these Raies, no lesse
        To quicken then refine:
You may by knowledge grow more bold.
And so more able to behold
        The bodie whence they shine.
[The first Dance followes.]
Now looke and see in yonder throne,
    How all those beames are cast from one.
        This is that Orbe so bright,
Has kept your wonder so awake;
Whence you as from a mirrour take
        The Suns reflected light.
Read him as you would doe the booke
Of all perfection, and but looke
        What his proportions be;
No measure that is thence contriv'd,
Or any motion thence deriv'd,
        But is pure harmonie.   (ll. 320-45)

The dancers are not to be stupefied at the vision of majesty: even though temporarily blinded by the light, as Dante in Paradise, they are not to neglect those acts of respect which will win them grace. By the perfection of their motions, they confess the power of this grace in them, which is also the means by which they may achieve knowledge of its source and the strength to emulate the perfection embodied there.

Admiration, or wonder, as an effect of a Jonsonian masque has, then, four aspects: it gives pleasure; it is a motive to knowledge; it is an incitement to respect; it is a basis of moral imitation. As spectators we admire and so understand; we respect and so imitate the king as the model of perfection. Wonder and respect, as specific effects, are to masque as pity and fear are to tragedy.

When I accord the praise of royalty this central position in the masque, I realize that I am asking for disagreement; for most critics seem certain either that we must look upon the complimentary element as inexcusable flattery or that we must patronize Jonson for it by citing historical circumstances to excuse his bad taste. Among the commentators, Professor D. J. Gordon is to my knowledge practically alone in taking seriously these characteristic passages. Writing of *The Masque of Blackness* and *The Masque of Beauty*, he very rightly concludes that there is profound substance within the convention of praising royalty:

> The central idea of these two masques is clear and simple: The King's presence turns Blackness into Beauty. . . . Compliments in this vein were, of course, quite in order. . . . But more is involved here than the formal, stereotyped gesture of the panegyrist; we are dealing here with notions more "remov'd" than the everyday apotheosis of the Crown. A grander apotheosis is adumbrated, in which James is given the position and function assigned to the Sun in the theory of Beauty held by the Florentine Platonists.[10]

Since I am chiefly concerned here with the fact that Jonson defined and practiced the masque as a literary form, I am not able to undertake a detailed analysis of recurrent imagery. Certainly the concept of kingship is frequently worked out in terms of the Sun-light symbolism, and Professor Gordon is altogether correct in recognizing its importance. For the present, however, I should simply question the wisdom of interpreting this symbolism solely in terms of neo-Platonic doctrines. Is it necessary to posit a strict parallelism with the Platonic commentaries of Pico della Mirandola and Ficino? Such terminology as "most formall cause of all dames beauties," for example, is not exclusively Platonic; and even if it were, was Jonson altogether dependent upon the compilations of Pico or Ficino for such knowledge? My brief analysis of the compliment to the king in *News from the New World* indicates what seems to me a more historically sound approach to the interpretation of the Sun-light imagery. With respect to the masques of *Blackness* and *Beauty*, it can, I think, be profitably argued that the transformation process is analogous to that Christian transformation of fallen human nature which was traditionally accomplished by the grace of God, whose special agent the

[10] "The Imagery of Ben Jonson's *The Masque of Blacknesse* and *The Masque of Beautie*," *Journal of the Warburg and Courtauld Institutes*, VI (1943), 129. See also his article, "*Hymenaei*: Ben Jonson's Masque of Union," *Ibid.*, VIII (1945), 107-45.

ruling monarch was generally acknowledged to be in Medieval-Renaissance political theory.[11]

But whether or not one agrees with Professor Gordon's interpretation of particular passages, one must applaud his service to Jonson criticism in undermining the unhistorical and altogether unsupportable prejudice against those praises of kingship which provide the ethical substance of the masque. For it may be said that the virtue of princes is to masque as the fall of princes is to tragedy.

To emphasize another very likely point of disapproval: I have argued that Jonson's use of comic materials was carefully regulated by the specific conditions of masque and was governed by clearly defined formal principles. I know it has been fashionable to see only another expression of Jonson's arrogance in his spirited defense of poetry against the demands of Inigo Jones's scenery and, consequently, to blame Jonson for the decay of the masque.[12] But I believe such an approach to be only another attack of critical arrogance upon Jonson's character. His prefaces and descriptions prove that he was fully alive to the respective beauties of spectacle, dance, and music; and his insistence upon the supremacy of poetry in the hierarchical arrangement of the several elements, far from breaking down form, was literally the only means of controlling the various materials and of shaping them into a meaningful and coherent whole. Jonson's preference for poetry is quite simply the logical outcome of what the masque is, for the appropriate effects of wonder and respect obviously cannot be achieved by spectacular stage sets. And, of course, Jonson thought highly of poetry in itself, though his critics often have not.

It is impossible for me to do battle here against the post-Romantic conviction that the truly poetical can have nothing to do with mere learning or with morality. Certainly neither Jonson nor his contemporaries shared this irrational view of poetry or this contempt for learning. And, in common with most of his old-fashioned compatriots, Jonson took for granted the ultimately moral purpose of all literature. To accuse him of pursuing the moral at the expense of the literary is only to reveal one's own confusion of ethical substance with overt didacticism and one's own failure to perceive that Jonson remained true to his form through symbolic development of a central theme.

It is certainly in order to urge that many currently held notions of the masque be subjected to careful study and revision in the light of what Jonson himself had to say. If we are to have a body of Jonson criticism worthy of its subject, the historical and aesthetic principles on which he

[11] See, among many discussions of this subject, L. C. Knights, *Drama and Society in the Age of Jonson* (Chatto and Windus, 1937) and Alfred Hart, *Shakespeare and the Homilies* (Melbourne University Press, 1934).

[12] Herford and Simpson, Vol. II, pp. 297 and 311.

worked must be taken seriously. For these principles—of decorum, of hierarchical unity, and of ethical purpose—are the principles of most Elizabethan literature and, according to his evidence, form the theory which Jonson followed in his efforts to establish the masque as a literary form.

Chronology of Important Dates

1572   Birth of Jonson.

c. 1583-89   Education at Westminster School, London.

c. 1589   Apprenticeship to his stepfather, a bricklayer.

c. 1595   Marriage.

1597   First recorded connection with the theater, as actor and playwright in the service of Philip Henslowe. Imprisonment for his share in a lost satiric comedy, *The Isle of Dogs.*

1598   *Every Man In His Humour,* played by the Lord Chamberlain's Company, with Shakespeare in a leading role. Arrest and imprisonment of Jonson after a duel in which he kills a fellow actor.

1599-1601   "The war of the theaters" between the select playhouses in the City and the public playhouses on the Bankside, to which Jonson contributes experimental plays labelled by him "comical satires."

1603   Death of Elizabeth I and accession of James I. Beginning of the era of court masques and entertainments, composed by Jonson for great state occasions.

1605   Imprisonment once again. Jonson this time voluntarily joins in prison his collaborators in the comedy *Eastward Ho,* found offensive for its mockery of the Scots.

1606   *Volpone,* acted at the Globe and at both Universities. Summons of Jonson and his wife—Roman Catholics at the time—before the authorities for failure to take communion in the Church of England.

1609   *Epicene, or The Silent Woman,* performed by the Children of the Queen's Revels.

1610   *The Alchemist,* at the Globe.

1614   *Bartholomew Fair,* at the Hope Theater.

1616   Publication of Jonson's collected plays in a folio volume entitled *The Works of Benjamin Jonson,* the first such collection in the history of English printing.

1618   Journey to Scotland on foot. Visit to the Scottish poet Drummond of Hawthornden, whose jotted record of Jonson's conversations is published in abridged form in 1711, and in its entirety in 1833.

1623   Destruction of Jonson's library by fire. Contribution by Jonson of commendatory verses to the first folio collection of Shakespeare's plays.

1625-32   Period of later masques and entertainments under Charles I and Henrietta Maria, and in circumstances of turbulent rivalry with the court architect, Inigo Jones.

1628   Jonson stricken by paralysis and confined to his chambers. Visited henceforth by a coterie of younger disciples, "The Sons of Ben."

1637   Death of Jonson. Burial in Westminster Abbey, under the epitaph, "O Rare Ben Jonson."

Notes on the Editor and Authors

JONAS A. BARISH, the editor, is Associate Professor of English at the University of California, Berkeley. He received his A.B. and Ph.D. from Harvard, and has taught at Yale. He is the author of articles on Jonson, and of *Ben Jonson and the Language of Prose Comedy* (1960).

T. S. ELIOT, perhaps the most distinguished man of letters in the English-speaking world today, makes his home in England.

L. C. KNIGHTS, of the University of Bristol, is Visiting Professor of English at the University of Pennsylvania. He is the author of a celebrated essay on Shakespeare, "How Many Children Had Lady Macbeth?" and of *Explorations, An Approach to Hamlet,* and *Some Shakespearean Themes.*

HARRY LEVIN is Professor of English and Comparative Literature at Harvard University. He has published on a wide range of subjects, including James Joyce in *An Introduction to James Joyce,* Christopher Marlowe in *The Overreacher,* Shakespeare in *The Question of Hamlet,* and American literature in *The Power of Blackness.*

EDMUND WILSON, America's most brilliant journalist-critic, has published hundreds of essays on literaure. His most important compilations include *Axel's Castle* (a study of symbolist literature), *The Wound and the Bow, The Triple Thinkers,* and *Classics and Commercials* (a collection largely of book reviews).

ARTHUR SALE is Lecturer at Magdalene College, Cambridge. He has edited *Volpone, All for Love,* and Crabbe's *The Village,* and published essays on Melville, Crabbe, and Emily Dickinson.

C. H. HERFORD, the senior editor of the Oxford edition of Jonson's works, also edited Jonson for the Mermaid Series, and wrote the entry on Jonson for *The Dictionary of National Biography.* He died in 1931.

PAUL GOODMAN, writer, has taught at the University of Chicago, Sarah Lawrence College, and New York University. He is a Fellow of the Institute of Gestalt Therapy, and the author of *The Empire City, Communities, Growing Up Absurd,* and *Utopian Essays and Practical Proposals.*

EDWARD B. PARTRIDGE is Associate Professor of English at Bucknell University.

RAY L. HEFFNER, JR., is Associate Professor of English and Associate Dean of the Faculties at Indiana University.

JOSEPH ALLEN BRYANT, JR., is head of the Department of English at The Women's College of the University of North Carolina.

DOLORA CUNNINGHAM is Assistant Professor of English at San Francisco State College, San Francisco, California.

Selected Bibliography on Ben Jonson

General:

Enck, John J. *Jonson and the Comic Truth*. Madison: The University of Wisconsin Press, 1957. An idiosyncratic, frequently perplexing, but nonetheless acute and original study of Jonson as playwright.

Hays, H. R. "Satire and Identification: An Introduction to Ben Jonson," *Kenyon Review*, XIX (1957), 257-283. An essay which combats certain sentimental prejudices, particularly damaging to Jonson, likely to be brought into the theater by playgoing audiences.

Herford, C. H., and Simpson, Percy. *Ben Jonson: The Man and His Work*. Oxford: The Clarendon Press, 1925. These two volumes of prefatory matter—biographical, critical, and documentary—to the complete edition of Jonson's works form an irreducible minimum for any serious study of their subjects.

Swinburne, Algernon Charles. *A Study of Ben Jonson*. London: Chatto and Windus, Ltd., 1889. Despite numerous eccentricities of judgment, and Eliot's unflattering opinion, this remains a highly attractive record of its author's enthusiasm for Jonson.

On Particular Aspects and Individual Works:

Barish, Jonas A. *Ben Jonson and the Language of Prose Comedy*. Cambridge: The Harvard University Press, 1960. A study of Jonson's prose style, and what it implies for his practice as a dramatist.

Bryant, Joseph Allen, Jr. "The Significance of Ben Jonson's First Requirement for Tragedy: 'Truth of Argument,'" *Studies in Philology*, XLIX (1952), 195-213. A lucid analysis of Jonson's theory of history, and its effect on his practice as a tragic playwright.

Campbell, Oscar J. *Comicall Satyre and Shakespeare's Troilus* and *Cressida*. San Marino, California: The Henry E. Huntington Library & Art Gallery, 1938. The most important study so far of Jonson's early comedy, and of the plays relating to the War of the Theaters.

Gordon, D. J. "Poet and Architect: The Intellectual Setting of the Quarrel between Ben Jonson and Inigo Jones," *The Journal of the Warburg and Courtauld Institutes*, XII (1949), 152-178. A learned, rewarding account of the philosophical background to the rivalry between Jonson and Jones in their capacities as masque-makers to the court.

Hollander, John. Introduction to *Ben Jonson*, The Laurel Poetry Series. New York: The Dell Publishing Co., Inc., 1961. An attractive and suggestive essay on Jonson's nondramatic poetry.

Levin, Harry. "Jonson's Metempsychosis," *Philological Quarterly*, XXII (1943), 231-239. An explication of the interlude in Act I of *Volpone,* becoming a wide-ranging discussion of Jonson's evolution as a comic playwright.

Ornstein, Robert. "Ben Jonson," in *The Moral Vision of Jacobean Tragedy*. Madison: The University of Wisconsin Press, 1960, pp. 84-104. A sensitive critical estimate of Jonson's two tragedies.

Waith, Eugene. "The Poet's Morals in Jonson's *Poetaster*," *Modern Language Quarterly*, XII (1951), 13-19. An acute discussion of some problems of interpretation raised by the play.

TWENTIETH CENTURY VIEWS

Other Titles